ASPECTS OF DONCASTER 2

ASPECTS *of* DONCASTER 2

Discovering Local History

Edited by
Brian Elliott

Series Editor
Brian Elliott

Wharncliffe Publishing

First Published in 1999 by
Wharncliffe Publishing
an imprint of
Pen and Sword Books Limited,
47 Church Street, Barnsley,
South Yorkshire. S70 2AS

For up-to-date information on other titles produced under the Wharncliffe imprint, please telephone or write to:

Wharncliffe Publishing
FREEPOST
47 Church Street
Barnsley
South Yorkshire S70 2BR
Telephone (24 hours): 01226 - 734555

ISBN: 1-871647-57-6

A CIP catalogue record of this book is available from the British Library

Cover illustration Doncaster Mansion House, from Miller's *History of Doncaster* (1804)

Printed in Great Britain by
Redwood Books, Trowbridge, Wiltshire

Contents

	Introduction	*Brian Elliott*	**6**
1.	Doncaster Rovers, 1962-64 An Apprentice's story	*Brian Elliott*	**8**
2.	Tom Puddings and the Waterways around Doncaster	*Mike Taylor*	**20**
3.	Wadworth and the Wordsworth family	*Ron Spensley*	**34**
4.	Elgar's visit to Doncaster, 1909	*Philip L Scowcroft*	**49**
5.	Doncaster Mansion House: An Anniversary Tour	*Brian Barber*	**53**
6.	Descent into Debt: The Corporation's finances, 1800-1838	*George Owen*	**69**
7.	The Doncaster Plant Churches: St James and St Judes	*Roger Glister*	**84**
8.	Jigsaws of Building History: Three Parish Churches in the Lower Don Valley	*Derek Holland*	**89**
9.	Remembered Forever: Church Monuments in the Doncaster Area	*Simeon Bennett & Tony Dodsworth*	**106**
10.	Denaby Main: The Development of a South Yorkshire Mining Village	*Melvyn Jones*	**123**
11.	Music in Doncaster during: The Napoleonic Wars	*Philip L Scowcroft*	**143**
12.	Some Women in Austerfield Wills and Inventories, 1658-1721	*Alice Rodgers*	**155**
13.	Bawtry: History in the Townscape	*Derek Holland*	**169**
14.	When Buffalo Bill Brought the Wild West to Doncaster	*Brian Elliott*	**175**
	Contributors		**183**
	Index		**189**

Introduction

by Brian Elliott

The first *Aspects of Doncaster* (1997) has been well-received by an increasing number of readers and researchers who have a keen interest in local and family history. It has also been welcomed by newcomers to the area who wish to get a flavour of their place of work or residence; and of course by many ex-Doncaster people with a genuine affection for their place of birth or upbringing. One regional journalist in a glowing review expressed a view that he hoped it would be a forerunner of further volumes. This second volume appears at the eve of the millennium - a most appropriate time to celebrate a historic Yorkshire town and its neighbourhood.

Currently the Aspects Series also has multiple or initial volumes available or forthcoming for Barnsley, Rotherham, Sheffield, Wakefield, Pontefract, Leeds, Huddersfield, Bradford, Hull and the Yorkshire Coast. Early volumes for Barnsley and Rotherham are already much sought after 'collectors items'. The acclaimed format which combines popular but original research and writing with high quality visual presentation, is also being piloted across the Pennines and in the Midlands, at Blackburn, Accrington and Birmingham. Nationwide coverage beckons.

In the 1882 edition of Murray's railway guide or *Handbook for Travellers in Yorkshire,* Doncaster is described as 'one of the cleanest and pleasantest towns in Yorkshire', echoing similar descriptions from earlier directories. Apart from the racecourse, 'Murray' concluded that the town's 'chief points of interest' were its modern churches and 'for those who care for machinery, the *plant* of the Great Northern Railway'. Roger Glister's article combines 'church' with 'plant' in a new account of St James and St Judes.

Derek Holland, whilst acknowledging the complexities of interpreting our medieval churches, also uses his observations relating to building materials and architectural features to provide us with an insightful appreciation of Kirk Sandall, Fishlake and Hatfield. A good range of medieval church monuments are extant in the Doncaster area and examples are explored and explained - with the benefit of superb illustrations - in the capable company of Simeon Bennett and Tony Dodsworth.

Ron Spensley's well-researched study of Wadworth and the

Wordsworth family involves the skilful use of a large variety of sources and also shows how local history can be purposefully and necessarily linked to national events; whilst Alice Rodgers makes excellent use of primary material from the Lumley Archive at Sandbeck for her innovative contribution on 'Austerfield women'.

Philip Scowcroft's wide-ranging historical interests are reflected in many published items and talks but for this volume he concentrates on two aspects of the town's musical heritage: first, Elgar's visit of 1909 and later he explores the extent of local music in the Napoleonic era. Similarly, Melvyn Jones's uses a variety of sources and methods so as to contribute to our better understanding of the sudden rise of mining communities, in particular Denaby Main. Another exemplar of research methods is evident in Mike Taylor's 'waterways' article featuring compartmental boats or 'Tom Puddings'.

Although now playing in the Football Combination - after the disasterous 1997-98 season - there has been a resurgence of interest in Doncaster Rovers under new ownership and management. Brian Elliott, a former Rover's apprentice, recalls the early 1960s when the club was the 'big spender' of the old Fourth Division and when a large Belle Vue crowd welcomed the return of Alick Jeffrey.

As very recent events have shown, managing local authority budgets by both elected members and officers is no easy task. George Owen provides us with a fascinating insight into the increasing complexity of Doncaster corporation finances during the first four decades of the nineteenth century, using hitherto little used sources.

Brian Barber, Principal Archivist at Doncaster Archives, takes us on a most timely tour of the most famous building of the town - the Mansion House - in celebration of the 250th anniversary of its opening, whilst, further afield, Derek Holland interprets some of the rich architectural history of Bawtry.

Finally, Brian Elliot celebrates the arrival of Buffalo Bill's Wild West Show, a forgotten event that thrilled thousands of people on the Race Common in 1903.

Once more sincere thanks are due to all contributors for compiling excellent studies relating to Doncaster and district history; and also for meeting editorial requirements and deadlines. If the Doncaster series continues it will provide an outlet for well-researched and well-written local history in a popular format. The book would not be possible without the support of Wharncliffe Publishing and in particular chief executive Charles Hewitt and Imprint Manager Mike Parsons. Thanks are also due to Paul, Roni and Jon Wilkinson, Barbara and Paula, and all the Pen & Sword team.

1. Doncaster Rovers, 1962-64: An Apprentice's story

by Brian Elliott

NEW ROVERS MANAGER OSCAR HOLD came to see my parents on 18 July 1962 with the intention of 'signing' me as an apprentice professional with the Fourth Division football club. We then lived on a small housing estate at Monk Bretton, near Barnsley. Oscar knew my father quite well because as young men they played football for the same Barnsley League amateur team. At the age of fifteen I had no hesitation in accepting his invitation - at a wage of £5 per week for the first year - despite several enquiries from 'more glamorous' clubs - and the possibility of 'staying-on' at my secondary modern school where a new fifth-form was due to be created. A few weeks earlier, accompanied by my father, we were given a tour of Belle Vue and introduced to its chairman, Jack Garnham.

I had always been interested in sport, especially football, at a time when when youngsters played games at every opportunity in all sorts of weather and on all sorts of surfaces. Our backyard and main street in the pit village of Carlton doubled as Lords and Wembley depending on the time of year, much to the annoyance of some residents, especially when windows were accidentally broken. I constantly wore out the toes of the most strongest of shoes, in fact I do remember my mother once getting a refund from a shop selling *Tuf* shoes (supposedly guaranteed for six months) after a few weeks usage; even short trousers had a very short life. Once I got a real leather 'casey' or football for Christmas which was such a prestigious and powerful gift that it gave a definite advantage when picking the best teams. I was, to use local lad Michael Parkinson's later phrase 'cricket mad' and 'football daft' for most of my waking hours. Like my dad - and because I was always 'big for my age' - I preferred to play in goal, so the 'daft' appellation was most appropriate.

Mick Mulligan, a year older and one of my best mates, lived next door but his elder brother, Peter, was a great role model for me, since he had played in the Barnsley Boys team that won the English Schools Trophy in 1958, the year of the Munich air disaster and had had an England Schoolboys trial. Peter, whilst a teenager, played for several seasons in Barnsley's reserves and first team, combining sport with teacher-training, the latter a rare local achievement in its own right.

As a schoolboy I must have had some footballing potential, selected to play for the Barnsley Junior Schools' team, the highlight being a game against Scunthorpe at the club's Old Show Ground. A temporary cross-bar was erected so as to lower the height of the goals! but I had no need of such an advantage. Whilst at secondary school I played for the town's Under 14 eleven. After a series of trial games I then became part of the highly successful 1960-61 Barnsley School Boys team (mostly as a reserve but still only aged thirteen/fourteen) that won the English Schools' Trophy, beating Liverpool in the two-legged final, with huge crowds at Anfield and Oakwell. The Barnsley team included a number of fifteen-year olds who became professional players: Jimmy Greenhoff (Leeds & Manchester United), Alan Woodward (Sheffield United), schoolboy international goalkeeper Alan Ogley (Barnsley & Manchester City) and John Hobson (Barnsley, Blackpool & Notts County). Centre-forward Ron Glover, a grammar school lad, completed his education for another year, joining Doncaster Rovers at the same time as myself (Figure 1).

During season, 1961-62 I was a permanent member of the Barnsley Boys' team which won the Yorkshire ('Wylie') Shield. It was a great evening at Oakwell in May 1962 when we beat Bradford Boys 4-0 in the second leg (7-2 on aggregate) before an appreciative 2,000 crowd. A few weeks earlier I was selected for the Yorkshire team, against Northumberland in a fixture played at Dunscroft Miners' Ground (Hatfield Welfare FC).

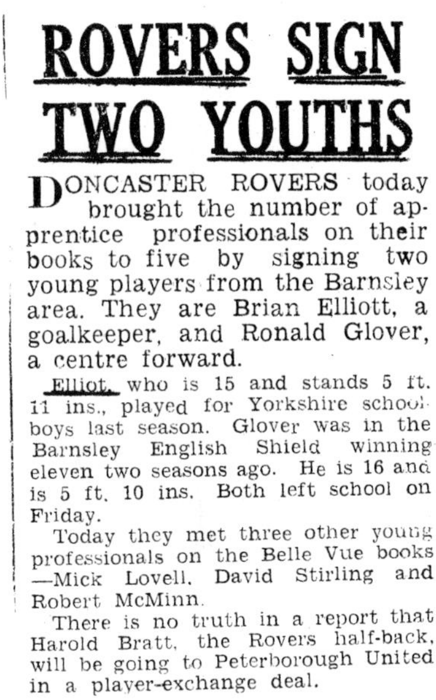

ROVERS SIGN TWO YOUTHS

DONCASTER ROVERS today brought the number of apprentice professionals on their books to five by signing two young players from the Barnsley area. They are Brian Elliott, a goalkeeper, and Ronald Glover, a centre forward.

Elliot, who is 15 and stands 5 ft. 11 ins., played for Yorkshire schoolboys last season. Glover was in the Barnsley English Shield winning eleven two seasons ago. He is 16 and is 5 ft. 10 ins. Both left school on Friday.

Today they met three other young professionals on the Belle Vue books —Mick Lovell, David Stirling and Robert McMinn.

There is no truth in a report that Harold Bratt, the Rovers half-back, will be going to Peterborough United in a player-exchange deal.

Figure 1. The 'signing' of Brian Elliott and Ron Glover brought the number of young apprentices to five for the start of season 1962-63, as reported in this local newspaper extract.

Travelling to Doncaster was via a bus from Monk Bretton to Barnsley, then a number 14 Yorkshire Traction bus that took the best part of an hour, terminating near the railway station in Doncaster. It was then another bus journey or a walk to the Belle Vue ground. Travelling with Ron put me at ease although he tended to sleep throughout most journeys, especially homeward, having an uncanny capacity to wake up just as the right time.

I soon found out what life as an apprentice footballer was really all about. Apart from Ron and myself the only other 'groundstaff lads' were Mick Lovell, David Stirling and Robert McMinn. On the whole we got on well together and also - despite some pranks- with physio/trainer Lew Clayton (ex-Barnsley) and his assistant the former Rovers player Frank Marshall. In the morning, from about 10 am we occasionally trained with the senior players and took part in practice games but most of the professionals (there were about 20) finished at lunch-time, only had light training Friday mornings and often a day off mid-week following a match. Not a bad life for them! We were on duty - or supposed to be - most of the time. Our main opportunity to train and enjoy ourselves was in the afternoons but 'groundstaff' was an appropriate word to describe our 'professional' duties which, during the season included a variety of practical tasks: putting players' kit out before they arrived, even sometimes assisting peeling off soaked shirts after training; cleaning the dressing rooms, baths and toilets (inspected by Frank or Lew) and assisting head groundsman Gordon Foster to prepare the practice and main pitch; and of course boot-cleaning. The ground was sacred turf for most of the time, probably the largest and one of the best playing surfaces in the Football League. One of our worst jobs was sweeping the terraces and grandstand after games. I also recall 'running errands' for General Manager/Secretary Tom Garnett's tobacco and for staff sandwiches.

Work-wise, I enjoyed the summer periods best of all. Again we helped (and sometimes annoyed) the groundsmen and spent a good deal of time applying red and white paint on wood, brick and metal - and a lot of it on ourselves. Training was very hard, especially pre-season which included what I then considered to be very long-distance runs. We used the large open-space area not far from the present Dome Leisure complex, near the airfield, but occasionally strayed on to Sandall Beat and part of the racecourse. The perimeter of the ground was used for sprint repetitions - and the stepped terrace of the steep Kop for strength training.

Rovers were obviously a small club that had seen better days but there was an evident sense of both pride and history amongst some of the backroom staff and certainly the loyal supporters. Long-service players such as Syd Bycroft, Clarrie Jordan and Bert Tindall were not that distant memories whilst stories associated with Charlie Williams were already legendary. Peter Doherty was talked about with affection whilst his predecessor, Jackie Bestall still had links with the club. The remarkable talent and demise of Alick Jeffrey who had played in the first team as a fifteen year-old amateur but whose future was curtailed when he broke his leg playing for the England Under-23 side in 1957 was often discussed.

Oscar Hold, the former Cambridge City manager, had been coaching in Turkey before his appointment at Belle Vue. I found him to be a very hard-working boss with ambitious plans for the long-term success of a club whose previous season had resulted in the ignomy of applying for re-election (even Accrington Stanley dropping out of the League didn't help). Oscar proceeded to almost replace an entire playing staff (Figure 2). We became the top-spenders of the division. Many new faces thus appeared during the first half of season 1962-63 and then came the dreadful winter when play was virtually impossible for two months.

I 'started work' on Monday 22 July 1962. The only players retained from the previous campaign (according to my diary) were Tony Wales (full-back), wing-halves Harold Bratt and John Fairhurst, wingers Phil Robinson and Fred Taylor, and inside-forwards John Ballagher and John Billings. Among the new players reporting for training were (from Aston Villa) Fred Potter (a

Figure 2. Doncaster Rovers parade their 'new look' playing staff before the start of the 1962-63 campaign. Note the new style first team shirts with an extra white half-circle band. **Front row:** (left to right): Stirling & McMinn (apprentices), Johnson, Ballagher, White (captain), Hale, Sambrook, Raine, Elliott & Glover (apprentices). **Centre row:** Frank Marshall (ass. trainer), Hinton, Lovell (apprentice, kneeling), Robinson, Wales, Windross, Bratt, Herrington, Hildreth, Thompson, Taylor, Oscar Hold (manager), Lewis Clayton (trainer). **Back row:** Wright, Billings, Helliwell, Potter, McCall, Fairhurst.
The only 'missing' player was Tony Conwell, the ex-Derby County full-back.

goalkeeper) and Irishman Alfie Hale, winger Mike Johnson (Fulham) and full-back David Raine (Port Vale) with new skipper and the former Liverpool centre-half and captain Dick White having put in several hours the previous week. I got on very well with Fred who, although only 21, seemed to me to be a very senior player. Dick White (Figure 3) certainly was a senior player, and although he struggled with injuries and pace was a good signing and always had a determined spirit. Dick always had some wisecracks to say in the dressing room and tried to keep up morale, even after bad results - and there were quite a few early ones. Alfie (Figure 4), of small stature, a forward, put a hundred per cent effort into games and was well-liked by the groundstaff lads.

Here is a record that I kept of the other 'new faces' of 1962-63:

Tony Conwell (ex-Derby County), full-back
Keith Ripley (Peterborough), wing-half
Dennis Windross (Darlington), centre-forward
Colin Booth (Nottingham Forest), inside forward
Bob Meadows (Northwich, Stoke), full-back
John Nibloe (Stoke City), forward
Bob Rooney (Sheffield United), inside-forward
Willie Purvis (Grimsby Town), centre-forward
Albert Broadbent (Lincoln - returning to Rovers, also ex-Sheffield Wednesday), wing or forward
Jimmy Wallace (Northwich), left-wing

What a job it must have been for the manager to achieve all these signings in such a short period of time. It was a record spending spree for the club. In particular the signing of Colin Booth (Figure 5) for £10,000 was then a substantial fee for a Fourth Division club. I liked Colin, he gave encouragement to the younger players and I can vouch that he could strike the ball with awesome power. Oscar meant business and despite ups and downs of the first eleven's form they were exciting times for fifteen year old apprentices. Beatlemania and the Merseysound was all the rage of course, though I had long arguments about the merits about a certain American singer called Elvis Presley. We were very fashion-conscious and £5 a week seemed to go a long way. I remember buying a Beatles-style light grey suit (no collar) from Burtons

Figure 3. Dick White leading the Liverpool team out at Anfield. Liverpool had just won the Second Division championship when Dick was transferred to Rovers.

and wearing it on a visit to the first-team dressing room on a Saturday match-day. You can imagine some of the reaction. Colin Booth pulled my leg a bit, showing his age a little by comparing my appearance to Paul Anka!

Figure 4. Alfie Hale, the former Aston Villa and Eire international.

The 1962-63 season started poorly but by Christmas the new players were playing much better as a team, with Booth, Nibloe and Hale combining well in attack; then the exceptional winter weather, the most severe since 1947, meant that only one game, on 9 February, was played between the end of December and the beginning of March - and this with grumbles from away team Stockport County who had the cheek to win the match 2-1. It had been a mammoth task to clear the snow and ice from the ground and involved many volunteers. During the Big Freeze training was very difficult though we did manage to make use of the RAF's large gymnasium at Finningley. The first fixture of the 'resumed season' took place at Torquay, resulting in a respectable 2-2 draw but match practice was badly needed. Again the RAF came to our rescue, offering their Bawtry ground for a mid-week full-scale practice match against Rotherham United. Just over sixteen years old, I found my name on the notice-board for this game (Figure 6). Perhaps it was too risky to play Fred Potter or

Figure 5. Colin Booth, born in Manchester, was a former schoolboy international who turned professional for Wolverhampton Wanderers in 1952 at the age of 17, eventually moving to Notts Forest.

Figure 6. Newspaper report of the Rovers v Rotherham United practice match, held just after the 'big freeze', March 1963.

Rovers and Rotherham teams in another practice game

By KEN MONTGOMERY

THE ROYAL AIR FORCE, which came to the aid of Doncaster Rovers earlier in the season when they put their spacious gymnasium at Finningley at the Belle Vue club's disposal, again gave the Rovers a helping hand today.

Looking for a ground where he could give his players a full-scale work-out, the Rovers' team-manager Mr. Oscar Hold, got in touch with R.A.F. Bawtry, who gave permission for a practice match with Rotherham United to be played there.

The Rovers fielded most of the team which drew 2-2 at Torquay, but not goalkeeper Fred Potter, who took a knock at Devon and wasn't risked. He was replaced by 16-year-old Brian Elliot.

Mr. Hold took the opportunity to field several of the younger players, with regular full-back Stewart Hildreth coming in on the second-half for Wright, who had started off as leader of the attack.

The Rotherham manager, Mr. Danny Williams, fielded his regular side, with Peter Madden, the Millmoor club's powerful pivot, standing out in defence and sharp-shooting centre-forward John McCole giving the Rovers' defence plenty to think about.

None of the Rovers' side which beat Scunthorpe United Reserves 1-0 in a North Regional League match under the Belle uVe floodlights last night, played in the match, alhough Dick White, Mike Johnson, and severad more watched the game, along wiht full-back Tony Conwell, who is making good progress in his fight back to fitness after breaking a leg last November.

Figure 7. Doncaster Rovers' Juniors (Nothern Intermediate team), taken before a game on Sandall Beat, 1963. Back row (left to right): David Stirling, Robert McMinn, Brian Elliot & Mick Lovell (apprentices), B Cook, D Whiteley and Harry Fellows (trainer). Front row: K Shaw, T Willis, Ron Glover (apprentice), B Hyde and P Wofindin.

the reserve-team goalkeeper! The Millmoor club, managed by Danny Williams, were a very good attacking side, two divisions above us - and it showed, since I was kept very busy retrieving the ball from the back of the Rover's net on several occasions. The extended season brought a halt to a downward trend for the first team, finishing in sixteenth position in the league, and Colin Booth scoring 34 goals. Attendances had also improved to an average of over 6,300 per home game.

The Reserves played in the North Regional League (after a season's absence). In December I was selected to play against Stockport County Reserves at Belle Vue but this was one of the first games postponed by the bad weather. Most of my 29 appearances were in the Northern Intermediate League and Cup (U19s) on good grounds against Yorkshire clubs and nearby towns such as Scunthorpe, Grimsby and Chesterfield but we also travelled to Newcastle, Sunderland, Middlesbrough and Wolverhampton, all usually under the experienced eye of our 'trainer', Harry Fellows (Figure 7). We only won about one in four games but the standard

Figure 8. Doncaster Rovers' squad pictured at the start of the 1963-64 season.

of play was understandably high against the top clubs. It was quite a contrast playing in the Doncaster Senior League, one of my earliest games being against Lundhill Athletic (Wombwell, Barnsley) on a terrible pitch where we won 4-2. I also had games against Ford United (3-2), Bawtry Town (5-0), Peglars Sports (3-1), Harvesters Recreation (6-4) and Rossington Rangers (1-0) who had ex-Rover's goalkeeper Ken Hardwick in their team; and I recall a DSL semi-final in which we lost by a single goal to Dearne Valley Colliery at the Peglars ground.

Figure 9. Dennis Crompton, age, 21, the former Burnley centre-half.

Despite a record loss of £43,683, thankfully reduced to just over £17,000 through various supporters' pools, there was considerable optimism at the start of the 1963-64 season (Figure 8). Money for new signings was obviously limited but included small fees for centre-half Dennis Crompton (Figure 9), from Burnley, right-half Colin Lambton (Figure 10) from Newcastle and young wing-half George Machin (aged 18) from Stoke. Other newcomers included three free-transfers, all forwards: Brian Westlake (19), from Stoke, Brian Moore from Notts County and Burnley's Alan Haspell (20). It was hoped that John Nibloe (Figure 11) who had now completed from his army duties would take some of the load from Booth who had amassed 38 goals the previous season - more than half of the club's total! Promotion was the main objective so the players' bonus system was reorganised with payments that peaked at £6 per player if the team was in the top four places. A far cry from modern-day incentives but at the time most of the first-teamers were receiving some of the best wages in the league.

Figure 10. Ex- Newcastle United right-half Colin Lambton, signed age 21.

The 1963-64 season started very well, with an opening draw and three wins, but this was followed by a more mediocre run of results. The highlight was the remarkable return of Alick Jeffrey, still only twenty-four, following a protracted period of legal and insurance negotiations. Hitherto not allowed to play in the league by the FA, Alick had made an impressive come-back with Skegness Town and then in Sydney, Australia. His first game, at Belle View for the reserves

Figure 11. Forward John Nibloe (ex-Sheffield United) was signed from Stoke City for £5,000. Always a cheerful and popular character, John was transferred to Stockport County in July 1964 but we were all very shocked at the Rovers to learn of his death in a car crash four months later.

against Crewe Alexandra on 14 December attracted a crowd of almost 3,000 and 11,719 attended for his first team 'debut' two weeks later when Rovers beat Southport 3-0, Colin Booth scoring a hatrick (Figure 12). Alick, though lacking in fitness and certainly needing to loose weight, had not lost his outstanding footballing skills. His arrival was a tremendous boost to the club though he didn't score in the league until March.

Figure 12. Alick Jeffrey heads the ball whilst challeged by a Southport defender, Belle Vue, 28 December 1963. Philip Robinson in the background.

A remarkable fixture took place in January 1964 when Rovers were leading Darlington 6-0 by half-time, adding four more goals by the close but at the end of the season the team finished with exactly the number of points as the previous campaign. There was better success in the FA Cup with victories against Notts County and Tranmere Rovers before loosing in a third-round replay at Bristol City. Colin Booth (23 goals) and Alfie Hale (20) were the leading scorers.

Most of my games continued to be in the Northern Intermediate League, my hopes for personal promotion dashed at the start of the season when Downie was signed on loan to cover an injury to Fred Potter. I was in good form in junior matches involving Middlesbrough (away,2-2), Sunderland (home, 1-1) and Leeds United (home,3-1: Figure 13). In one game, because of an arm injury, I swopped shirts with an outfield player and scored.

Leeds Js. v. Doncaster Js.

N. INTERMEDIATE LEAGUE

Fast end-to-end play characterised the earlier exchanges with most of the Leeds attacking coming from the left wing pair, Winspear and Hibbert.

Hawkins tested Elliott with a rasping shot from 20yd. which the keeper fielded cleanly.

After good work by Holmes, who forced a corner on the left, Harvey failed to complete a clearance and HYDE was on the spot to ram the ball home to give Doncaster the lead.

Hawkins ended a fine run with a well-placed shot which Elliott saved, but offside was ruining most of the Leeds forward moves.

Fighting back hard Leeds drew level with a nicely-judged lob from GREY, but Doncaster added further goals through HOLMES and JOHNSON.

RESULT:	Gls.
DONCASTER JUNIORS	3
LEEDS UNITED JUNIORS	1

Figure 13. Newspaper report of Rovers' Juniors match v Leeds United Juniors.

The resignation of Oscar Hold was both a surprise and, for myself a personal disappointment. Writing to me in 1994, Oscar described some of the boardroom politics that resulted in his decision to go. Within a week he was back coaching a top Turkish side that went on to win their league and therefore qualify for the European Championship.

Hold's successor was Bill Leivers, the former Manchester City full-

Figure 14. The new Rovers' players at the start of season 1964/65.
Back row:(left to right): Lovell, Stirling, Ricketts, Billings, McMinn.
Middle row: Lew Clayton (trainer), Fairhurst, Watton, Oxford, Elliott, Potter, Marsden, Ripley, Frank Marshall (ass. trainer).
Seated: Robinson, Tait, Hale, Henderson, Leivers (player-manager), Jeffrey, Broadbent and Taylor.

back who was appointed as player-manager. There was yet another great clear-out of players prior to the start of the 1964-65 season, including the departure of fellow apprentice and travelling companion Ron Glover. Even prolific goalscorer Colin Booth was transferred, but at a proft, to Oxford United. New players included centre-forward Alex Tait (Bristol City), centre-half Jack Marsden (Carlisle) and ex-England winger Colin Grainger.

Leivers also brought in veteran goalkeeper Ken Oxford from Derby

'oncaster v Darlington

(NORTH REGIONAL)

DONCASTER ROVERS RES.—Elliott: irling. Meadows: Lovell, Davey, achin; Downing. Billings, Kelly. Hyde. obinson.

DARLINGTON RES.—Fleming: Carter, eavisides: Gibson. Robson, M Donald; oole. Maltry. weddle. Conlon, urbeck. Referee: H. Williams(Sheffield).

Rovers were a goal down in e 5th minute, but hit back to ke the lead by half-time.

Visiting centre forward 'EDDLE ran through unchal-nged and whipped the ball ist Rovers' teenage goalkeeper lliott, who was playing in his st reserve team match.

Hyde went near for Rovers llowing a corner on the left, ıd only minutes later Lovell ove a free kick over the bar llowing a foul on Downing.

Play was held up for several inutes while the winger ceived attention.

ROBINSON levelled the score ter 27 minutes from close in ter a shot from kelly had been ocked on the goal-line.

After 40 minutes Rovers took e lead when Robinson played free kick at DOWNING'S feet ıd the winger made no mis-ke.

Half-time:—Doncaster R. R. 2
Darlington R. ... 1

Figure 15. Newspaper report of first half of reserve fixture versus Darlington.

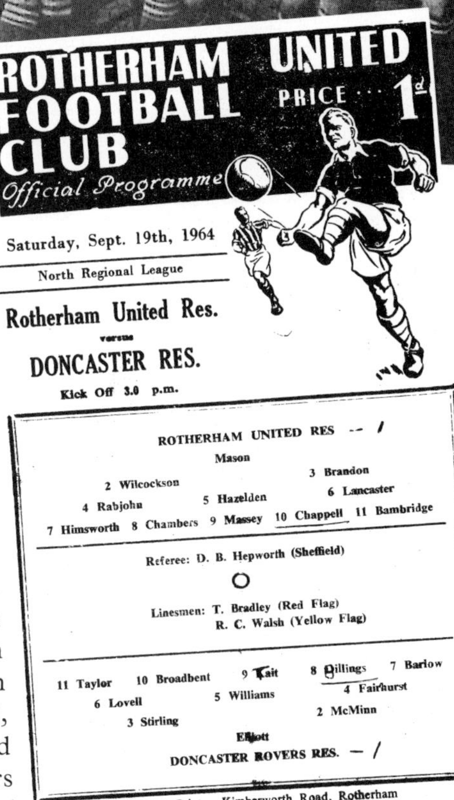

ROTHERHAM UNITED FOOTBALL CLUB
PRICE ... 1d
Official Programme

Saturday, Sept. 19th, 1964

North Regional League

Rotherham United Res.
versus
DONCASTER RES.

Kick Off 3.0 p.m.

ROTHERHAM UNITED RES -- 1

Mason
2 Wilcockson 3 Brandon
4 Rabjohn 5 Hazelden 6 Lancaster
7 Himsworth 8 Chambers 9 Massey 10 Chappell 11 Bambridge

Referee: D. B. Hepworth (Sheffield)

Linesmen: T. Bradley (Red Flag)
R. C. Walsh (Yellow Flag)

11 Taylor 10 Broadbent 9 Tait 8 Billings 7 Barlow
6 Lovell 5 Williams 4 Fairhurst
3 Stirling 2 McMinn
Elliott

DONCASTER ROVERS RES. — 1

L. G. Wooller, Printer, Kimberworth Road, Rotherham

Figure 16. Programme for reserve team fixture between Rotherham and Doncaster. The game resulted in a 1-1 draw.

County so opportunities for me to progress under the new management were limited (Figure 14). 'The Boss' took me on one side during an early season practice match and informed me that a professional contract would not be forthcoming, and advised that it would be best for me to look for a job. It was a great blow. This left only a few weeks of my apprenticeship to run, leaving me on the dole

Figure 17

The Rovers for 1962-63

FRED POTTER (Goal). A newcomer from Aston Villa. Only 21, he is 5 ft. 11 ins.

REGGIE BRAIN (Goal). Last season with Rossington Miners Welfare. A young 'keeper of great promise.

KEITH HELLIWELL (Goal). Showed good form last season. Comes from Great Houghton.

BRIAN ELIOTT (Goal). A former Yorkshire Boys' 'keeper.

TONY WALES (Right Back). Secured a first team place last season. Is an England Youth player and toured Austria with that team.

TERENCE BEILBY (Right Back). In his fourth season and a former Doncaster Schoolboy.

TONY CONWELL (Left Back). Secured from Derby County and was formerly with Huddersfield Town.

STUART HILDRETH (Left Back). Another former Doncaster Schoolboy and in his fourth season.

DAVID McCALL (Full-Back). Signed last season and son of the former Nottingham Forest defender. An excellent cricketer.

JOHN FLETCHER (Full-Back). A Sheffield lad who had a run with the League side last season. Also plays wing half.

ROBERT McMINN (Full-Back). A member of last season's Doncaster Schoolboys eleven.

DAVID RAINE (Wing-Half). Recently transferred from Port Vale where he has spent seven seasons. Born at Stone, Staffordshire.

DAVID WRIGHT (Wing-Half). Joined us two seasons ago from Leeds United. Former Doncaster Schoolboy.

HAROLD BRATT (Wing-Half). Joined us last season from Manchester United, and hails from Salford.

JOHN FAIRHURST (Right-Half). A former member of the Doncaster Schoolboys XI and in his fourth season. Made a number of appearances with the League side last season.

DICK WHITE (Centre-Half). A newcomer who was captain of Liverpool for the past three seasons. Is 5 ft. 11 ins. and 12 stone 1 pound. Also had experience with Scunthorpe United.

ERIC THOMPSON (Centre-Half). Another recruit from Leeds United, a former England International Schoolboy.

26

DAVID STIRLING (Wing-Half). A member of the Doncaster Boys' XI last season.

RON HINTON (Half Back). Plays in many positions and was formerly the Doncaster Boys' leader. An excellent shot.

ERIC HERRINGTON (Left-Half). A great little worker who had a run with the League side last season. Another former Doncaster Schoolboy.

KEITH RIPLEY (Left Half). Recently secured from Peterborough United. Formerly with Leeds United.

MIKE JOHNSON (Outside Right). A close season capture from Fulham, where he had considerable First Division experience. Formerly with Gloucester City.

PHILIP ROBINSON (Outside Right). A young player who joined us from Huddersfield Town last season and played mainly with the League side.

JOHN RAMSHAW (Outside Right). A Doncaster lad who played with Retford Town last season.

JOHN BALLAGHER (Inside or Wing Forward). Secured from Sheffield Wednesday early in 1961, and has played in all forward positions.

ALFIE HALE (Inside Right). An experienced young forward secured from Aston Villa. Formerly with Waterford. An international with Eire.

DENNIS WINDROSS (Centre Forward). Transferred from Darlington this summer and was the former Middlesborough and Brighton leader. Is 5 ft. 10 ins and 11 stone 8 pounds.

RONALD GLOVER (Centre Forward). A newcomer and formerly with Barnsley Boys, who won the English Schools' Shield. Is 5ft. 10in. in height.

JOHN BILLINGS (Inside Left). In his fourth season and also a former Doncaster Schoolboy.

MIKE LOVELL (Inside Left). One of last season's Doncaster Boys' XI and a promising youngster

RAY SAMBROOK (Outside Left). Secured from Manchester City this summer and the former Coventry City winger. Is 5 ft. 11 ins. and 11 st. 10 lbs.

FRED TAYLOR (Outside Left). Joined us from the 1958-59 Doncaster Boys' team and made a few appearances with the League side last season.

27

Figure 18

The Rovers for 1963-64

Goalkeepers:—

FRED POTTER—In his second season and was formerly with Aston Villa.

KEITH HELLEWELL—Hails from Great Houghton, and had some League experience last season.

*BRIAN ELLIOTT—In his second year and was the former Yorkshire Boys' 'keeper.

Full Backs:—

TONY CONWELL—In his second season and had considerable experience with Derby County and Huddersfield Town.

DAVID RAINE—Formerly with Port Vale; joined the Rovers in June, 1962.

BOBBY MEADOWS—Came to Rovers last November from Northwich Victoria and was formerly with Stoke City.

RODNEY MYERS—Joined Rovers last season and was formerly with H.M. Forces.

*ROBERT McMINN—A young defender who was with Doncaster Schoolboys eleven two years ago.

Half Backs:—

DENNIS WINDROSS—Came to Rovers from Darlington last season and was formerly with Brighton and Middlesbrough as a centre-forward.

HAROLD BRATT—In his third season and was formerly with Manchester United.

JOHN FAIRHURST—A former Doncaster Schoolboy and starting his fifth season.

DICK WHITE—The former Liverpool and Scunthorpe United centre-half who joined Rovers last season.

DENNIS CROMPTON—A newcomer from Burnley F.C., where he has been for four seasons.

KEITH RIPLEY—Joined us last season from Peterborough United, and has also seen service with Leeds United and Mansfield Town.

COLIN LAMBTON—A recent acquisition from Newcastle United, where he was for three seasons.

GEORGE MACHIN—A young half-back who joined Rovers in July from Stoke City.

*DAVID STIRLING—In his second season and a former Doncaster Schoolboy.

*MIKE LOVELL—Two seasons ago was a Doncaster Schoolboy. In his second year.

Forwards:—

BRIAN MOORE—A winger who is a newcomer from Notts County. Is well built and 24.

PHILIP ROBINSON—In his third season and an ex-Huddersfield Town winger.

ALAN HASPELL—A young player who was for five seasons with Burnley. Is 20 years old.

COLIN BOOTH—Secured last season from Nottingham Forest, and was formerly with Wolverhampton Wanderers.

JOHN NIBLOE—The former Stoke City and Sheffield United forward who joined Rovers during last season.

*RONALD GLOVER—A young forward who was a former Barnsley Schoolboy.

JOHN BILLINGS—In his fifth season and a former Doncaster Schoolboy.

BRIAN WESTLAKE—Secured from Stoke City this summer—a 19-year-old leader.

ALFIE HALE—In his second season and was formerly with Aston Villa. An Eire international.

GEORGE MANSELL—A young inside forward who was formerly in local football.

ALBERT BROADBENT—An experienced player who re-joined Rovers from Lincoln City. Also been with Sheffield Wednesday, Rotherham United and Notts County.

FRED TAYLOR—Joined Rovers in 1958-9 from the Doncaster Boys' team.

* Apprentice professionals

Amateurs:—

TERENCE TWELL (Goalkeeper)
BRIAN COOPER (Half Back)
PETER GREENWOOD (Goalkeeper)
ROGER SLACK (Full Back)
ROBERT W. BENNETT (Centre Half)
JAMES TAYLOR (Outside Right)
WILLIAM R. WILLS (Full Back)
JOHN WILLIS (Inside Forward)
MICHAEL J. COLE (Inside Forward)
ARTHUR CHARLTON (Half Back)
JACK CLAY (Inside Forward)
ADRIAN HARVEY (Wing Half)
DEREK HYDE (Wing Half)
DAVID WILLIAMS (Centre Half)

The Rovers for 1964-65

	Height		Weight		Previous clubs	Birthplace
Goalkeepers:—						
Fred Potter	5	11	12	4	Aston Villa	Cradley
Ken Oxford ...	5	10	11	2	Derby Co. and Norwich C.	Middleton
Brian Elliott ...	5	11	12	0	Yorkshire Boys	Barnsley
Full Backs:—						
David Raine ...	5	9	11	1	Port Vale	Stone, Staffs.
Rodney Myers ...	5	8	11	2		Sheffield
James Watton ...	5	8	10	12	Port Vale	Wolverhampton
William Leivers .	6	2½	14	7	Manchester C. & Chesterfield	Clay Cross
David Stirling ...	5	8	10	5	Doncaster Boys	Doncaster
Robert McMinn ..	5	9	9	12	Doncaster Boys	Doncaster
Half Backs:—						
Graham Ricketts .	5	10	11	7	Stockport Co. & Bristol Rovers	Oxford
Jack Marsden ...	6	0	12	0	Carlisle Utd. & Leeds United	Leeds
John Fairhurst ...	5	9½	11	0	Doncaster Boys	Doncaster
Mike Lovell	5	11	11	10	Doncaster Boys	Doncaster
Keith Ripley	6	0	12	6	Peterboro' Utd. & Mansfield T.	Normanton
David Williams ..	5	9	10	8	Felkirk Boys	Shafton
Forwards:—						
Philip Robinson ..	5	5	10	0	Huddersfield T.	Doncaster
Alfred Hale	5	6½	10	6	Aston Villa	Waterford
John Billings	5	10	11	0	Doncaster Boys	Doncaster
John Henderson .	6	0	12	0	Exeter City & Charlton Ath.	Johnshaven
Alex Tait	5	9	11	1	Bristol City & Newcastle Utd.	Bedlington
Derek Hyde	5	11	11	0	Doncaster Boys	Doncaster
Alec Jeffrey	5	11	13	9	Yorkshire Boys	Rawmarsh
Albert Broadbent	5	11	12	8	Lincoln City & Sheffield Wed.	West Bromwich
Fred Taylor	5	10	10	11	Doncaster Boys	Doncaster

Figure 19

Figure 20

for my eighteenth birthday. Ironically I began playing particularly well and was chosen for a couple of reserve games (Figures 15-16), but like the vast majority of ground staff lads, my professional career had well and truly ended. The most notable feature of the season for the club was the outstanding form of Alick Jeffrey who scored 39 goals in league and cup games.

Later, in February 1965, I wasn't too surprised to learn that Leivers had left the club 'for personal reasons' at a time when the Rovers were pressing for promotion, but under able caretakers went on to win the Fourth Division championship.

Despite the disappointment of not 'making the grade' I would have certainly regreted not signing that apprentice professional contract for Doncaster Rovers Football Club back in 1962.

Appendices

(I) Players listed in the official club handbook for seasons 1962-63, 1963-64 and 1964-65 (Figures 17-19):

(II) Front cover (Figure 20) of the Doncaster Rovers Official Handbook for the 1964-65 season. The cover photograph was taken during the previous end of season's league fixture against Tranmere Rovers on 25 April 1963 when Rovers won 2-1 before a 5,928 Bellue Vue crowd. Colin Booth, who scored both goals, can be seen behind the Tranmere goalkeeper Harry Leyland. Eight league games had to be played during April (4 wins, 2 draws, 1 lost) and a further five up to 18 May due to the fixture backlog arising from winter postponements.

2. Tom Puddings and the Waterways around Doncaster

by Mike Taylor

SURPRISINGLY, MOST CHANGES MADE TO WATERWAYS in the Doncaster area (Figures1-2) during the first half of the twentieth century were initiated by the Aire & Calder Navigation (A&CN) Company whose waterway linked Leeds, Wakefield, Goole and Selby. Prior to about 1890, that company had had few dealings with the owners of navigations connected to the river Don and its most profitable operation was the Tom Pudding system.

Tom Puddings

Compartment boats, usually called Tom Puddings - supposedly due to their shape - were introduced on the A&CN in the late 1860s. Measuring 20ft (6.1m) x 15ft (4.6m) with a depth of 9ft (2.7m), each boat was loaded with about 35 tons of coal at one of the waterside collieries in the Castleford, Leeds and Wakefield area before being towed in a train by steam tug to Goole (Figure 3). Here,

Figure 1. Part of the Sheffield & South Yorkshire Navigation during the middle decades of the twentieth century.

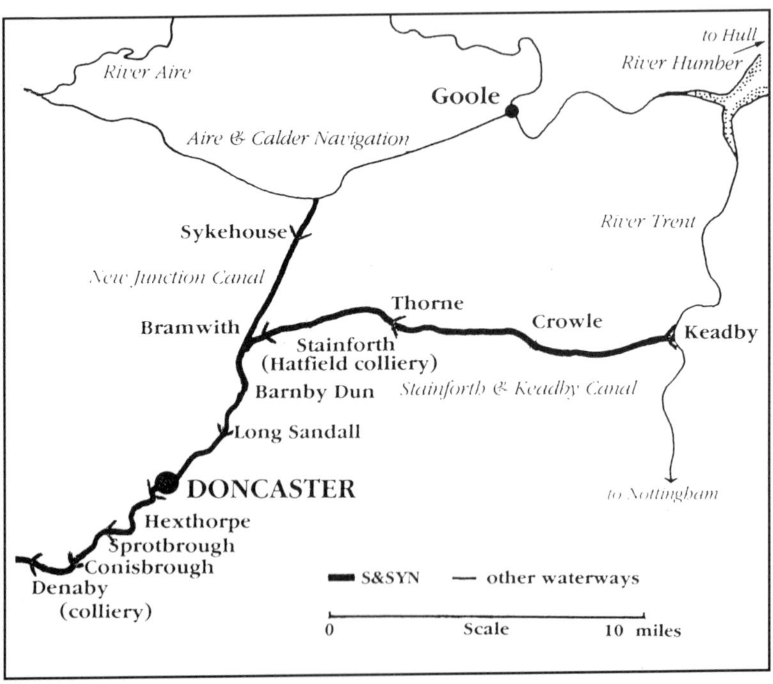

1889	Sheffield & South Yorkshire Navigation (S & SYN) Company formed.
1891	Bill, promoted by the Aire & Calder Navigation (A & CN) Company, to construct, jointly with S & SYN Company, the New Junction Canal received Royal Assent.
1895	S & SYN Company took over its four waterways from the Manchester, Sheffield and Lincolnshire Railway and began operations.
1905	New Junction Canal opened. Milethorn cut made.
1907	Sprotbrough cut widened above road bridge and upper entrance improved.
1909	Doncaster lock lengthened.
1914	Ladies' Harbour cut made.
1932	Bramwith lock lengthened. Staithe and canal lay-by built near Stainforth for loading coal from Hatfield Main Colliery into canal craft.
1933	Puddings began collecting Hatfield coal for delivery to Goole.
1934	Gashouse cut made.
1948	Nationalisation of inland waterways, including S & SYN and A & CN.
1959	New Lock completed at Sandall.
1972	Conisbrough lock eliminated by raising Sprotbrough weir.
1973	Hatfield staithe closed.
1979	S & SYN Improvement Scheme began.
1981	Denaby staithe closed.
1983	Improved S & SYN opened.
1986	End of Tom Pudding operation.

Figure 2. A chronology .

each unit was lifted in turn by one of the port's distinctive hydraulic hoists (Figure 4) and its cargo tipped into ships bound for ports in either South-East England or mainland Europe.

Doncaster Waterways in the nineteenth century

In 1843, the waterway route for trading vessels passing through Doncaster itself had assumed its present path with the opening of a one-thousand yard (915m) long canal cut between Newton Farm and Dockin Hill containing a lock close to the site that the Great Northern Railway would choose to bridge the navigation a few years later. The previous route for craft, via a lock at Mill Bridge, was then closed and a still water link was thus produced between the town and the river Trent at Keadby. This comprised the meandering, former

Figure 3. A train of loaded Tom Puddings heading for Goole behind one of the A&CN Company's steam tugs. The jebus or cutwater immediately behind the tug lifts the first vessel and deflects the tug's wash beneath the train. *British Waterways*

Figure 4. One of the Tom Pudding tipping hoists at Goole with the ship *Mary Anderson* being loaded.

course of the river Don between Doncaster and Sandall, a canal cut of 1823 from Sandall to Stainforth and the Stainforth & Keadby Canal of 1802.

With a view to making Doncaster a seaport, two of the tortuous ex-river sections, near Sandall, had been by-passed by short lengths of canal, banks had been raised to increase the depth of water and all bridges had been made to swing, resulting in the first fixed-masted seagoing vessel arriving at Doncaster in 1845.

Unfortunately, the navigation fell under control of railway interests in 1850. Few changes were made, maintenance work was neglected and little money invested in the waterway during the subsequent 45 years. Seagoing craft were persuaded to load coal at Thorne instead of Doncaster and subsequently in the Trent at Keadby as railway lines were progressively extended from Doncaster to wharves at these places.

In 1889 however, following pressure from Sheffield's industrial interests, the Sheffield & South Yorkshire Navigation (S&SYN) Company was formed to make Sheffield accessible to seagoing craft via Doncaster. Financial problems meant that the company was unable to take over its four waterways (the Don navigation, the Dearne & Dove Canal, the Stainforth & Keadby Canal and the Sheffield Canal) until 1895. Even then, the former railway company owners had to accept shares in the new company as payment, leaving it with little working capital and equal numbers of railway and non-railway directors on the board.

Plans for the S &SYN Company's Ship Canal were published in 1889 and the project resurfaced at intervals over the next 40 years as, across the Pennines, the Manchester Ship Canal prospered. Perhaps the final time that it received serious consideration was at a conference held in Doncaster during November 1926 when the subsequent press statement pointed to the conflict between a stable waterway and an active coalfield necessitating many millions of tons of coal being left in situ to support the canal and prevent subsidence if it were built.

Twentieth century alterations to the S&SYN owed little to the Ship Canal for which the company was originally formed and more to the A&CN Company's desire to maintain coal supplies for its Tom Puddings as the collieries in west Yorkshire threatened to become worked out.

The New Junction Canal

In 1890, the two navigation companies, encouraged by the owners of Denaby Main Colliery who were anxious to sell their own coal and that from their nearby soon-to-be-sunk Cadeby Colliery, began planning a 'Junction Canal' (Figure 5). This was to link the S&SYN at Bramwith with the A&CN at Southfields, enabling the Puddings to reach Goole with coal loaded on the S&SYN.

A major problem was that dimensions of locks on the A&CN had been steadily increased over the years, whilst those on the S&SYN had remained at Sheffield size (61ft 6ins [18.8m]) x 15ft 6 ins [4.7m]) for decades. Consequently, Pudding trains could pass through A&CN locks in one or two pennings but the S&SYN locks were able to accommodate only three Puddings at a time.

In 1898, as construction of the New Junction Canal proceeded apace, the S&SYN Company proposed to lengthen its locks to 140ft (42.7m). This was greeted with dismay by W H Bartholomew who had been responsible for introducing the Tom Pudding operation on the A&CN and who had recently retired as 'Chief Engineer and General Manager' with that company to become a 'Consulting Director' with responsibility for overseeing construction of the new canal. Bartholomew advised his company to abandon the canal

Figure 5. Construction, circa 1902, of the aqueduct to carry the New Junction Canal over the river Don at Bramwith. *British Waterways*

Figure 6. A train of empty Tom Puddings bound for Doncaster to be loaded passing through Sykehouse lock on the New Junction Canal in two sections (tug, jebus and seven pans followed by the other ten pans).

unless the S&SYN Company were prepared to make their locks at least 215ft (65.6m) long up to Denaby.

Similarly, the General Manager of the S&SYN had earlier stated that 'unless proper facilities are provided, it would be better that the Joint Canal should not be constructed'.

Nevertheless, despite these reservations, the canal was built at a cost of about £300,000, shared equally between the two navigation companies. Comprising five and a half miles (8.9km) of waterway, one 215ft (65.6m) long lock (Figure 6), together with several aqueducts and movable bridges, the canal was opened with little ceremony on 2 January 1905.

By this time the S&SYN Company had begun to make improvements to their waterway, as promised, with the building of a canal to cut off another of the ex-river meanders at Milethorn, near Doncaster's Strawberry Island, itself formed by an earlier cut-off.

A letter from Bartholomew, dated 10 July 1905 was received by the S&SYN Board:

> *It was pointed out to our board at their meeting on the 3rd inst. that your company had accomplished a very necessary improvement in their waterway below Doncaster by the diversion they have made at Mile Thorn and I was desired to ask you to bring before your committee the importance of making a similar diversion of the present circuitous waterway immediately to the westward of that referred to and thus remove a serious navigational difficulty in the working of general traffic and the introduction of compartment boats.*

Always the dominant partner by virtue of its superior financial resources and lifetime independence from railway control, the A&CN Company offered a loan for this improvement.

At a meeting between the two companies on 29 November 1905, less than a year after the new canal had been opened, the Leeds-based company produced the following list of work plus estimates of cost that they considered necessary before the Puddings could work to Denaby:

Lengthening Sandall lock	£6,000
Straightening below Doncaster	£1,800
Lengthening Doncaster lock	£12,000
Lengthening Sprotbrough lock	£.8,000
Sprotbrough new cut	£3,000
Lengthening Conisbrough lock	£5,000
Contingencies	£3,600
	£39,400

Figure 7. A Sheffield size keel (61ft 6ins [18.8m]x 15ft 6ins [4.7m]), almost certainly loaded with coal from a South Yorkshire colliery, heading down Sprotbrough cut towards the lock via the narrow 18ft (5.5m) channel adjacent to the mill before the 1907 improvements.

An alternative and cheaper course of action was also suggested. This involved lengthening Sandall lock, straightening the canal below Doncaster and making a new cut at Sprotbrough. The cost of this less satisfactory measure was estimated to be £11,000 and, if adopted, was to involve horse haulage of three Puddings at a time from Denaby, and hopefully, collieries further up the navigation such as Manvers Main and Roundwood, through the existing locks to Doncaster where they would be made up into trains and hauled to Goole by steam tug.

Bartholomew considered it absolutely essential that the new cut at Sprotbrough should be constructed before any attempt was made to work Puddings above Doncaster, as there was great danger of them being carried over Sprotbrough weir.

Above Doncaster, the navigation up to Denaby comprised mainly the river Don, with a short canal cut at Conisbrough and a longer one at Sprotbrough. There had been few changes for over a century but, in 1907, the canal by Sprotbrough mill (Figure 7) was widened

Figure 8. A horse-drawn keel entering the upper end of Sprotbrough lock cut from the river Don to pass buildings that are now part of the *Boat Inn*. In the 1907 improvements, the 90 degree turn was eliminated by excavating land to the left of the vessel's position, producing a straighter canal and a river/canal junction further upriver away from the weir which lies out-of-shot, just to the right of the view.

Figure 9. Loaded keels moored above the original Sheffield size lock at Doncaster circa 1905 before the North Road bridge had been built. *Alan Oliver Collection*

from 18ft (5.5m) to 38ft (11.6m) and the upper entrance to the lock cut (Figure 8) was improved by eliminating the 90° junction with the river and moving it further from the weir.

In 1908, plans were made to lengthen Doncaster lock (Figure 9) and the Puddings made a trial trip to Denaby, collecting 330 tons of coal in eleven Puddings. Five pennings were needed for the train in each direction at Sandall, Doncaster, Sprotbrough and Conisbrough locks, making the whole operation very time-consuming and unprofitable.

The lengthening of Doncaster lock to 215 ft [65.6m] (Figure 10) took place in 1909. At the same time and on virtually the same site, Doncaster Borough Council were building the new North Road Bridge to eliminate the railway level crossing and the Great Northern Railway were widening their bridge to accommodate an extra track. Legal arguments abounded. The S&SYN Company's worry concerned the large cylindrical columns supporting the road bridge which were being built on their land close to the canal and lock. The disputes were eventually resolved by arbitration and all three projects were completed, leaving the waterway with Sandall lock as a 61ft 6ins (18.8m) bottleneck below Doncaster.

In 1913 another of the meanders near Doncaster was cut off by-

Figure 10. A 1909 view of work to lengthen Doncaster lock and build the new North Road bridge. The Great Northern Railway bridge is also visible.

passing Ladies' Harbour with a canal adjoining the one at Milethorn made in 1905.

Puddings abandon Denaby

Bartholomew died in 1919, aged 88. His influence on the S&SYN lived on however and Henry Pickard, the A&CN Company's Engineer, who had designed the 1909 new lock at Doncaster, produced plans in 1929 for 215ft (65.6m) x 22ft (6.7m) locks at Sandall, Sprotbrough and Conisbrough. These were never built and nor was the long lock suggested in 1931 to replace both Sprotbrough and Conisbrough locks to facilitate passage of the Puddings to Denaby. What was built however, was the last of the Bartholomew-suggested canal cuts to the west of the Don's old meandering course. This, the 185 yard (169m) long Gashouse cut, was completed in 1934 by Doncaster Corporation in return for some land and a cash payment from the S&SYN Company as part of the 'Doncaster

Figure 11. Gashouse cut, the final one of five such canal cuts made to the western side of meanders in the former course of the river Don below Doncaster. The photograph was taken in 1954 after the upper end of the former waterway route had been sealed off.

North-West Development Scheme'. Until this time, the gasworks had been alongside the main line of the navigation but now they were sited on a side-arm (Figure 11).

In the event, apart from trial runs, the Puddings never did work to Denaby, though vast quantities of coal were taken away from the staithe here by Sheffield size craft until it closed in 1981.

Puddings to Hatfield

In 1930, the A&CN Company shifted its attention away from Denaby as a source of coal for its hoists at Goole in favour of Hatfield Main Colliery, near Stainforth. They entered into an agreement with the S&SYN Company and Hatfield Main Colliery Company to lengthen Bramwith lock and construct a lay-by where vessels could be loaded at the rail-fed staithe built adjacent to the Stainforth &

Figure 12. Hatfield Main Colliery staithe in 1932, just before the Puddings began to load here. *British Waterways*

Keadby Canal, some distance from the colliery. Estimated to cost £20,000 and, amazingly costing £19,855, the project was funded by the S&SYN Company (£8,000) with loans from the A&CN Company (£8,000) and the colliery company (£4,000) in return for certain toll concessions.

Tonnage figures for the New Junction Canal demonstrate the impact of the Hatfield-Goole Pudding traffic: In 1931, before loading at Hatfield was possible, 1133 vessels carried 105,332 tons on the waterway: by 1936, 1313 vessels carried 129,711 tons but, additionally, 5969 Puddings delivered 211,606 tons of coal loaded at Hatfield for tipping at Goole, a grand total of 341,317 tons.

Nationalisation

Nationalisation of the waterways in 1948, eventually led to yet another of Bartholomew's suggestions being implemented in 1959, forty years after his death, by construction of a new 215ft (65.6m) x 22ft (6.7m) lock at Sandall. Seventeen-pan trains could then pass between Goole and Doncaster wharf with only two pennings at each of the two locks encountered (Sykehouse and Sandall). Prior to 1959, they had

Figure 13. A Pudding being loaded with coke ex-lorry in the shadow of St George's Church at Doncaster *British Waterways*

Figure 14. The diesel tug *West Riding*, launched at Dunston's yard, Thorne, in 1958, hauling a train of empty Puddings through Bramwith whilst en route for Hatfield staithe. It was customary, as here, for the jebus to be pushed in front of the tug when handling a light train and for it to be positioned as in Figure 3 when loaded. *Norman Burnitt/Waterways Museum, Goole*

begun working to Doncaster (Figure 13) to load coal brought by lorry from collieries some distance away when a seventeen-pan train needed seven pennings at Sandall lock.

The late 1950s saw steam tugs replaced by new diesel-engined units (Figure 14) in an attempt to keep the Pudding system up to date. However, the coming of North Sea gas in the late 1960s led to a spectacular fall in demand for coal by London gasworks and this cargo had finished by 1971, though pitch and coke replaced it to some extent.

Ironically, after 1979, the Puddings ceased loading on the A&CN after over a century of successful operation but continued on the S&SYN until 1986, collecting smokeless fuel destined for Scandinavian blast furnaces loaded from lorries at Doncaster.

In a move originally planned in 1939 when Conisbrough mill and its water rights were purchased by the S&SYN Company, Conisbrough lock was eliminated in 1972 by raising the weir at Sprotbrough. Sprotbrough lock itself, however, like all those above Doncaster, remained Sheffield size until the £16 million improvement scheme of 1979-1983 produced locks of dimensions 254ft (77.5m) x 23ft (7.0m) up to Rotherham (Figure 15). The Puddings could now have come to Denaby with ease!

Figure 15. An aerial view of the new lock under construction at Sprotbrough in 1980 as the Improvement Scheme was in progress. A motor barge laden with coal from Denaby is approaching the old Sheffield size lock. *British Waterways*

Sources

The story was traced using the S&SYN Directors' Minute books held at the PRO, Kew (RAIL 866 1-12), the S&SYN Board Minutes at Sheffield Archives (SYN 2/1 -76), copies of the *Doncaster Gazette* in Doncaster Archives and material discovered and collected by Malcolm Fielding of the Inland Waterways Association from the former S&SYN Head Office at Sheffield.

3. Wadworth and the Wordsworth Family

by Ron Spensley

THE WORDSWORTH FAMILY of Penistone and Wadworth, distantly related to the famous Lake District Wordsworths, figured in Brian Barber's excellent survey of the landed gentry of the Doncaster District in the first volume of *Aspects of Doncaster.* The present article traces the circumstances which enabled the family to purchase its Wadworth estate in 1748, and looks at its involvement with local and national issues during the next three-quarters of a century.

The Penistone Origins

In the reign of Henry VIII, according to the early nineteenth century antiquarian, Joseph Hunter, the Wordsworth family lived at Water Hall, Penistone.[1] The Hall, or rather its successor, is still there: in the early 1980s the South Yorkshire County Archaeology Service surveyed the house and concluded that it was most likely built in the first half of the seventeenth century, replacing in two stages a

Figure 1. Water Hall today, much as it was when it was occupied by the Wordsworths. *The Author*

medieval house which was probably moated.[2] As Figure 1 shows, subsequent changes in detail have left its traditional form largely intact.

The rebuilding of Water Hall may have been a consequence of the increase in the family's landed wealth which occurred when Ralph Wordsworth (1591-1663) married Elizabeth (1607-1665), the coheiress of Richard Micklethwaite of Swaithe Hall, Worsbrough.[3] The marriage may have taken place in the mid-1620s, which is within the period suggested above for the rebuilding of the Hall. But it is just possible that Ralph's son, Josias, who inherited the estate in 1661, had some hand in it. The Hall may seem too old-fashioned for this later date, but the new classical style made little impact in the upland areas of the West Riding before the end of the seventeenth century; mullioned windows, for example, were still being put into some houses in early Georgian times.[4]

Very little is known about the Wordsworths' exploitation of their estate; presumably, they leased much of it and lived on their rents. They may also have been involved in the cloth trade, the variety known as 'ordinary Penistones' being supplied from local wool.[5] There is no *direct* evidence of involvement, but

1) the younger sons who migrated to London may have been involved in the cloth trade there (see below)

2) one younger son became a mercer in Sheffield and

3) in the 1760s Josiah Wordsworth of Wadworth built a cloth hall in Penistone which still belonged to the family in 1825.[6]

The London Adventure

The Penistone Josias already referred to (Josias I) died in his eighties in 1709, and his eldest son John in the same year. Many years previously, possibly as early as 1680, Josias I's second son (Josias II) had moved to London where he became a 'merchant' in Mincing Lane, in the City.[7] At the north-eastern end of Mincing Lane stood the Hall of the Cloth Workers' Company, one of the twelve great London Livery Companies. Did Josias II make his fortune there ? Research in the Livery Companies' archives might well cast more light on the matter.

Josias I was clearly successful in his enterprises, eventually becoming a director of the East India Company, which was then by far the largest trading organisation in the country. At some stage he was joined in London by his nephew, Josias III, but whether this was before or after the latter inherited the Penistone estate from John in 1709 is unknown. When, however, his Uncle died without a direct male heir in 1736, Josias III inherited the bulk of his wealth. He also inherited the possessions of his cousin, Samuel, another member of the family who had moved to London, also inspired, perhaps, by Uncle Josias's success. By a mixture of enterprise and good fortune, therefore, Josias III had inherited by the 1740s much of the wealth of the previous generation of Wordsworths, including an estate at Sevenscore near Minster (Thanet), and property in Reigate.[8]

The decision of the younger sons of Josias I to go into trade in the late seventeenth century was not unusual. Under primogeniture, younger sons of prosperous farmers/lesser gentry stood to inherit very little of their father's fortune. Consequently an appreciable number chose (or more likely were directed to) commercial apprenticeships.[9] They hoped, of course, eventually to accumulate enough wealth to establish themselves or the next generation among the landed gentry, and this was probably the long-term aim of Josias II and his younger brother, Elias. But their intentions were thwarted, by the simple failure, in each case, to produce a male heir, and it is somewhat ironical that their strenuous efforts to improve their lot should simply benefit the branch of the family which already had the lion's share.

After his uncle's death, Josias III appears to have lived on in Mincing Lane. He too became an East India Company Director and has been described as a 'Russia Merchant'. Both he and his uncle appear to have held the chairmanship of the East India Company's Court of Directors at various times, and one of them is known to have represented the Company's interests in discussions with Sir Robert Walpole, the leading politician of the times.[10] Towards the end of his life, however, Josias III must have decided that his fortune was sufficient to enable his eldest son, yet another Josias, to return to south Yorkshire to live in style among the landed gentry.

The Wadworth Estate

According to Edward Miller, writing at the beginning of the nineteenth century, there existed at Wadworth, before the Wordsworth's arrival, an Old Hall which was '...formerly inhabited by the families of Copley, Battie, Higgins and Arthur.' The Wordsworths, Miller says, purchased the estate from John Arthur and built a new hall 'adjoining the old one.' Hunter's version, written about twenty years later later, is simply that John Arthur sold to the Wordsworths and that Josias (Hunter conflates father and son) 'much improved the house and estate.'[11]

It was on the basis of these sources and an engraving of Wadworth

Figure 2. Wadworth Old Hall, the Jacobean - possibly Elizabethan - mansion which stood next to the present Hall until the late nineteenth century.

Old Hall (Figure 2) reproduced in John Wainwright's *History of Strafford and Tickhill* (1826) that Marc Girouard wrote the introductory paragraphs of his well-known account of the purchase and building of Wadworth Hall.[12] Girouard stated that the Jacobean Hall illustrated in Wainwright had once (long before the Wordsworths' arrival) belonged to the Copley family, and that its subsequent owner, whom he thought to be John Arthur, sold it to the Wordsworths, together with the rest of the estate, in the mid-eighteenth century. Girouard also believed, unsurprisingly, that this Hall stood on the very site where the Wordsworths were shortly to build their new house.

It is easy to see how Girouard reached these conclusions, but, unfortunately they were incorrect. His error stemmed directly from Miller, who implies that the Copley, Battie, Higgins and Arthur families occupied at different times, the same house and estate, and that the last of these, the Arthurs, sold it to the Wordsworths. But this is not so; there were in fact two quite separate houses and estates and two quite separate set of owners. Visual evidence of this is provided by the Yorkshire sketchbook of the topographical artist, Samuel Buck.[13] In the early 1720s Buck sketched the two halls; they stand only a few yards from each other, very close to the site of the present Wadworth Hall (Figure 3). One is a Jacobean house, immediately recognisable as the illustration in Wainwright. Immediately to the east, however, is another large house, elements of which appear to date from the later seventeenth century. Buck provides two explanatory captions: the Jacobean house is part of Lionel Copley's estate, the second house part of William Arthur's.

There is other evidence, in addition to Buck's drawing. The Jacobean house is known to have been occupied by the Wadworth branch of the Copley family in the first half of the seventeenth century. After the Restoration of the Monarchy in 1660, the family, which had supported the Parliamentary cause, managed nevertheless to hold on to its Wadworth estate. For the next hundred years there was a succession of Lionel Copleys until the death of the last of them, without a direct male heir in 1766 - long after the Wordsworth's arrival. The estate then passed to Godfrey Higgins, the nephew of the last of the Lionels, and remained in his family until the mid-nineteenth century.[14]

The house which the Wordsworths purchased was not, therefore, the Copleys' Jacobean house but the one next door. Since 1741 it had been owned by John Arthur, the son of the William referred to by Buck. The estate appears to have been owned by the Arthurs since the late seventeenth century when the last of the Wadworth Batties - the fourth of the families so misleadingly strung together by Miller - died without an heir.[15] There is good evidence that John Arthur I, the father of the William referred to by Buck, was the first Arthur to own this estate, and it seems reasonable to assume that he purchased it when the last Wadworth Battie died in 1682.[16]

John Arthur I was an 'attorney' (i.e. solicitor) who from 1688 served as Town Clerk to the Corporation of Doncaster. His eldest son, William, was also a prominent member of the Corporation; in 1721, as Recorder, he travelled to London with the Town Clerk to represent Doncaster's interests in connection with a bill for the navigation of the river Don.[17] Given his grandfather and father's involvement in administrative and legal matters, it is no surprise that John Arthur II became a lawyer, being described in one document as 'a Special Pleader of the Middle Temple, London'.[18]

The Arthurs held the right of presentation to the vicarage of Wadworth, and a younger brother of William Arthur was the incumbent from 1711 to 1748. The right then passed to the

Figure 3. Buck's drawing of the two Halls at Wadworth in the 1720s, some thirty years before the present Hall was built. *Wakefield Historical Society Publications*

Wordsworths, who were similarly to use it to the advantage of a member of their own family in the early nineteenth century, when one of Josias IV's grandsons, Charles Arthur Verelst, became vicar.[19] It was all a part of the then universal system of patronage and nepotism.

How the Wordsworths came to choose Wadworth is unclear. John Arthur's younger brother, William, is said to have obtained a place with the East India Company and married a Director's daughter.[20] There is no evidence, as far as I know, that she was a Wordsworth, but the Company may have served as a channel of communication between the Wordsworths and Arthurs.

The estate was purchased in April 1748. In February 1749 Josias III settled it and all his other possessions in Yorkshire on his son, Josias, who was about to marry Ann Robinson, daughter of Arthur Robinson, Collector of the Customs at Sunderland. The settlement was confirmed in his will two months later, shortly after the marriage had taken place. The will also specified that, should Josias IV have no son, his daughters (if he had more than one) were to hold his Yorkshire estates 'in common'.[21] Less than a year later Josias III died and he can never, therefore, have seen the new Wadworth house in its completed state. He was buried in London at St Dunstan's in the East, a few hundred yards from Mincing Lane.[22]

The Building of Wadworth Hall

Given the date of purchase, building cannot have begun until mid-1748 at the earliest. The completion date is unknown, but as James Paine was ordering plaster for the interior in 1750, it was probably no later than 1751.23 The architectural historian, Peter Leach, attempted to link the building of the Hall with the Platt family, Rotherham architect-masons who were involved in the early 1740s in the building of Cusworth Hall, about four miles to the north of Wadworth. On the basis of certain stylistic parallels, Leach concluded that Wadworth, like Cusworth, was begun to a design by George Platt and that, as happened at Cusworth, James Paine was brought in to finish the task.[24]

Interesting as his stylistic comparisons are, there is a chronological problem with Leach's argument. George Platt died in 1743, five years before the Wordsworths purchased Wadworth. If he was responsible for the initial design of Wadworth, it or some version of it is more likely to have been worked upon or brought to Paine's attention by George's son, John, who continued successfully in his father's profession.[25] And here the evidence is tantalisingly circumstantial. John Platt worked for or with Paine at Ormsby Hall after 1750, as Leach says, but there is no evidence that before this he worked at Wadworth. In the early 1760s, as his own notebook shows, he designed Josias Wordsworth's Penistone Cloth Hall and visited Wadworth Hall to discuss the commission with him, but again this has no bearing on the issue under discussion.[26] The only safe conclusion is that Paine and John Platt knew each other, were at times involved in the same project, and probably had some influence on each other's architectural ideas.

The Quality and Style of the Hall

One well-known architectural dictionary applies epithets such as 'solid', 'conservative', 'dignified' and 'conventional' to James Paine and the buildings which he designed.[27] But is this a fair assessment of Wadworth Hall ? 'Solid' - if by that we mean 'durable' - it has certainly proved to be, but what of the rest?

Since the 1950s a number of social and architectural historians have written in praise of the Hall, stressing its artistic unity, its elegance and a quality which several have called 'movement'.[28] By this they mean the way in which the various elements of its external design contrast with or complement each other to produce a lively and dramatic effect. This quality is often associated with the work of the celebrated Scottish architect, Robert Adam, whose reputation in the eighteenth century subsequently eclipsed that of Paine and still stands much higher today. A house like Wadworth, however, which is externally as striking and innovative as anything built by Adam, shows how misleading such conventional judgements can be.

Wadworth (Figures 4 & 5) is best seen as a classical house which synthesises elements of various traditions: the Palladian (the Venetian window, the overall balance between wall and window space), the Baroque (the movement), and possibly the Vernacular (the bold use of dormer windows at a time when they were largely, though not

Figure 4. Wadworth Hall from the south (the entrance front). *Brian Elliott 1994*

Figure 5. The Hall from the West, showing the Venetian or Palladian window which lights the main staircase. *Brian Elliott 1994*

entirely, absent from fashionable architecture). An architect's ideas were being continually modified, especially by his patrons who might or might not require particular features. It seems that the Wordsworths did not, for instance, wish their new house to have the typically rusticated basement floor which would normally contain the offices and kitchen, but that they did want dormer windows in the attic storey.

The Wadworth Enclosure of 1766

The Wadworth Enclosure award involved, as often in the Midlands and North, the abolition of tithes, the holder receiving as compensation part of the land which was enclosed. Tithe owners generally welcomed this change as they had always found it difficult to secure their dues. In Wadworth, Josias Wordsworth, who held the right of presentation to the vicarage, possessed as was normal in such situations the important corn tithes, and this was reflected in his allocation under the award. He received 584 acres of the total 2057 acres enclosed - nearly 30 per cent. As the map of the award indicates his previous holdings of land in Wadworth were

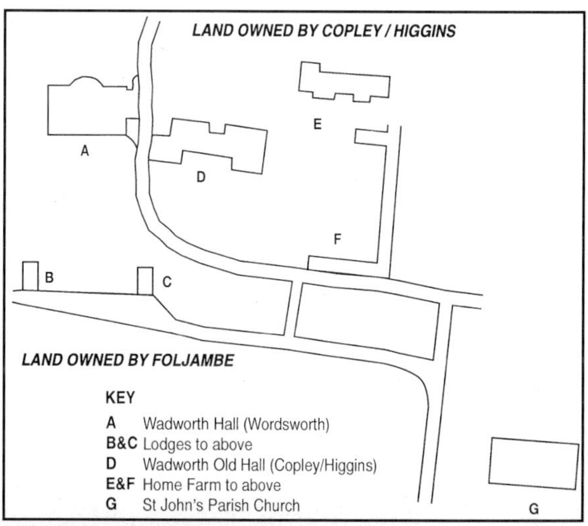

Figure 6. Reconstruction of the neighbourhood of Wadworth Hall in the second half of the eighteenth century, based on the Enclosure Map of 1766.

comparatively small; following the enclosure they were much more in keeping with his fine house, and would, of course, greatly increase his income from rent. The main drawback was that the land was not in a block, but scattered over different parts of the parish, as was the case with the land of the other three major landowners. But although it was unlikely that the Hall would ever stand at the centre of a unified estate (Figure 6), the award of 58 acres to its immediate north and west was at least a step in the right direction.[29]

The Next Generation - The Kents and Verelsts

With the Wordsworth name and fortune so strongly invested in the senior branch of the family, their failure to produce a son must have been a major disappointment to Ann and Josias Wordsworth; the gentry and nobility always placed great importance on the continuance of the family name and the 'honour' associated with it.

Nevertheless, the Wordsworths must have been very pleased at the time with the marriages which they were able to arrange for their daughters, Mary and Ann. Mary was born in 1751, at about the time when the new Hall was completed and Ann a year or so later.[30] There is no record of the births of either daughter in the Wadworth parish records and they probably took place in London. Nothing is known about their childhoods but they appear in the records in 1771, when they were married, on the same day, at St John's, Wadworth.[31]

Mary Wordsworth married Sir Charles Kent of Fornham St Genevieve, in Suffolk, the son of Charles Egleton, a London merchant. Egleton served as Sheriff of London in 1743, was knighted the same year, and in 1744 married Sarah Kent the only daughter of Samuel Kent who at that time owned the estate at Fornham. When Sarah's only brother died childless in 1766, it passed to the Egletons.[32]

On Sir Charles' death in 1769, his son, the Charles who was to marry Mary Wordsworth, inherited the Fornham estate. It was a condition of the inheritance that he changed his name from Egleton to Kent, and unsurprisingly he complied. Two years later and by then married to Mary Wordsworth, he was knighted. It took him some time, apparently, to make his mark, but in 1781-2 his willingness to serve as Sheriff of Suffolk seems to have done the trick. The position of county sheriff was generally unpopular among the gentry - it was essentially ceremonial and involved a good deal of expensive entertaining, the cost of which fell largely upon the post-holder himself. Kent appears, however, to have been rewarded for his pains, and in 1782 he became a baronet, this being the highest title a

Figure 7. 'Mrs Verelst', George Romney's portrait of Ann at the time of her marriage. Clifton Park Museum. *Courtesy of Rotherham Metropolitan Borough Council*

commoner could hold. Baronetcies could be bought, but the recommendation of a powerful patron was required too. In Kent's case this was the Duke of Grafton, owner of an estate to the south of Thetford, only a few miles from Fornham. The Duke controlled the Parliamentary seat of Thetford, and eighteen months later Kent was returned as one of its two Members. It was a contested election (many were not), but the Duke had only to exercise his influence over or generosity towards the voters to produce the 'right' result - after all there were only twenty-one of them![32] Kent remained the Member for Thetford until 1790, when he chose not to stand again. There is no record of his ever speaking in Parliament, but no doubt he could be trusted upon to vote the 'right' way when occasion demanded.

In the same year (1784) the Kents' only son and heir, another Charles, was born. As far as is known they lived either on their Fornham estate, near Bury St Edmonds - well known as a town to which the gentry resorted [34] - or in their house in Chandos Street, Cavendish Square, one of the most fashionable areas of London. Their son was baptised at St George's Church, Hanover Square, only a few hundred yards away. In London they would have been neighbours to the Verelsts, since the latter occupied a house in the Parish of St James, Westminster, in the same fashionable area.[35]

Ann Wordsworth married Harry Verelst, the former Governor of Bengal. Verelst's ancestors were Dutch portrait and flower painters who came to England after the Restoration. Born in 1733 - nothing seems to be known about his parents - he was brought up by his uncle, Willem, a portrait painter. Among the latter's patrons was the East India Company, and it was possibly on his recommendation that Harry entered the Company's service in Bengal in about 1750.[36]

He rose spectacularly and in 1767 was appointed Governor of Bengal, a position which he held for the next two and a half years. He then returned to England with, according to one modern biographer, 'an easy fortune'.[37]

Back home, Verelst was labelled by the jealous and resentful as a 'nabob' - an upstart, a man of obscure family origins who had made a fortune in India and now intended to establish himself in the upper ranks of the gentry or even creep into the nobility.[38] Ex-governor Robert Clive, for example, managed to become a Viscount. Verelst, however, with a smaller fortune than Clive and a family pedigree which was obscure even by nabob standards, must have known that an alliance with another family on the rise would provide the best basis, in the long term, for social advancement. Money could buy style, and style, given time, would overcome prejudice. He and Josias must have been well-informed about each other's affairs as a consequence of their common involvement with the East India Company, and Verelst's choice is a good indication of just how rich the Wordsworths were at this time.

At first everything went well. Ann Verelst's new status was strikingly commemorated in her full-length, larger-than-life portrait by George Romney, one of the foremost painters of the time. This painting is now on display at Clifton Park Museum, Rotherham, and is undeniably impressive (Figure 7). At about the same time, the Verelsts purchased Aston Hall estate near Rotherham from the Earl

Figure 8. Aston Hall, near Rotherham, designed for the Verelsts by the York architect John Carr. *Brian Elliott*

of Holderness, and commissioned a new house which, in size, though not necessarily in architectural merit, visibly surpassed Wadworth Hall(Figure 8).[39] Unfortunately, however, Verelst was about to become embroiled in a bitter legal dispute which would soon put paid to all his personal hopes and ambitions.

By 1772 the affairs of the East India Company were under parliamentary scrutiny following a collapse in the value of its stock and allegations of administrative corruption during a famine in Bengal.[40] Much criticism focussed upon the role of the Directors of the Company and Robert Clive, the Governor before Verelst, but Verelst himself was pursued in the courts by William Bolts, an adventurer whom Verelst had had imprisoned and then deported from Bengal on a corruption charge. From 1774 onwards Verelst lost a series of court cases over his actions in Bengal, and was required to pay damages and costs running to many thousands of pounds. Financial ruin eventually forced him to leave the country and he died in exile at Boulogne in 1785.[41]

After her husband's death, Ann Verelst succeeded in the Chancery Court in establishing a claim to Aston Hall, and although, as Hunter indicates, it was briefly advertised for sale, she was able to repossess it herself under favourable terms.[42] There is no evidence, however, that she, or her eldest son, had the resources to reside at Aston until the 1820s and it appears to have been leased until then. The Wederburn-Websters, an ill-assorted couple who leased the house during the latter part of the Napoleonic Wars were acquaintances of Byron, who visited on occasion and seems to have had a very brief, half-hearted affair with Lady Frances.[43]

During this long period Ann Verelst lived in various places in the South of England: at 'The Cottage', Old Windsor - a small Georgian villa rather than a cottage in the modern sense of the word; at Shurton Court, a few miles from Bridgewater in Somerset; and (by 1819) at Holywell House, a few miles west of Southampton. She and her son frequently borrowed money at this time; loans of £150 in 1810, £600 in 1812 and £900 in 1819 are recorded and there were presumably others.[44]

In 1803 her eldest son, Harry, married Amelia Herbert, of Muckross in County Kerry. In the context of the Verelsts' fortunes in the previous twenty years or so this was, socially, something of a recovery. Amelia's father was a distant relative of the Earls of Pembroke and had himself married the daughter of a Viscount. Amelia, however, was not his heir, and her marriage portion would be restricted as Herbert had two sons to provide for.[45]

The Estate after Josias's Death

When Josias died in 1780, aged 61, his daughters inherited both the Wadworth and Penistone estates, holding them 'in common' as required by their grandfather's will.[46] Under this arrangement all transactions concerning the two estates had to be undertaken jointly by the Kents and Verelsts; for example their redemption of the land tax on both estates, which was effected by 1802 under a scheme introduced by William Pitt the Younger in 1798 as a means of financing the wars with France.[47]

The early years of peace after 1815 were difficult for landlords and tenant farmers alike. Previously high wartime food prices fell drastically and farming became a more than usually uncertain business. By the early 1820s, when prices were at their lowest, it became impossible for landlords to find tenants in some cases, and in others tenancies had to be agreed on a short-term basis. This is probably the background to an agreement in 1822 between Joseph Seels, a tenant farmer, and the Kents and Verelsts that Seels would in future rent his land (194 acres) on a yearly basis.[48] Further insight into the instability of tenant farming at this period can be obtained by comparing the names and holdings of the principal tenants in 1800 (recorded in connection with the redemption of the land tax) with those in 1825 (the year of the sale of the estate).[49] No name is common to both periods; in 1800 the principal tenants were said to be James Green - 174 acres, John Shaw - 124 acres, Thomas Parkinson - 94 acres and Thomas Shaw - 61 acres, whereas in 1825 they were Lawrence Smith - 228 acres; Joseph Seels - 194 acres; the Bletchers - 113 acres; John Elvidge - 62 acres; Joseph Surr - 11 acres.

Ann Wordsworth, Josias's widow, continued to live at the Hall until her death in 1814, aged ninety-three.[50] The following year her daughters leased it to Sir William Lumley, a younger brother of the Earl of Scarbrough (the Earl resided at Sandbeck Park, only five miles to the south of Wadworth). Lumley had served as a commander of cavalry under Wellington in Spain and Portugal during the Napoleonic Wars. He returned to England in 1811, was promoted in 1814 to the rank of Lieutenant General and knighted the following year. Wadworth became available at just the right time, enabling him to settle within easy distance of his titled brother's main residence. The patronage of an influential relative mattered far more than it does today and the Earl's influence may have been a factor in Sir William's eventual appointment in 1819 to the post of Commander in Chief and Governor of Bermuda.[51]

The Kents and Verelsts received £241 annually for the leasing of the Hall and grounds, and Sir William undertook to put and maintain in good order the Hall and other buildings mentioned in the agreement (maintenance of the roof excepted).[52] Important though the rent itself may have been, the benefits gained from no longer having to maintain and run the Hall must have been considerable. The words 'put in good order' may be significant too; it is difficult to imagine that the Hall would have been modernised to any extent during the last years of Mary Wordsworth's long life.

After Sir William Lumley's departure in 1819 the next tenant of the Hall was probably Sir George Scovell. Scovell, like Lumley, had served as a cavalry officer in Spain and Portugal during the Napoleanic Wars, and had also taken part in the Waterloo campaign.[53] It is not known whether he immediately replaced Lumley at the Hall, but he appears to have been there in 1822.

The last tenant of the Hall before its sale in 1825 was the Rev William Ewbank, the son of the Rev Andrew Ewbank who was Rector of Londesbrough (part of the Yorkshire estates of the Dukes of Devonshire) and Burghwallis (north of Doncaster). None of William's own rectorships - Kirklington, Bolton Percy - explain why he wished to live at Wadworth, but he was also chaplain to Earl Fitzwilliam, whose main residence was only a few miles away.[54] This was, of course, the last great age of pluralism and substitution by curate in the Anglican Church, when many clergymen lived anywhere but in the parish for which they were supposed to be responsible. The Wadworth parish records, incidentally, show that Ewbank officiated just once at St John's, Wadworth, when (perhaps in an emergency) he took a burial service in 1823.[55] He continued to lease the Hall during James Owen's brief ownership and is last recorded as tenant in April 1826.[56]

In addition to holding the house, grounds, and various outbuildings connected with it, Ewbank also tenanted the home farm, opposite the western lodge of the Hall on the other side of Stubbin Lane, a twenty acre field known as Wike Field, and a cherry orchard of four acres, extending to the south of the home farm as far as Church Road.[57]

The Sale of the Hall

With their real income from tenancies probably in decline over a number of years, it is not surprising that by 1825 the Kents and Verelsts had decided to sell their Yorkshire estates. Both families were probably in need of capital: Harry Verelst to develop his Aston estate after the years of uncertainty, Sir Charles Egleton Kent to maintain at Poynton House in Lincolnshire and no doubt at his London residence the lifestyle appropriate to one who had married the daughter of an earl.[58] Wadworth Hall was a fine house in itself but fashions had changed, and it was still hemmed in by land and buildings belonging to the Foljambe (increasingly) and Higgins families.

The sale - 'to take place by auction on 11 June 1825 or to be agreed by private treaty before that date' - was advertised in the Doncaster Gazette. The house, the notice says, would be of interest to 'a family of rank' or 'a farmer of superior fortune' - an uneasy compromise, perhaps, between dignity and realism.[59]

As matters turned out, an auction was not necessary. The Bawtry solicitor, James Owen, made an offer of £25,000 for everything and this was accepted - we still have the written agreement.[60] Within a few months the Hall and part of the land were back on the market as Owen, like any enterprising man of the law, sought to make his profit.[61] But that is another phase of their history.

Notes and References

1. Hunter, Rev J *South Yorkshire: The History and Topography of the Deanery of Doncaster,* vol 2, London, 1831, p 335.
2. South Yorkshire County Archaeological Service, *Report on Water Hall, Penistone for the County Monuments and Sites Record,* ref PI/2195, 1983.
3. Addy J (ed) *A Further History of Penistone,* Penistone WEA, 1965, p 67: Wordsworth G G, *Some Notes on the Wordsworths of Penistone,* Ambleside, St Oswald Press, 1929, p 13 & 18.
4. Pevsner N *The Buildings of England: Yorkshire, The West Riding,* 2nd ed, London, Penguin Books, 1967, pp 41-42.
5. Addy *op cit,* p 54.
6. Hunter *op cit,* p 335.
7. Bedford E G *Genealogical Memoranda Relating to the Family of Wordsworth,* London, Mitchell and Hughes, 1881, p 27.
8. Doncaster Archives, DX/BAX/D/24/2/2, Will of Josias Wordsworth the Elder.
9. Sharpe, J A, *Early Modern England: A Social History, 1550-1760,* London, Edward Arnold, 1987, p 174.
10. Chaudhuri K N *The Trading World of Asia and the East India Company 1660-1760,* Cambridge, CUP, 1978, p 394.
11. Miller E *The History and Antiquities of Doncaster and its Vicinity* etc, Doncaster, W Sheardown, 1804, p 255; Hunter *op cit,* vol 1, 1828, p 253.
12. Girouard M 'Wadworth Hall, Yorkshire, The Property of the West Riding County Council', *Country Life,* 104 (1 Sept 1966), 494f. The engraving is in Wainwright G *Yorkshire, An Historical and Topographical Introduction* etc, Sheffield, J Blackwell, 1829.
13. *Samuel Buck's Yorkshire Sketchbook,* Wakefield, Wakefield Historical Publications, 1979, pp 70-71.
14. Goodchild J 'Lionel Copley, 17th Century Capitalist', in Jones M (ed), *Aspects of Rotherham 2,* Barnsley, Wharncliffe Publishing, 1996, p 28; Hey D 'The Ironworks at Chapeltown', *Transactions of the Hunter Archaeological Society,* vol 10, 1979, pp 252-53; West Yorkshire Archives: Registry of Deeds, BF/367/531, Higgins to Tofield. For recent independent confirmation of the separate identities of the two Halls and estates see Alan Harvey's unpublished study *The Church of St John The Baptist,* Wadworth, April 1997, pp 66-67 & 71-72.
15. Burke J & Burke J B *A Genealogical and Heraldic Dictionary of the Landed Gentry of Great Britain and Ireland,* vol 2, London, Henry Coburn, 1846, p 1645.

16. Wakefield Registry of Deeds, YY/506/624, Arthur to Wordsworth.
17. *A Calendar to the Records of the Borough of Doncaster: Courtiers of the Corporation,* Doncaster, 1902, p 187.
18. *An Index to the Archbishop of York's Marriage Bonds and Allegations 1735-1749,* compiled by E B Newsome, Borthwick Lists and Indexes, 15, 1996.
19. Clay J W (ed) *Joseph Hunter, Familiae Minorum Gentum,* London, The Harleian Society, 1894-96, vol II, p 632. Charles Arthur Verelst was Vicar of Wadworth from 1820 to 1837.
20. Doncaster Archives, DZ/SYK/5, p 173; SYK/19, p 53.
21. Doncaster Archives, Baxter Papers, DX/Bax D/24/2/2, Abstract of the Title to Wadworth Hall and Estate 1748-1825.
22. Sheffield Archives, LD/136.
23. Doncaster Archives, Battie-Wrightson MSS, BWA/22.
24. Leach P *James Paine,* London, A Zwemmer, 1988, p 212.
25. Potts J D *Platt of Rotherham: Mason-Architects 1700-1810,* Sheffield, 1959, p 4.
26. Potts *op cit,* p 10.
27. Fleming J, Honour H & Pevsner N *The Penguin Dictionary of Architecture* (4th ed), London, 1991.
28. See, for example, Hey D *Buildings of Britain 1550-1750: Yorkshire,* Ashbourne, Moorland Publishing, 1981, p 115.
29. Doncaster Archives, P21/9/A1 & A2, The Wadworth Enclosure Award and Map.
30. *Burke's Complete Baronetage,* vol V (1707-1800), Exeter, William Pollard, 1906, p 225.
31. Doncaster Archives, P/21/1/A/3, Parish of St John's, Wadworth: Baptisms, Marriages and Burials 1749-1790.
32. Coppinger W A *The Manors of Suffolk,* vol VI, Manchester, privately printed, 1910, p 269.
33. *Bury Free Post,* 25 March, 1 April and 25 April 1782. For the political background, see Namier L & Brooke J *The History of Parliament: The House of Commons 1754-1790,* vols I & III, London, HMSO, 1964.
34. Defoe D *A Tour through the Whole Island of Great Britain,* London, Penguin Classics, 1986, pp 73-74.
35. For these and other details about the Kents, see *Complete Barontage,* loc cit, and Sheffield Archives, LD/1358; for the Verelsts, Sheffield Archives, LD/136.
36. Woodruff P *The Men Who Ruled India: The Founders,* London, Jonathan Cape, 1953, p 119.
37. *The Dictionary of National Biography from the Earliest Times to 1900* (hereafter DNB), vol XX, Oxford, OUP, 1917, pp 248-49. For an estimate of the fortune which Verelst may have made in Bengal, see Marshall P J *East India Fortunes: The British in Bengal in the Eighteenth Century,* Oxford, Clarendon Press, 1976, 1976, p 190 & 239.
38. For hostility to the 'nabobs', see Edwardes M *The Nabobs at Home,* London, Constable, 1991.
39. Hunter, *op cit* (vol 2), p 165.
40. Edwardes, *op cit,* p 55f
41. DNB, *loc cit.*
42. Rotherham Archives, 0301/F/Verelst & Wordsworth Papers.
43. Quennell P *Byron, the Years of Fame,* London, Reprint Society, 1943, p 147f.
44. See note 42.
45. For the Herberts, see Burke's Irish Family Records, 5th ed, London, 1976.
46. See note 21.
47. Sheffield City Archives, LD 1359.
48. Doncaster Archives, DX/Bax/S/61227.
49. Doncaster Archives, DX/Bax/S/61219, June 1825 Sale Notice.
50. *Doncaster Gazette,* 25 November 1814.
51. DNB, vol XII, p 276.
52. Doncaster Archives, DX/Bax/S/61217.
53. DNB, vol XVII, p 1061. My thanks to Alan Harvey for the information about Sir George's occupancy of the Hall.
54. *Burke's Landed Gentry,* 18th ed, London, vol III, 1972, p 304f.
55. Doncaster Archives, P21/1/C1, St John's Wadworth Parish Register: Burials.
56. The last assessment of his Poor Relief contribution, based on his tenancy of the Hall, was made in April 1826 (Doncaster Archives, P21/6/B1/8).
57. See note 48.
58. He had married Sophia, a younger daughter of William Lygon, 1st Earl Beauchamp *(Complete Baronetage, loc cit).*
59. *Doncaster Gazette,* 6 May 1825.
60. See note 47
61. Doncaster Archives, DX/Bax/61219, November Sale Notice.

4. ELGAR'S VISIT TO DONCASTER, 1909

by Philip L Scowcroft

Figure 1. Elgar: A portrait from around the turn of the century.

DONCASTER IS, AND PROBABLY has always been, a provincial town of less than first importance, musically speaking. During the nineteenth century it had its share of the celebrity concerts so common in that period and often featuring eminent instrumentalists and singers. French-born Louis Jullien, who created the promenade concert in this country, had brought his orchestra to the Mansion House in 1844 and three more times to the town between 1849 and 1858. The charismatic violinist Niccolo Paganini had paid a visit in 1833[1] and the equally charismatic pianist Franz Liszt in 1840.[2] Other important composer-performers came to the town in later years.[3] But even more outstanding than any of these occasions was the concert just five years before the Great War in which Sir Edward Elgar (Figure 1) conducted the London Symphony Orchestra. The *Doncaster Gazette* described this as 'one of the most notable ever held in the town', a frequently overdone phrase in local newspapers, but surely justified in this case.

Elgar's association with the LSO, an orchestra founded in 1904, was a close one and lasted the best part of thirty years. He took it on its first provincial tour in November 1905 - travelling tired him and gave him headaches but he needed the money at that time (later he was to conduct the orchestra, several times, for nothing, when its funds were low or during the Great War). The LSO gave the first performances of several Elgar compositions, notably the *Introduction* and *Allegro* and the *Second Symphony*, and the first London performance of the *First Symphony*, and much later made many recordings of his works under the composer's direction. In 1911, on the retirement of Hans Richter, it invited Sir Edward to become its permanent conductor.[4]

Two years before that invitation, the LSO's autumn tour of the provinces included Doncaster on its itinerary, in fact giving the first of the 1909-10 series of Subscription Concerts at the Corn Exchange at 8pm on Thursday 28 October 1909 (Figure 2). Although doubts were expressed by the *Doncaster Chronicle,* even after the event[5], as to the concert being 'too severely musical for a popular gathering who like broad and telling effects rather than the delicate interpretation of subtle melody' (a somewhat circumlocutory way of suggesting that Doncaster was, unjustly in this writer's view, an unmusical town), attendance was happily 'very good indeed', despite the high prices, for those days of 7s(35p) and 5s (25p) of reserved seats - unreserved seats could be had for 2s. (10p) and 1s. (5p).

The programme was mainly devoted to Elgar's own music, but it began with a 'spirited' account if Weber's *Euryanthe* overture, in which, continued the *Gazette* critic, 'the dramatic passages and charming melodies...received full justice from the orchestra'. The principal work in the first half was Sir Edward's *First Symphony,* which the printed programme accorded an enormous note several pages long, boasting a number of musical examples. Doncaster thus heard one of the hundred-odd performances this symphony enjoyed during the first year or so after its premiere (surely a record for any symphony), being, according to the *Chronicle,* only the ninth provincial town to hear it.[6] The *Gazette* noted that this performance was 'a magnificent volume of sound - which even the bad acoustics of the Corn Exchange could not seriously impair[7] - and a rendering in which every tone, every shade of meaning...was brought out to the full'. Interestingly, the report felt it necessary, even as late as 1909, to say that 'it is making a large demand upon the artistic appreciation of an ordinary concert audience to place the whole of [a symphony] before them at a sitting'. The *Chronicle,* whose correspondent appeared to believe the symphony was in three movements (admittedly the scherzo and slow movement are played without a break) spoke of its 'majestic beauty' and the 'intense feeling' of the reading. The audience heard it throughout (said the *Gazette*) with 'rapt attention' and greeted it at the end with 'an enthusiastic burst of applause'.

After the interval Elgar introduced three movements from his second *Wand*

MM. GEORGE & BROMLEY BOOTH'S
FIRST
DONCASTER
SUBSCRIPTION
CONCERT.
TENTH SEASON.
CORN EXCHANGE, OCT. 28, at 8.
SIR EDWARD ELGAR
AND
THE LONDON SYMPHONY
ORCHESTRA.
The Programme will include ELGAR'S NEW SYMPHONY; and "SEA PICTURES" sung by Miss
PHYLLIS LETT.
PRICES: 7s. and 5s. (Reserved); 2s. and 1s. (Unreserved). 1s. Tickets sold only at the Hall at 7.45. Early door at 7. 6d. extra. Ordinary doors, 7.30. Concert at 8.
Plan and Bookings at Messrs. Meacock's, High Street, Doncaster. Tel. 211. 4629

Figure 2. Advertisement for Elgar's concert in Doncaster (from the *Doncaster Gazette,* 22 October 1909). Note the significance of 'Early' and 'Ordinary' doors in ticket pricing. Meacock's was Doncaster's leading music shop for over half a century.

of Youth suite: *Little Bells, The Tame Bear* and *Wild Bears,* the last of which had to be encored, and the *Elegy* from Tchaikovsky's *Serenade for Strings* which featured, as the *Gazette* noticed, 'very delicate work...its pathos and restrained sentiment were beautifully handled'.

The soloist was a popular contralto, Phyllis Lett, who had been heard several times before in the town. In the first half she had warmed up with Handel's *Ombra mai fu* - the so-called *Largo* - 'with splendid feeling and rich ripe tone' and compared by the *Chronicle* to that of Clara Butt, a frequent visitor to Doncaster before and after 1909, though the *Gazette* stressed that Elgar 'happily does not believe in the over sentimentalising of this familiar work'. Now she tackled three of the five *Sea Pictures* (originally written indeed for Clara Butt in 1899), *Sea Slumber Song, Where Corals Lie* and *The Swimmer,* and apparently did so with considerable sympathy. A long programme by present day standards concluded rousingly with Elgar's then relatively new fourth *Pomp and Circumstance* march.

Both newspapers remarked on Elgar's conducting technique, the *Chronicle* contenting itself with referring to his 'nervous energy and directive genius', the *Gazette* saying it was 'a study in itself...his manner is nervous and forceful, almost jerky, but entirely free from fuss or violence', an appreciation confirming other more sophisticated contemporary accounts.

The concert was a landmark in Doncaster's musical history. Sir Edward never returned, but his music has retained its popularity in the town.[8]

Notes and References

1. 18 October, at the New Concert Room in High Street, whose Ionic pillars still stand. Two singers shared the programme with him. Paganini played his own *Prelude e Rondo Brillante, Sonata Militaire* and his Variations on *Nel Cor Piu* and *The Carnival of Venice.*
2. 7 December, at the Mansion House. Liszt was assisted by another pianist, W F Lockwood (who promoted the concert) in a Duet by Thalberg and three vocalists, Miss Bassani, Miss Steele and John Orlando Parry. Liszt's solos included the *Grand Galop Chromatique.* His 'brilliancy and rapidity of touch and tone combined with exquisite delicacy and feeling' was noted by the *Doncaster Gazette* correspondent of the day.
3. Among these we may instance the violinist Henri Vieuxtemps (1863), harpist John Thomas (1873), pianist Cecile Chaminade (1895), conductor John Philip Sousa with his band (1905), cellist W H Squire (1908-10), pianist Ferruccio Busoni (1908), pianist Rutland Boughton (1917), conductor Hamilton Harty (1923), organist Louis Vierne (1925) and pianist Benjamin Britten (1946).
4. He declined the invitation. For Elgar's work with the LSO, see Michael Kennedy, *Portrait of Elgar* (Oxford, 1968, subsequently revised).
5. Both *Gazette* and *Chronicle* reports appeared on 5 November 1909.
6. Its premiere was at the Free Trade Hall, Manchester on 3 December 1908.
7. In the latter part at least the Corn Exchange's musical career - the last concert took place there in 1967 - its acoustics were generally reckoned to be very good. It has recently been rebuilt after a disastrous fire in 1994.

The writer promoted an Elgar Festival in Doncaster in May 1974 and has compiled a list of local Elgar performances since 1900 with hundreds of entries.

5. Doncaster Mansion House: An Anniversary Tour

by Brian Barber

THIS YEAR DONCASTER MANSION HOUSE CELEBRATES the two-hundred and fiftieth anniversary of its official opening on 15 April 1749.[1] (Figure 1) In the mid-eighteenth century, Doncaster was a medium-sized market town with about two and a half thousand inhabitants and was a local social centre, having as its focus the already-famous race course. It was governed by a corporation which could trace its documented history back over six hundred years. The corporation had acquired a town hall by converting the former church of St Mary Magdalene, in the market place, which it had purchased in 1557.[2] By the 1730s, it was considering how it could provide a more suitable place for civic entertaining - its 'public feasts' - than its customary practice of hiring houses or rooms in inns and transporting a growing accumulation of cutlery and tableware around the town.[3] In 1738, the council decided to find a permanent solution by providing a municipal mansion house, following the example of York, begun in 1725, although the earliest civic mansion house was built by the corporation of Newcastle-upon-Tyne in 1691, London (1739) and Bristol (1783) followed. In these major towns, there were also assembly rooms financed by private subscribers, but in a much smaller town like Doncaster, there was probably not sufficient private wealth at this period to finance assembly rooms by subscription, and so the mansion house fulfilled the role of both.[4]

The corporation purchased

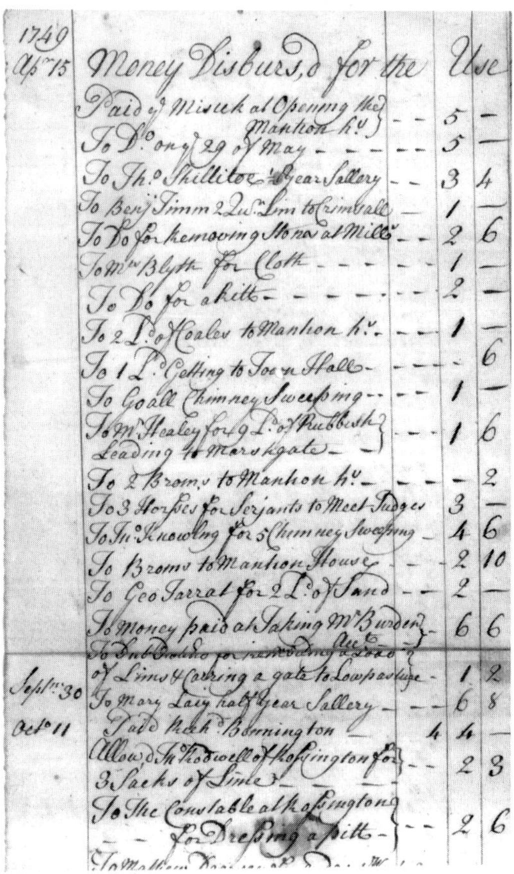

1749 Ap. 15 Money Disburs'd for the Use

Paid ye Musick at Opening the Mansion ho.	5	—
To Do. on ye 29 of May	5	—
To Tho. Shillitoe ½ Year Sallery	3	4
To Benj. Simm 2 Qu. Lime to [illegible]	1	—
To Do for Removing Stone at Mill	2	6
To Mr Blyth for Cloth	1	—
To Do for a Kitt	2	—
To 2 Ld of Coales to Mansion ho.	1	—
To 1 Ld Getting to Town Hall		6
To Goall Chimney Sweeping	1	—
To Mr Healey for 9 Ld of Rubbish Leading to Marshgate	1	6
To 2 Brooms to Mansion ho.	—	2
To 3 Horses for Serjants to Meet Judges	3	—
To Jn. Knowling for 5 Chimney Sweeping	4	6
To Brooms to Mansion House	2	10
To Geo Jarrat for 2 Ld of Sand	2	—
To Money paid at Taking Mr [illegible]	6	6
To [illegible] of Lime & Carrying a gate to Low pasture	1	2
Sept. 30 To Mary Lacy half Year Sallery	6	8
Oct. 11 Paid Rich. Bonnington	4 4	—
Allowd Jn [illegible] for 3 Sacks of Lime	2	3
To The Constable at [illegible] for Dressing a pitt	2	6

Figure 1. This account of 'Money Disburs'd for the Use of the Corporation' is the only document to preserve the date of the official opening of the Mansion House.

part of a garden on the west side of High Street in 1739 for £170. It had been part of the site of the Carmelite Priory, established by 1346 and dissolved, along with other religious houses, by order of Henry VIII in 1538. The priory had been a place of pilgrimage, the home of the miracle-working image of 'Our Lady of Doncaster'. The grounds of the priory took up two and a half acres within the defences of the town from Hallgate, where there was a 'great gate house' opposite Scot lane, westward to what is now Duke Street.[5]

The designer of the building which was finally completed in 1748 was James Paine (1717-1789, Figure 2), although, as we shall see, with some assistance from a very distinguished source. He was appointed in 1744 and the mayor laid the 'first stone' on 26 March of that year. In the corporation records the architect is described as 'Mr Pain of Wragby'[6] as he was then superintending the rebuilding of Nostell Priory (in the parish of Wragby, near Wakefield for Sir Rowland Winn. Paine's success with the Doncaster mansion house led to offers of work from the local gentry, and he was involved in the building or alteration of Hickleton, Cusworth, Sandbeck and Wadworth Halls. It was the beginning of a long and successful career which was to see him designing or remodelling over thirty country houses and fulfilling a score of London commissions.

Paine publicised his Doncaster commission in 1751, with the publication in London of his *Plans, Elevations, Sections and other Ornaments of the Mansion House belonging to the Corporation of Doncaster.*[7] The elements of his plan were simple. On the ground

Figure 2. James Paine aged thirty-four as he appears, drawn by Francis Hayman, on the title page of his published Plans of the Mansion House of 1751. An architect whose work can be found across England from Northumberland to Wiltshire, he and his contemporary, Sir Robert Taylor, had few competitors before Robert Adam appeared on the scene in the 1760s.

floor, the entrance hall and staircase were flanked by two rooms on each side (with a butler's room and backstairs) and on the first floor there was a reception room, running the entire width of the building, and adjoining it, an anteroom on each side of the staircase. The first floor plan conforms to that for assembly rooms already in general use: a set of three rooms, comprising a ballroom, tea room and card room (Figure 3). In the published work, the mansion house is shown as flanked on each side by two houses, one supposedly for the mayor and one for the recorder, who was judge of the borough court. These are very unlikely to have formed part of the design approved by the corporation, not least because it did not own the land which would have been needed to build them (Figure 4).

Figure 3. The plan of the principal storey shows the simple plan of the first floor: a double-cube room, the 'banquetting room' in Paine's description, and two rooms flanking the staircase. The room on the right is smaller to accommodate the siting of the backstairs, which subsequent alterations, probably in 1806, removed to the west end of the new dining room.

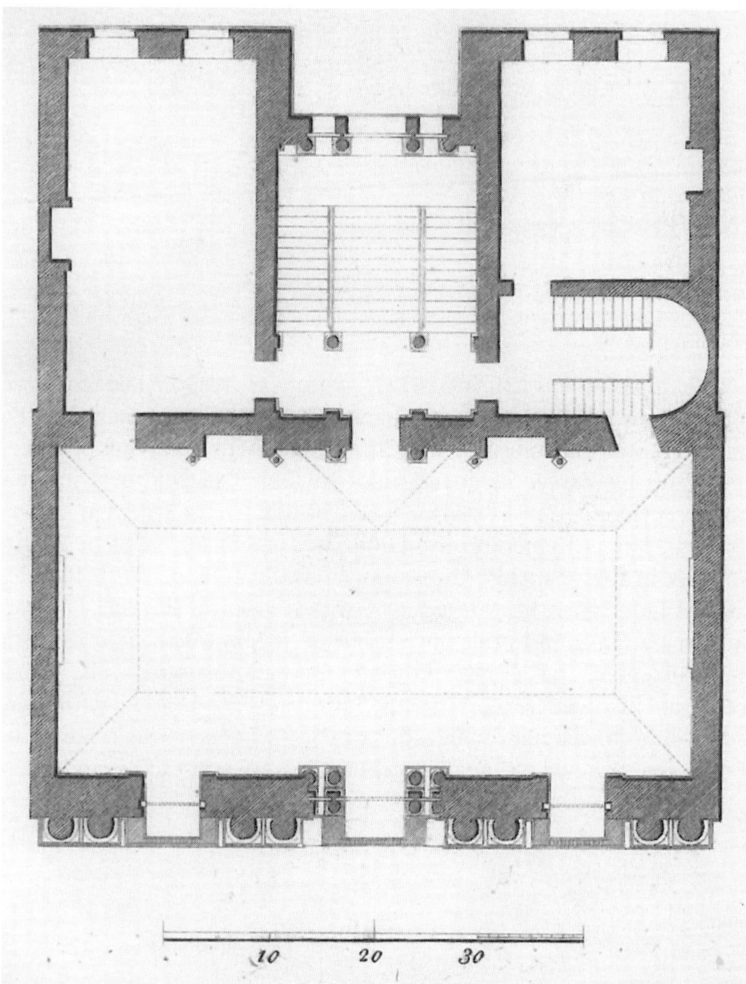

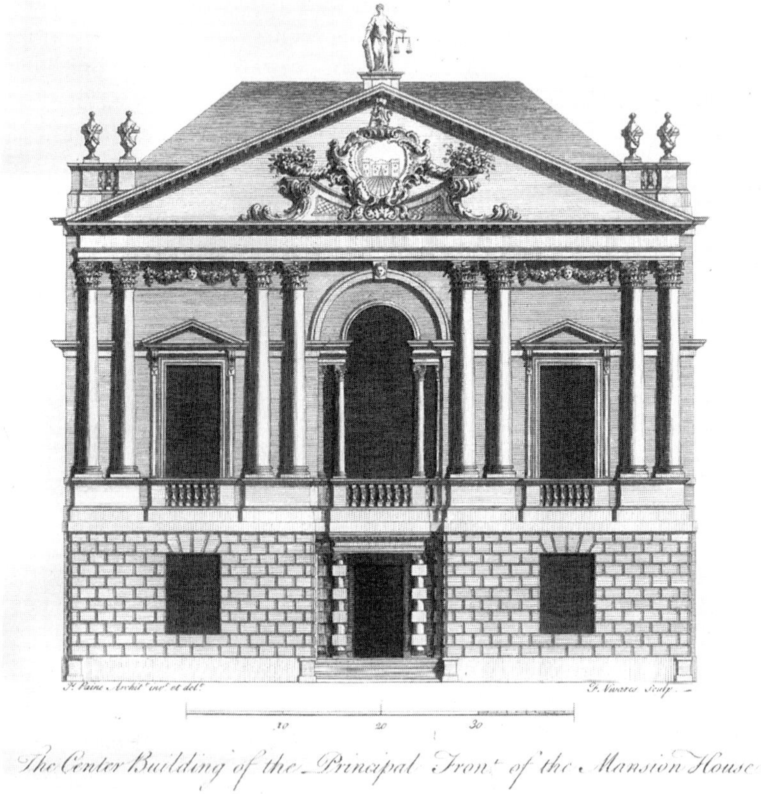

Figure 4. The 'Centre Building' as it was named in the Plans was in fact all that the corporation commissioned and all that was built, despite the implication of the published plans.

William Lindley (c1739-1818), who was responsible for two programmes of alterations, was hardly of the eminence achieved by Paine, but was a distinguished local architect with a thriving practice. Beginning his career as an assistant to John Carr of York, he had moved to Doncaster by 1783, when he became a freeman of the borough. His influence on the Doncaster townscape is to be found not only in the Mansion House but in Hallgate and South Parade. Beyond Doncaster, he worked on Cantley, Hooton Pagnell, Owston and Serlby Halls and built the church of St John, Wakefield to form the centrepiece of a splendid late Georgian suburb. The third architect involved was William Hurst (1787-1844), who was responsible for extensive alterations in 1831.[8] Hurst was a native of Doncaster, the son of an innkeeper, and an apprentice and then

Figure 5. Alderman Hurst, the architect, not only worked on the Mansion House but designed other buildings in the vicinity. The Subscription Rooms, obstinately known by their unregenerate title of the 'Betting Rooms', were designed by Woodhead and Hurst in 1826. The main room was 90 feet by 20 feet. Regrettably, the pillared portico alone remains now.

partner of Lindley. He was also a member of the corporation, becoming a councillor in 1814, alderman in 1828 and mayor later in the same year. Locally, his principal buildings are Christ Church, Priory Place Chapel, and the Subscription Rooms (Figure 5); he also designed the new town of Goole for the Aire and Calder Navigation Company. Since the social life of the town was dominated by horse-racing, it is natural that the racing-calendar exerted an influence over the history of the mansion house. It seems possible that the building of the new dining room in 1806 formed part of the preparations for the visit to the races in the September of that year of the Prince Regent, the future king George IV, and his brother, the Duke of Clarence, who succeeded him as William IV. Significantly, the royal brothers stayed at Lindley's home in South Parade.[9] The motive for the 1831 extension was explicitly 'for rendering sufficient accommodation to the Nobility and Gentry attending Doncaster Races'.[10]

The building, decoration and furnishing of the Mansion House was the work of a variety of craftsmen, some of whose names have gone entirely unrecorded and some of whom are no more than names. However, we know that amongst them were the distinguished plasterers Thomas Perritt and Joseph Rose, who were not local men, although Rose worked locally at a number of houses, including Cusworth and Sandbeck. John Thompson (1714-1771), the 'bricklayer', or building contractor, was succeeeded in his business by his great-nephew William Anelay, whose name continues in use today by the firm of Anelay of York, building craftsmen.[11] The carpenter, William Rickard (1727-1809) was a member of the corporation, chosen as a councillor in 1756, alderman in 1773 and twice mayor in 1774 and 1782.

The first reference to furnishing the house dates from 3 November 1748, when it was decided that there was to be:

> *for the great room, Deal Benches covered with red of green Bays* [ie baize] *and two large stove Grates for ye great room*[;] *for ye drawing room one Stove Grate Walnut Tree Chairs with Spanish Leather Bottoms*[;] *for ye low rooms plain grates and Elm Chairs*[;] *four Glass Chandeliiers for ye Vestibule*[;] *Ranges for ye Kitchen and Back Kitchen and such other Kitchen furniture as Nanny Smith shall advise.*[12]

Few of the original furnishings now remain.[13] These comprise six mirrored sconces (wall-mounted candle-holders), purchased for £60.18s. (£60.72 pence) and six mahogany card tables. There are also three clocks (one of them a modern purchase) by George Hallifax (c1726-1811). A migrant from a clock-making family in Barnsley,[14] he was admitted a freeman in 1750. Like Rickard, and equally long-lived, he also was a member of the corporation, becoming a councillor in 1755, alderman fifteen years later and mayor in 1775 and again in 1791. More survives from the furniture commissioned after the extensions of 1806. There are twenty-seven mahogony dining chairs, which cost a total of £66.14s.(£66.60 pence), and three large mahogany sideboard tables, which cost £49.8s.6d.(£49.42 pence), all by William Lilley of Doncaster (c1753-1816). There is also a fine carved mahogany chair purchased in 1779 for use by the mayor at the corporation's manorial court at Rossington.[15] (Figure 6) In the last two centuries, the contents of the house have been augmented by purchases and gifts, some, but unfortunately not all, chosen because they are contemporary in style with the period of the house, others because they have particular relevance to the history of the town. Amongst this latter group is a long-case clock by Benjamin Huntsman who, before moving to Sheffield and becoming one of the pioneers of steel-making, lived nearby on Hallgate, on the site of Priory Place.

The cost of the mansion house is not ascertainable. The anonymous author of a mayoral chronicle of 1779 gave the cost as

Figure 6 (a) The handsome chair commissioned for the corporation's manorial court room at Rossington, and now kept at the Mansion House, was first used at the court held on 1 November 1779. The occasion was clearly used for the entertainment of the corporation's tenants in Rossington (probably a rent-day dinner), as this bill for the festivities shows. Over 300 pints of ale, 12 bottles of wine and 4 of each of rum and brandy were drunk to the music of the borough band or 'waits'.

Figure 6 (b) The Rossington court chair was described by its makers, Stokes and Stacey as 'A Mahog: Cabriolet chair With a Rampt: Lyon Carvd: on back & Ribbd: on Top'. It cost £3.13s.6d. (£3.67p) amd a further 1s.6d. for a man to carry it to Rossington. Nothing is known of the makers; if they were local, as seems likely, no record of them has survived.

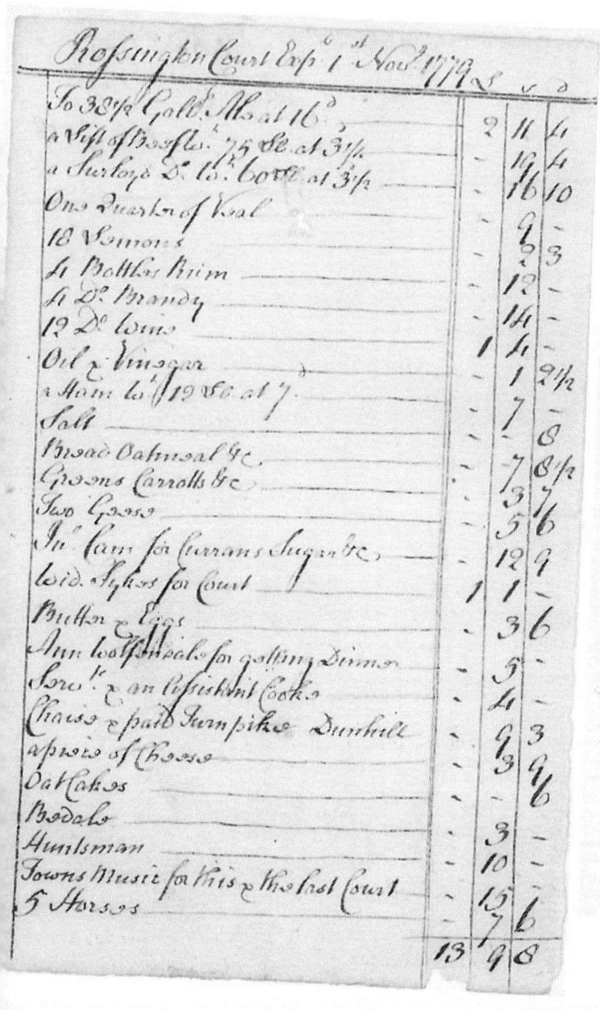

Rossington Court Exps 1st Novr 1779

	£	s	d
To 38½ Gallns Ale at 16d	2	11	4
a Sift of Beef lbs 75 lb at 3½	-	16	4
a Surloyn Do lb 60 lb at 3½	-	16	10
One Quarter of Veal	-	9	-
18 Lemons	-	2	3
4 Bottles Rum	-	12	-
4 Do Brandy	-	14	-
12 Do Wine	1	4	-
Oil & Vinegar	-	1	2½
a Ham wt 19 lb at 7d	-	7	-
Salt	-	-	8
Bread Oatmeal &c	-	7	8½
Greens Carrotts &c	-	3	7
Two Geese	-	5	6
Jno Cam for Currans Sugar &c	-	12	9
Wid. Sykes for Court	1	1	-
Butter & Eggs	-	3	6
Ann Wolfendale for getting Dinner	-	5	-
Servt & an Assistant Cooks	-	4	-
Chaise & paid Turnpike Dunhill	-	9	3
a piece of Cheese	-	3	9
Oat Cakes	-	-	6
Bedals	-	3	-
Huntsman	-	10	-
Towns Music for this & the last Court	-	15	-
5 Horses	-	7	6
	13	9	8

£6,000 and Edward Miller in 1804 claimed the cost of building and furnishing to be 'upwards of £8,000'. There now appears to be no way of confirming this. In February 1746, the corporation approved Paine's estimate of £4,523.4s.6d. clearly for the fabric alone. In 1831, an examination of municipal finances over the previous century estimated a total of around £5,600 before the alterations of the nineteenth century. The alterations of 1801 were contracted for at £950, but no accounts survive; nor do they for the substantial works of 1805-6. The alterations of 1831 cost not less than £1,800 but, again, there are no accounts.[16] As problematical as the cost is some of the building history of the house. The absence of much documentation and the absence of any early plans apart from those published by Paine have led vital parts of this history to rely solely on informed deduction, much of it based on the inventories.[17]

Three features are notable about the exterior. The first is that of the scale of the building. At the time of its construction, Hallgate, although one of the principal streets of the town, would have had a much more modest appearance that it now has. There would have been none of the three-storied Georgian town houses or Victorian banks and commercial premises. Instead, typical buildings would have been traditional two-storey cottages, the sole remaining

Figure 7. This view of the Mansion House published in September 1804 in Miller's *History* shows a later eighteenth century three-storied town house to the left and to the right an older two-storied building. The latter was probably typical of the buildings on High Street at the time the Mansion House was built.

Figure 8. One of the unrealised drawings for a facade for the Palace of Whitehall by Inigo Jones shows clearly the source of Paine's design for Doncaster Mansion House.

example of which is to be seen across the road near Baxtergate. In this context, the mansion house would have seemed an even more imposing structure that it does to-day.[18] (Figure 7)

The second is that the building is not entirely as Paine designed it. The building was originally topped by a giant pediment spanning the entire facade. The parapet is the result of alterations carried out in 1801, when it is also likely that the stonework was given its present facing of stucco. The new pediment was topped by a lion, a symbol which the borough took from one of the heraldic badges used by king Edward IV. Edward granted the borough its charter of incorporation in 1467, and the lion badge adorns the margin of the charter.[19] The white lion was a badge of the earls of March, through whom Edward claimed his right to the throne, although when he became king, the lion became golden.

The third, and most notable feature is that the design of the facade is not by Paine at all. It is a copy of a facade which was originally intended for the royal Palace of Whitehall by Inigo Jones, the most important British architect of the early seventeenth century. Jones spent many years fruitlessly redesigning the Whitehall palace for James I and his son Charles I. His famous banqueting hall, from which king Charles I stepped to execution, is now the only complete building to survive from the palace, which was destroyed by fire in 1698, its site gradually colonised by government offices. Paine decided to carry out part of Jones' scheme in his work in Doncaster, so providing the borough with a building of even more distinguished origin than it could have expected.[20] (Figure 8)

The ground floor is in 'rusticated' stone, that is with each block carved with recessed edges. This was a traditional means of indicating the lower status of this floor compared with the first, or principal floor, which contains the main rooms of the house. The importance of the first floor is emphasised externally by its height, accentuated by the tall central Venetian window, (its design not finalised until February 1748),[21] the four pairs of Corinthian columns and the elaborate carving in between them. Entry is through the deeply-recessed front door, another detail copied from Inigo Jones.

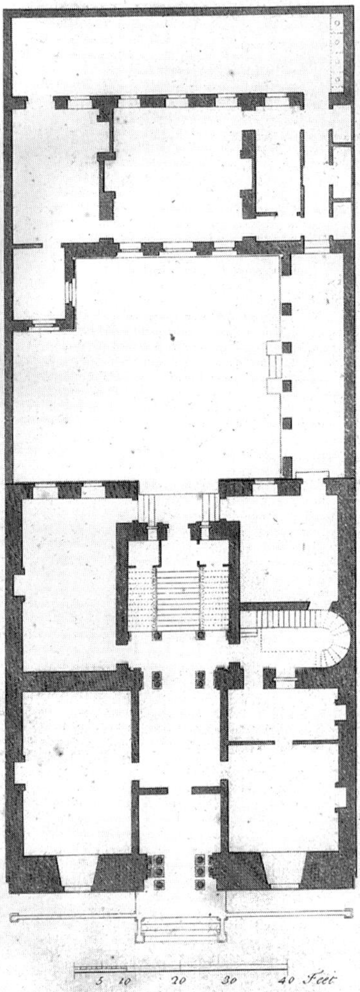

Figure 9. The plan of the 'rustick story' or ground floor shows the four rooms arranged around the vestibule and staircase and, on the right centre, the butler's room and backstairs. Beyond are the kitchens and domestic offices joined to the main building by a colonnade.

A tour of the interior of the building thus takes us through the front door and into the ground floor. In Paine's scheme, there were four principal rooms on this 'rustick storey' (Figure 9). The published plans give no indication of the use of these rooms, but the inventories of the house, regularly made by the mansion house committee from 1756 to 1908, allow us to discover the use to which the rooms were put and how they were furnished (Figure 10). In the mid-eighteenth century, the ground floor housed the grandly-titled 'court of judicature' where the mayor and the three alderman-magistrates held the magistrates (petty sessions) court each Monday morning, the gentlemen's dining room, the aldermen's room and the councillors' room. By October 1826, the court room had ceased to appear in the inventory, but there was a committee room and, by December 1835, a ground-floor room had been allocated to the mayor. There was also the butler's room (now the attendants' room) and the back stairs, by which the servants gained access to the two floors. The back stairs were relocated during the alterations carried out in 1806.

Behind the mansion house was a court yard. A colonnade (converted into a closed passage in the mid-1820s) along the north side joined the house to the single-storied domestic range of buildings: a little back kitchen, larder, back kitchen, grand kitchen and pastry larder and behind these a back yard where poultry was reared. Underneath the ground floor in the brick-built vaults were the servants' hall and keeping cellars, which in the 1820s housed prodigious quantities of port: 1,380 bottles in 1828.

The vestibule contains a wall-clock in a japanned oak case by George Hallifax, originally valued at seven guineas (£7.35 p) which he provided for the Mansion House as part of the condition for his admittance as a freeman.[22] There are also four dining chairs from the set supplied by William Lilley in 1801 and two mahogany card tables dating from about 1755. To the left of the front door is the front committee room. Amongst the contents are twenty-one chairs from the Lilley set, a second wall clock by Hallifax, originally acquired for the kitchen in 1770 and a portrait in oils of Frederick Fisher (1794-1850) of Westfield House, Balby. He was a solicitor, and town clerk until displaced in 1836 after the reform of the corporation. He returned to the council, this time as a councillor, in 1838 and became mayor in 1848. He was also a landowner, selling some of his

Figure 10. The first page of the inventory of the Mansion House taken in October 1781. The inventories from 1756 to 1909 provide invaluable information on the contents of the rooms, their changing uses and alterations to the building.

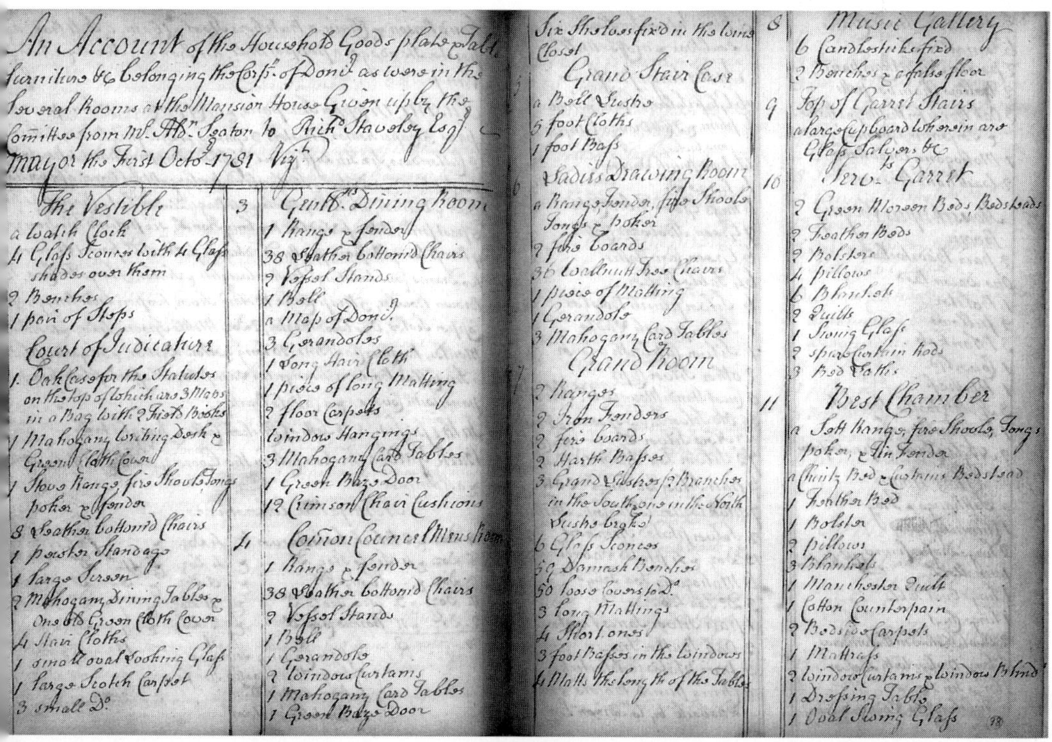

An Account of the Household Goods plate & Table furniture &c belonging the Corpn. of Doncr. as were in the several Rooms at the Mansion House Given up by the Comittee from Mr. Aldn. Seaton to Richd. Staveley Esqr. Mayor the First Octo. 1781 Vizt.

The Vestible
a Watch Clock
4 Glass Sconces with 4 Glass shades over them
2 Benches
1 pair of Steps

Court of Judicature
1 Oak Case for the Statutes on the top of which are 3 Maps in a Bag with 2 Field Books
1 Mahogany Writing Desk & Green Cloth Cover
1 Stove Range, fire Shovel Tongs poker & fender
8 Leather bottomd Chairs
1 pewter Standage
1 Large Screen
2 Mahogany Dining Tables & one old Green Cloth Cover
4 Stair Cloths
1 small oval Looking Glass
1 Large Scotch Carpet
3 small Do.

3 Gentln. Dining Room
1 Range & fender
38 Leather bottomd Chairs
2 Vessel Stands
1 Bell
a Map of Doncr.
3 Gerandoles
1 Long Hair Cloth
1 piece of long Matting
2 floor Carpets
Window Hangings
3 Mahogany Card Tables
1 Green Baze Door
12 Crimson Chair Cushions

4 Comon Council Mens Room
1 Range & fender
38 Leather bottomd Chairs
2 Vessel Stands
1 Bell
1 Gerandole
2 Window Curtains
1 Mahogany Card Tables
1 Green Baze Door

Six Shelves fixd in the Wine Closet

5 Grand Stair Case
a Bell Leash
5 foot Cloths
1 foot Bass

6 Ladies Drawing Room
a Range, fender, fire Shovel Tongs & poker
2 fire boards
36 Wallnutt tree Chairs
1 piece of Matting
1 Gerandole
3 Mahogany Card Tables

7 Grand Room
2 Ranges
2 Iron Fenders
2 fire boards
2 Harth Basses
3 Grand Lustres 2 Branches in the South one in the North Leashs broke
6 Glass Sconces
59 Damask Benches
50 loose Covers to Do.
3 Long Mattings
4 Short ones
3 foot Basses in the Windows
4 Matts the length of the Tables

8 Music Gallery
6 Candlesticks fixd
2 Benches & a false floor

9 Top of Garret Stairs
a large Cupboard wherein are Glass Salvers &c

10 Servts. Garret
2 Green Moreen Beds Bedsteads
2 Feather Beds
2 Bolsters
4 pillows
6 Blankets
2 Quilts
1 Swing Glass
2 spare Curtain Rods
3 Bed Mats

11 Best Chamber
a Stove Range, fire Shovel, Tongs poker, & tin fender
a Chintz Bed & Curtains Bedstead
1 Feather Bed
1 Bolster
2 pillows
3 Blankets
1 Manchester Quilt
1 Cotton Counterpain
2 Bedside Carpets
1 Mattrass
2 Window Curtains & Window Blind
1 Dressing Table
1 Oval Swing Glass

land for the building of 'Plant Town' (now part of the site of Hyde Park flats) to house the newly-arrived railway plant workers in the early 1850s.[23] There are also photographs of the mayors of Doncaster since local government reorganisation in 1974. The mayoral portraits from 1835 to 1974 are now held at Doncaster Archives.[24] The contents of the back committee room include a fine nineteenth century dining table and a set of twenty-five dining chairs and three carvers and a wall clock by Richard Holt of Newark.

The mayor was not allocated a room of his (later, but only on five occasions before 1974, was it her) own until 1835. In the mayor's parlour, on the right of the front door, is an arm-chair elaborately carved from bog oak by C Collinson of Doncaster and exhibited at the Great Exhibition of 1851. There is also a long-case clock by John Philip of London. This is the only room specifically allocated to the mayor. Unlike the other municipal mansion houses, Doncaster's was not intended as an official residence for the mayor. Not until 1779 do bedroom furnishings appear, one the 'best chamber' and the other for the housekeeper, both probably in the garret. The best chamber continues to appear until, in 1834, its contents became those of a storeroom, and in the following year it was demoted to the 'spare bedroom'.

Behind the mayoral parlour is the site of the former backstairs of the Paine building now a corridor, and contains the Rossington manorial court chair and a portrait of John Whitaker, in whose first mayoralty the chair was made. He was mayor in 1778 and again in 1784. The adjacent members' room has a long-case clock by George Hallifax and two of the Lilley set of chairs.

The grand staircase is in the imperial style, that is dividing into two separate flights at an intermediate landing. Above this landing to the left and the right are two cast metal life-sized 'Italian pages with lights', which first appear in the inventories in 1865. The flight of stairs on the left has plasterwork topped by the head of Minerva, the goddess of wisdom and that on the right has over it the head of Mercury, the god of commerce. Originally, the staircase was lit by a Venetian window (no doubt intended as symmetrical with that at the front of the building) directly above it. When the gallery allowing direct communication between the drawing room and the banqueting room was created in 1864, the window was moved to the new external wall.[25] In 1986, its glass was replaced by the new panes of a specially-commissioned 'peace window' to commemorate the International Year of Peace. On the landing are two more of the six card-tables of about 1755 and two of the six rococo mirrored sconces supplied in 1755. The remaining four hang on the walls in the gallery of 1864. The brass candle-holders are recent replacements as the originals had been removed at some time in the past.

What has been known as the ballroom since 1826 is the principal room of the Mansion House in every sense. Originally known as the 'Grand Room' it is a double cube: its dimensions are sixty feet in length, thirty in height and thirty in width. Almost certainly Paine is again paying homage to his great predecessor, Inigo Jones, amongst whose works is a double-cube room at Wilton House, Dorset, for the Earl of Pembroke.[26] The 'Grand Room' occupies the entire first floor of the front of the building. Paine, to judge from his published plans, intended the ceiling and wall panels to have paintings (Figure 11). These were not carried out, and the decoration of the room is instead in plaster-work of a remarkable quality, some of it now painted in unauthentic colours. The room is lighted by three crystal chandeliers, which the corporation decided to buy in 1750 for about £140.[27] There is a musicians' gallery over the principal entrance doors. The oil paintings include portraits of three of the owners of Wentworth Woodhouse: the Marquess of Rockingham, briefly prime minister before his early death in 1782, and the fifth and sixth earls Fitzwilliam, who succeeded the marquess at Wentworth Woodhouse. The portrait of a youthful king George III was presented by Lord Eardley in September 1804.[28] To the right and left of the staircase are the two other first-floor rooms of Paine's original plan, although one

Figure 11. The 'Window Side of the Banquetting Room' as shown in the Plans was as much wishful thinking by Paine, no doubt with an eye to impress potential clients, as his elevation showing the 'center building' flanked by two subsidiary ones. By the time his Plans were published, the fine plasterwork had been completed, but decoration as shown in the engraving had never been planned or executed.

has been radically altered. The drawing room, once called the ladies' dressing room, is as Paine designed it. The portraits, apart from a copy of that of the actress Sarah Siddons by Sir Joshua Reynolds, are of local notables: T B Mason, town clerk in succession to F W Fisher, from 1836 to 1867; Archdeacon Sandford, vicar of Doncaster from 1905 to 1928, and the second viscount Halifax, father of the Foreign Secretary in Chamberlain's government, whose family lived at Hickleton Hall from 1830 until after the Second World War.

It is likely that what is now known as the Ladies' Room was radically altered in works carried out in 1806 and 1831. In Paine's original scheme, the room was much smaller, as the passage containing the back stairs separated it from the Great Room. In 1806 new back stairs were built at the west end of the dining room, to allow direct communication with the kitchens. The space formerly occupied by the old back stairs on the first floor was absorbed into the new ladies' room. The building of the dining room beyond the west wall would have deprived this room of natural light, and so roof-lighting of some description must have been installed in 1806. In 1831, council agreed to spend £250 so that 'the card room be raised as high as the supper room' [29] and the present handsome rectangular roof lantern was probably constructed at this time.

The room is hung with eight portraits in oils. Five of these are royal portraits, spanning the twentieth century from Edward VII to Elizabeth II. Five others are locals, and include Sir William Bryan Cooke (1782-1851), the owner of the Owston estate and, as a local supporter of moderate reform, the first mayor of the reformed corporation in 1836,[30] and Sir Edmund Beckett (1787-1874), better known by his former surname of Denison. Resident in South Parade, he was an MP for the West Riding parliamentary division from 1841 to 1859 and the chairman of the Great Northern Railway Company. It was he who was responsible for arranging the transfer of the company's locomotive plant from Boston, Lincolnshire to Doncaster in 1852, so radically changing the character of the town.

Figure 12. This view of the Mansion House was taken at the beginning of 1999, shortly after exterior renovation work was completed. Amongst those involved was the firm of William Aneley of York. This firm, formerly based in Doncaster, was founded by John Thompson, a master bricklayer who worked on the building 250 years earlier.

He also had the more dubious distinction of lending to Sir Robert Peel, former prime minister and creator of the modern Conservative party, the horse from which he fell to his death in 1850. Like many prominent nineteenth century businessmen, Beckett failed to receive an entry in the original Dictionary of National Biography, but the omission is to be repaired in the forthcoming new edition.[31]

What is now the council chamber formerly had a more convivial use. The principal purpose of the extensions of 1806 was to provide this handsome new supper or dining room, superseding the small gentlemen's dining room on the ground floor. Its dimensions echo those of the Grand Room, for it is sixty feet long, but three feet shorter in both height and width, which helps to make this room appear less forbiddingly lofty than the other. Like the Grand Room, it also has a musicians' gallery. The room was certainly altered, although unfortunately to an indefinable extent, in 1831. The inventory of 1834 (the first since 1830) mentions a 'new orchestra', or musicians' gallery and in 1831, £130 was spent on a mirror and fifty guineas (£157.50 pence) on two chandeliers.[32] The description of this as the 'banqueting room' first appeared in 1865.That this room has been used since 1914 as the council chamber is indicative of the increasing adoption of the mansion house as a municipal building which has superseded its social role. As we have seen, three rooms in the mansion house were in use as a court room and rooms for elected members of the council from the beginning. Doncaster demolished its sixteenth century town hall in 1847 to make way for the new covered market, and the guildhall, built in the following year, was not large enough to meet the expanding needs of even nineteenth century local government. Visitors to the mansion house today (Figure 12) are more likely to be answering a summons to business than an invitation to pleasure.

Figure 13. William Brooke, a mercer, was mayor of Doncaster three times. The Mansion House was being built during his second term in 1746-47. He was wealthy enough to be able to commission three family portraits from the young Joseph Wright of Derby in the early 1760s: of himself, his daughter Elizabeth (his wife had died in 1743) and his son-in-law William Pigott, the son of the vicar of Doncaster. By a happy coincidence, all three portraits were acquired by Doncaster Museum and Art Gallery in 1999. *Reproduced by permission of Doncaster Museum Service, Doncaster MBC.*

Notes and References

1. The date does not appear in the corporation's act books, and is preserved only in an account of disbursements: '1749 Apr 15 Paid ye Musick at Opening the Mantion hs. 5 shillings' (Doncaster Archives, reference: AB/6/1/6).
2. Doncaster Archives, AB/7/4/50.
3. See G H Martin and others, *Doncaster: A Borough and Its Charters* (Doncaster, 1994), pp 81-83.
4. See M Giroud, *The English Town* (London, 1990), chapter 7. T Oliver, *A New Picture of Newcastle upon Tyne* (Newcastle upon Tyne, 1831), pp 55-56, records that the cost of the mansion house there was £6,000.
5. Doncaster Archives, AB/2/3 page 721, and DZMD/51. The museum at Kings Lynn has a pilgrim badge from the priory (Doncaster Archives, DZMZ/81).
6. P Leach, *James Paine* (London, 1988), pp 99-101 and 182-183. Doncaster Archives, AB/2/1/3, p 755 and AB/3/4/1, entry for 1744.
7. Doncaster Archives, AB/ENG/1/1.
8. H Colvin, *A Biographical Dictionary of British Architects, 1660-1840* (London, 1978) for both Lindley and Hurst and D Lindstrum, *West Yorkshire Architects and Architecture* (London, 1978), pages 103 and 192 for Lindley.
9. Doncaster Archives, reference AB/2/1/4, p 263.
10. Doncaster Archives, reference AB/2/2/3/3, 11 Feb 1831.
11. H E C Stapleton (ed), *A Skilful Master-Builder* (York,1975), pp 5-6.
12. Doncaster Archives, AB/2/1/3, p 788. *A Calendar to the Records of the Borough of Doncaster* (Doncaster,1902), p 220, mistranscribes this entry.
13. These are discussed in C Gilbert, 'Furniture by local makers at Doncaster mansion house', *Regional Furniture,* volume II, 1988, pp 23-32.
14. Information on his origins kindly provided by Brian Elliott.
15. Doncaster Archives, AB/3/4/1, entry under 1778 John Whitaker, May 31 (1779).
16. Doncaster Archives, AB/3/4/1, entry under Peter Carr 1748; E Miller, *History of Doncaster* (1804), p 140; Doncaster Archives, AB/2/1/3, p 768; AB/6/1/12; AB/2/2/3/1, 2 Dec 1800; AB/2/2/3/3, 11 Feb 1831, 4 May 1831, 10 Aug 1831.
17. Doncaster Archives, AB/2/25. Reference is not given to the inventories where the year is given in the text.
18. See the plate in E Miller, *History of Doncaster* (1804), facing page 140, which shows a typical traditional cottage to the right of the mansion house.
19. Doncaster Archives, AB/1/4 and E A Danbury, 'The Decoration of the Doncaster Borough Charters', pp 32-35 in G H Martin and others, *Doncaster: A Borough and Its Charters* (Doncaster, 1994).
20. J Summerson, *Architecture in Britain 1530 to 1830* (Harmondsworth, 1970), pp 138-139.
21. Doncaster Archives, AB/2/1/3, p 783.
22. Doncaster Archives, AB/2/1/3, p 792.
23. Doncaster Archives, AB/4/10; AB/CLERK/27/1; DY/TB/4/63.
24. Doncaster Archives, AB/MAYOR/1-111.
25. This minor improvement (which can have cost no more than £375, according to the published accounts of the corporation, 1863-1864 and 1864-1865, Doncaster Archives, reference AB/TREAS/1/3) was the work of the borough surveyor (see the *Nottingham, Lincolnshire and Doncaster Gazette,* 20 Jan 1865, p 7, col 2)
26. Summerson, *op cit,* pp 142-144.
27. Doncaster Archives, AB/2/1/3, p 792.
28. Doncaster Archives, AB/2/1/4, p 248.
29. Doncaster Archives, AB/2/2/3/3, 4 May 1831.
30. An obituary appeared in the Liberal-supporting *Doncaster Gazette,* which was reprinted as a pamphlet accompanied by four sonnets, a memorial sermon and other items. A copy is amongst the Cooke of Wheatley client papers of J Dawson, Doncaster Archives, reference DY/DAW/12/3.
31. The author is Professor I McLean of Nuffield College, Oxford.
32. Doncaster Archives, reference AB/2/2/3/3, 10 Aug 1831.

6. Descent into Debt: The Corporation's Finances, 1800-1838

by George Owen

AT THE BEGINNING of the nineteenth century the Corporation of Doncaster owned considerable property. In addition to houses and buildings and a modest amount of land in Doncaster itself, it owned some 1900 acres in Balby, Hexthorpe and Sandall, and another 2571 acres in Rossington, almost the entire village.[1] The Corporation drew rents from these properties and had other income from such assets as the grandstand at the racecourse, its shares in the River Dun Company and interest from loans made to two turnpike trusts. An estimate put the value of the Corporation's estate, even before the end of the eighteenth century, at more than £100,000. This was far greater than that of some larger towns.[2]

The day to day management of the Corporation's finances was in the hands of their steward. He collected rents and other receipts, settled bills and made other disbursements. Stewards had been employed to manage the finances since 1752.[3] In November 1801 George Burks, formerly a woollen and linen draper, was appointed as steward. Although he had no obvious qualifications for the post he left ledgers which are models of neatness and accuracy. Highly respected for his integrity, he held the post for nearly a quarter of a century. After his death in 1824 his place was taken by his son Henry and then in 1827 by Richard Dennison, the Corporation's land agent.

This account of the Corporation's finances during the early nineteenth century begins with an analysis of Burks' receipts and disbursements during the financial year 6 April 1805 to 5 April 1806 since this happens to be unusually well documented. During the year, disbursements were greater than receipts and the Corporation had recourse to borrowing to make up the deficit. This pattern was constantly repeated during the next thirty years and led to the growth of a very large debt and correspondingly high interest payments to the Corporation's creditors. In 1838 a newly-elected Town Council chose to meet a growing financial crisis by selling off its most valuable property, the Rossington estate, in order to reduce its debts.

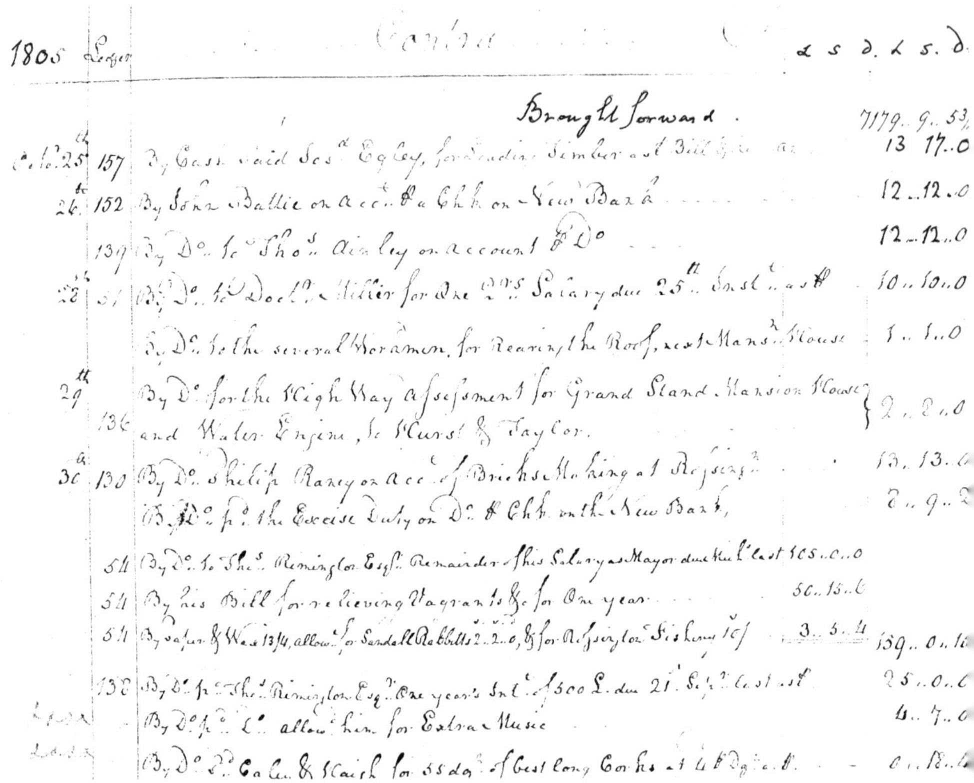

Figure 1. Extract from George Burks' cash book showing daily entries of transactions for 25-30 October 1805. *Doncaster Archives AB6/1/7/4.*

Burks' first duty was to make daily entries of all transactions, whether receipts or disbursements, in his cash book (Figure 1). [4] He then entered receipts in a second account book, his 'rental'

(Figure 2).[5] At the end of each financial year he submitted his cash book, rental and other accounts to a committee appointed by the Corporation. In practice checking was generally done by the Mayor and one or two senior members of the Corporation. After 1814 a Finance Committee was appointed each year, meeting monthly to check the accounts and issuing an annual report.

Burks showed rent receipts of £7,285 (to the nearest £) in his 1805-6 rental. A curious feature of this total was that it included items which were not rents of land or buildings but were forms of investment or trading income. They included the dividends paid on shares held by the Corporation in the River Dun Company, the interest on loans made to turnpike trusts and receipts from the sale of timber from the Corporation's woodlands at Sandal and Rossington. Other items included the 'water rents' paid by householders supplied with water from the Corporation's waterworks and receipts from the sale of tickets to the grandstand. There was also a 'rent' of £100 a year due from Alderman John Robinson, a timber merchant and wharfinger. This was in return for the lease of the Corporation's right to charge a toll of twopence a ton on goods carried on the river through the town.

These non-rent items in Burks' list of rent receipts came to £2,823 in 1805-6, leaving £4,462 as the actual amount paid in rents on land and property. The importance of the Rossington estate is shown by its contributing £1,520, or more than a third of these rent receipts. The Corporation's rental income was very substantial for a town of fewer than 6,000 inhabitants. The Corporation of York drew only some £2,000 in rents, whilst that of Leeds none at all.[6]

At the end of his rental account Burks added a list of other receipts

Figure 2. Extract from George Burks' 'rental', Oct 26-Nov 2 1805. *Doncaster Archives AB6/1/7/4*

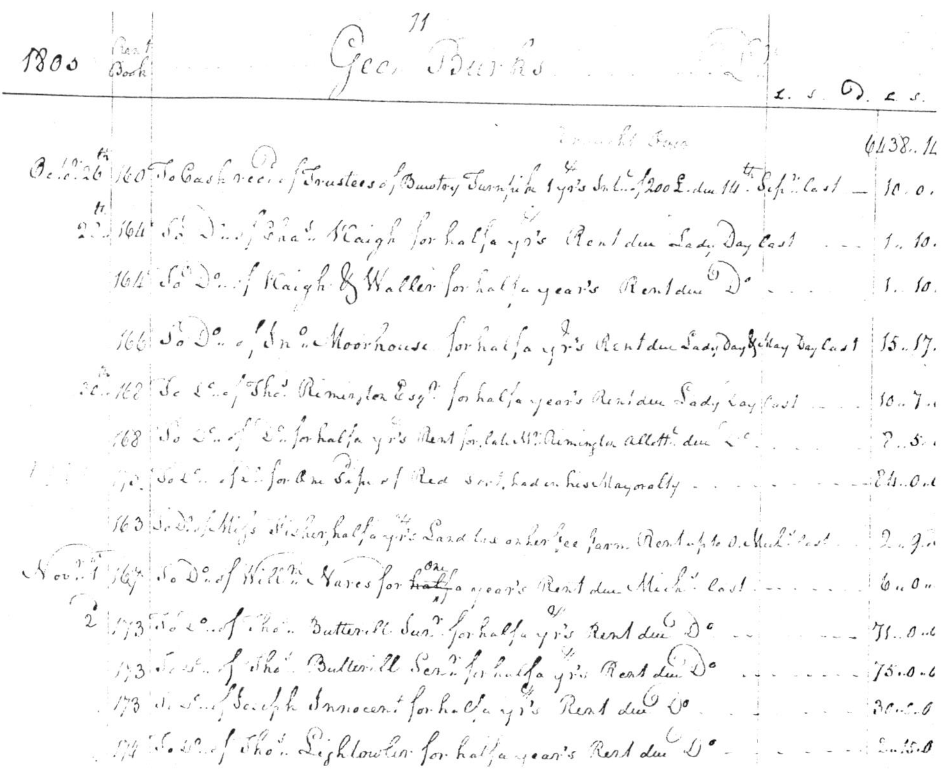
1805 Rent Book Geo. Burks Dr. £. s. D. £. s.
6438..16
Octr 26th 160 To Cash recd of Trustees of Bawtry Turnpike 1 yr's Intt of 200 £ due 14th Sepr last — 10. 0.
27th 164 To Do of Richd Haigh for half a yr's Rent due Lady Day last ... 1.. 10.
164 To Do of Haigh & Waller for half a year's Rent due Do ... 1.. 10.
166 To Do of Jno Moorhouse for half a yr's Rent due Lady Day & May Day last 15..17.
30th 162 To Do of Thos Rimington Esqr for half a year's Rent due Lady Day last ... 10..7..
168 To Do of Do for half a yr's Rent for late Mr Rimington allott due Do ... 7..5..
170 To Do of Do for the Sale of Red Stuff had in his Mayoralty ... 24..0..
163 To Do of Miss Fisher half a yr's Land tax on her fee farm Rent up to Mich. last 2..9..
Novr 1 164 To Do of Willm Nares for one year's Rent due Mich. last ... 6..0..
2 173 To Do of Thos Butterill Senr for half a yr's Rent due Do ... 75..0..0
173 To Do of Thos Butterill Senr for half a yr's Rent due Do ... 75..0..0
173 To Do of Joseph Innocent for half a yr's Rent due Do ... 30..0..0
174 To Do of Thos Lightowler for half a year's Rent due Do ... 2..15.0

under the heading of 'Sundries'. These included fines paid by those responsible for breaking street lamps, a payment of £31.10s. made by a man purchasing his freedom of the borough, and the proceeds from the sale of 'old boulders' - possibly cobblestones taken up when streets were resurfaced. Many of these receipts were forms of trading income, only distinguished in some arbitrary way by Burks from those he included with rents. Indeed, he entered under 'Sundries' a receipt for £325, an instalment of a payment for timber sold to a Grantham merchant although an entry for other wood sales had already appeared among his rent receipts. Miscellaneous 'Sundries' receipts of £1,205 and the non-rent receipts of £2,823 together amounted to £4,028 and with the actual rents of land and property brought the Corporation's current income for the year to £8,490.

The 'Sundries' account also showed further receipts of £2,920. These were loans made to the Corporation, acknowledged by Burks as 'by my hand' or 'by note'. His note was a simple receipt undertaking to repay the loan at interest on demand. Other loans, usually for larger sums, were 'by bond'. A bond was a formal document setting out the terms on which the loan was made, the interest which the Corporation promised to pay and the notice the lender was required to give when he (or she) wished their money to be repaid. A number of lenders, more especially the town's friendly societies, treated loans to the Corporation as a convenient way of holding their savings, rather than use one of the town's banks, which would not as a rule pay interest on their deposits. Such bodies as the Mutual Society, the Gardeners' Club and the Women's Tea Club, lent their balances at 5 per cent interest in 1805. Burks was often directed by members of the Corporation to borrow for some specific purpose. This might be to repay a loan made earlier or to finance some project such as the purchase of property. In these circumstances he often seems to have made the first approach to potential lenders. In 1805-6, loans to the Corporation, often referred to by Burks as 'principal money', were £2,920, making total receipts from all sources £11,410.

Burks entered disbursements in his cash book, settling smaller bills himself and larger ones when payment had been authorised by the Finance Committee.[7] When recording disbursements the nearest equivalent to Burks' rental was his so-called 'ledger'.[8] This did not show total disbursements: instead it showed a number of separate accounts, some for the tradesmen regularly employed by the Corporation, some for the Corporation's salaried officers, others for individuals and organisations who had lent money to the

Corporation and were recipients of interest payments. Burks' cash book shows that total disbursements in 1805-6 were £12,805, nearly £1,400 greater than total receipts.

An analysis of the disbursements entered in the cash book shows that many were regular salary payments to Corporation officers. These included a yearly 'salary' (really an entertainment allowance) of £630 to the Mayor. In return he was required to provide two dinners a year for the gentlemen of the town and neighbourhood. He was also expected to entertain distinguished visitors, including the judges when they passed through the town twice a year on their way to the assizes at York. Burks himself had a salary of £84 a year, raised in December 1805 to £120; the town clerk's salary was £105 a year but he was also paid for any legal work done for the Corporation. The gaoler and his assistant and the sergeants at mace were other prominent salaried servants of the Corporation.

The Corporation also took upon itself responsibility for paying a salary of £52.10s. a year to the master of the grammar school, another £42 to the organist at the parish church and £10 a year to the schoolmaster at Rossington to supplement the few pence paid each week by his pupils. In addition there were regular payments to humbler servants, to Sarah Winterbotham, the so-called 'fat cook at the Angel' who had been persuaded to leave her kitchen at the inn to work at the Mansion House instead, and to the waits, who provided music on civic occasions. Outdoor employees included the pinder, the bellman, the woodman, the gamekeepers and the neatherd who controlled the grazing on the Low Pasture. Apart from the woodman, these were paid very low wages but often had other duties for which they received extra payments. The Corporation paid Thomas Marriott and his wife 8s. a week for acting as caretakers at the grandstand and a yearly payment of £10; Marriott and several others were also paid when on duty during the races.

Members of the Corporation were proud of their readiness to contribute to charitable and other worthy causes. They made a regular donation of £100 a year to the trustees of the Dispensary and £21 to the Sunday School. Britain was at war with the French and the Corporation subscribed fifty guineas to a fund for the widows of men killed at Trafalgar, as well as making payments to the families of members of the Volunteer Infantry and the Volunteer Cavalry Yeomanry. All these donations in 1805-6 totalled £472.

Burks paid interest at 5 per cent to those who had lent money by note or bond to the Corporation. Interest payments in 1805-6 amounted to £1,407, indicating debts of more than £28,000. The debts of the borough of Nottingham, a town considerably larger than Doncaster, caused great alarm there on reaching £20,000.[9]

Efforts to maintain and improve Corporation property gave rise to far the largest amount of expenditure. Payments ranged from sixpence (for mending a clothes horse at the Mansion House) to very considerable sums. For work on the roads and pavements during the year, paviours, workmen and labourers were paid £131 10s. 3d. Burks hired labourers by the day to cut hedges, clean ditches and to clear rubbish. 'Six men for delivering the Betsy and Nancy, Mr Robinson's vessels, of boulders, £1.12s.' was a typical entry. Women too were hired on a casual basis to clean the Mansion House and to wash and iron linen. One woman, a chimney-sweep's widow, was in constant demand. She took over his trade and swept fourteen chimneys of property belonging to the Corporation between June 1805 and January 1806 at a shilling each.

It is difficult to distinguish between current and capital items when dealing with expenditure on maintaining and improving Corporation property. The expense of having chimneys swept or the Mansion House repainted may be regarded as current expenditure on keeping property in good order. Building work on the rectory at Rossington, however, increased the value of the Corporation's estate. The cost of it was capital expenditure, the equivalent of purchasing additional land or property. Payment for several thousand young trees in 1805-6, the beginning of an extensive scheme for replanting woodlands at Sandall and Rossington, was clearly another form of capital expenditure. An analysis of the cash book suggests that total expenditure under the heading of maintaining and improving the Corporation's property was more than £7,000 a year.

Another important capital transaction involved the repayment of loans. From time to time the Corporation's creditors presented their bonds or notes of hand for repayment. In April 1805, for example, the executors of Robert Robinson asked for a loan of £100 made in 1764 to be repaid, and an officer of the Mutual Friendly Society for £28.8s. During the year, total repayments were £2,256, the largest single repayment one of £1,400 in August 1805 to the executors of Richard Jennings. At the same time Burks issued a bond for £1,400 to Miss Elizabeth Jennings, part of the £2,920 of principal money borrowed appearing in his 'Sundries' receipts. This transfer of debt from one creditor to another left the Corporation's financial position unchanged, but had the effect of increasing the totals both of receipts and disbursements for 1805-6 by £1,400. Repayments during the year were £664 less than the new borrowings.

On 5 April 1806 Burks closed his accounts of the years' receipts and disbursements.[10] Making allowance for a balance of £1,399 held over from the previous year, he presented his accounts as follows:

Receipts	Disbursements
£11,410	£12,805
To balance of GB's last account £1,399	Due to Corpn from GB on this account £4

During the year total receipts had fallen short of disbursements by £1,395. Current receipts of £8,490 had probably been close to meeting current disbursements but were not large enough to include the capital costs of improving and extending Corporation property as well. The difference had been made up by borrowings and by a fortunate surplus carried over from the previous year. Borrowings had exceeded repayments of principal money by £664 so increasing the Corporation's debts. This pattern of disbursements exceeding receipts and of new borrowings providing some of the Corporation's financial needs, had been established long before 1805-6 and was now to be repeated with occasional exceptions for each of the next thirty years.

During the years between 1805-6 and the late 1830s the pattern of current receipts and disbursements remained broadly the same, but the size of most items increased. Rents increased only slowly; many properties were on long leases and rents could only be increased when these came to an end. There were substantial increases in the Rossington rents in 1811 and in 1817 those of the 270 acres of 'accommodation lands' let to members of the Corporation at low rents as a perquisite, were raised by 30 per cent. In 1821 many tenants found themselves in difficulty as agricultural prices fell and members of the Finance Committee commented on 'the depression among that class of persons from which the revenues of this body are mainly derived'. There were piecemeal increases in other rents, including that of the sailcloth factory which was raised from £45 a year to £70. Income from the rents of land and property, which had been £4,462 in 1805-6, rose to £5,081 in 1827 and to £5,733 in 1832. [11]

Some current receipts increased as a result of capital expenditure on income yielding assets. Receipts from the sale of tickets to the grandstand, for example, had been £291 in 1805-6. They rose sharply to more than £2,000 a year after improvements had been made in 1823 and 1824. Income from investments rose substantially, partly because traffic increased on the roads and on the Don, partly because shares had been purchased in two more canals and in the town's newly established gas works and further loans made at interest to turnpike trusts. By 1827 investment income had risen to £1,215 and by 1832 to £1,756. The charge levied on those purchasing the freedom of the borough rose by stages until it was three times what it had been at the beginning of the century.

On the disbursements side, expenditure on salaries did not substantially increase, although members of successive finance committees called for cuts in both staffing and salaries. The steward's salary was increased in 1827, and a new chief gaoler was appointed at a higher salary, but the mayor's salary was halved. Salaries were £1,313 in 1832 and pensions £157.

Members contributed to a wider range of charitable causes: to funds set up to relieve hardship in the town in 1816 and in 1831 when severe weather created unemployment amongst the poor, and during the cholera epidemic. They contributed to relief in Ireland and in the manufacturing districts, to funds for the restoration of York Minster and of the bells and organ of the parish church. They also supported the newly established National and British schools, the Lying-in and Warm Clothing charities and the Deaf Institution.

The Corporation increased its contributions of prize money to the organisers of the races from £92 in 1800 to £260 in 1832. This was successful in attracting more spectators, but the costs of policing the increased numbers rose during the same period. Legal expenses continued to be an important though not a constant item of expenditure. They varied from £58 in 1827 to £599 in 1832 and then rose to £1,938 in 1835 as the result of members' efforts to oppose the passage of the Municipal Reform Bill, which threatened them with the loss of their powers and privileges.

The central feature of the Corporation's finances during the early years of the century was the heavy capital expenditure which took place during this period. This sometimes led to increases in the Corporation's receipts from property and income-yielding assets, but since it was financed to a considerable extent by various kinds of borrowing, it led to increases in interest payments to the Corporation's creditors which eventually, in 1838, forced the Corporation to reduce its debts.

The Corporation had financed some of its expenditure by borrowings at least as early as 1629. [12] Proposals to cut expenditure to avoid the need to borrow were made in the 1680s without result. By 1714 members were expressing alarm at what they called 'the great debt', then more than £1,000. They urged the need for economies. Instead, within a few years, the Corporation went ahead with a series of projects intended to make Doncaster a social centre rivalling York: building a Mansion House, laying out a new race course and commissioning Carr of York to design a grandstand (Figures 3). A theatre was built in the market place and other projects included a new gaol and a factory building intended to create a sailcloth industry in the town. Efforts were made to improve the town's amenities, widening and paving the streets and rounding off street corners. In 1775 the Corporation purchased the town's waterworks for £2,300 and at the beginning of the nineteenth century paid nearly £2,000 to redeem the Land Tax falling on

Figure 3. The Grand Stand, from Miller's *History of Doncaster,* 1804

property in the town. The greater part of the expenditure involved in this ambitious programme of town improvements was financed by money borrowed largely from townsmen and women. Some of it, like that on the grandstand or on the waterworks yielded income to the Corporation, but much of it did not.

The second report of the Finance Committee, issued in August 1815, confirmed that expenditure had continually outstripped receipts during the preceding fourteen years.[13] The report identified some £23,139 capital expenditure in this period. More capital expenditure took place after 1815 with the largest ever single outlay by the old Corporation in 1817. This was the purchase of the tithes on the Corporation's property in the town and neighbourhood for £10,900. Tenants now began to pay their tithes to the Corporation instead of to the original lessee. Much of this capital expenditure could only be financed by borrowing and so led to further sharp increases in debt.

The additional funds required to finance these capital projects varied from year to year. As lord of the manor of Rossington, the Corporation had the right to 'present' or appoint the incumbent to the rectory there: in 1820 the sale of a presentation provided the Corporation with a much-needed windfall of £5,250. More was borrowed: members came increasingly to rely on the sale of annuities to supplement the usual method of borrowing by issuing notes of hand or bonds. There had been only one annuitant in 1805-6, receiving £20 a year; soon afterwards Dr Chorley, an alderman and the town's leading physician, paid £2,000 for an annuity of £200 and another alderman purchased an annuity of £500 in 1818 for £5,634. Most members of successful finance committes were senior members of the Corporation, among them men with considerable financial expertise: James Jackson, then Leonard Wallbank Childers and later Edward Tew, for example, were all partners in the town's banks. They were supported by other professional men of considerable standing, including the architect, William Hurst, who served for many years on successive committees. They repeatedly drew attention to the growth of debt, from £54,399 in 1817 to £64,247 in 1819 and to nearly £85,000 in 1831. They called for 'economies and retrenchment', for an end to new building projects and fresh borrowing.

Details of the Corporation's finances became more widely known in 1833 when a public enquiry into its affairs was held as part of the Royal Commission's investigation of municipal corporations. [14] When the town clerk was questioned during a three-day hearing, he relied heavily on the report drawn up earlier by the so-called 'Stock'

STATEMENT

OF THE

INCOME AND EXPENDITURE OF THE LATE CORPORATION OF DONCASTER,

IN THE YEARS 1832, 1833, 1834, & 1835.

PARTICULARS OF INCOME RECEIVED.	1832. £. s. d.	1833. £. s. d.	1834. £. s. d.	1835. £. s. d.
Rents received	5732 18 5	7035 9 8	5601 2 6	6771 3 3
Interest	271 3 4	167 4 9	421 17 4	332 16 10
Tithes	648 0 0	461 0 7	550 1 2	527 11 8
Land Tax	76 4 0	73 5 2	64 12 1	76 2 0
Canal Shares	1302 0 0	1349 0 0	1080 0 0	1601 0 0
Grand Stand	1453 4 0	1522 10 0	1719 18 0	1975 1 0
Booths on Race Ground	141 15 0	147 0 0	154 17 6	154 17 6
Wood sold	680 17 7	563 10 0	313 5 9	621 15 4
Weighing Machine	14 2 6	13 3 0	14 15 9	16 14 6
Tolls at Statutes	2 0 0	3 8 6	2 2 9	2 5 6
Water Rents	471 8 10	463 5 1	457 0 7	470 5 1
Butcher and Market Stalls	145 5 11	85 5 6	65 10 9	126 18 2
Gas Dividends	183 4 0	133 4 0	145 13 0	133 4 0
Discount on Gas Payments	....	14 4 3	11 12 6	12 1 6
Chief Rents	11 14 0	2 6 0	4 2 2	25 18 11
Manure	101 13 0	79 2 0	57 0 0	163 17 6
Ground Rents	0 5 0	7 0 0	....	0 18 2
Bark	104 4 0	113 8 0	131 13 0	129 17 0
Car Drainage	29 14 7	29 1 4	39 0 1	2 18 9
Bricks, Tiles, &c.	39 0 0	....	16 10 4	....
Tenant Right	70 0 0	70 0 0	264 11 0	231 19 7
Rent of River and Wool Tolls	....	....	....	627 5 6
Purchase Money of Hall Gate House	....	....	....	500 0 0
Purchase Money of Land at Hexthorpe	....	....	....	42 0 0
Library and News Room Shares	....	26 5 0	....	....
Lamps sold	....	6 2 0	....	....
On purchase of two Freedoms	....	126 0 0	....	....
Sundries	....	57 17 6	....	56 10 0
£	11478 14 2	12548 12 4	11115 6 3	14603 1 9

THE PRESENT DEBT OF THE CORPORATION.

	£. s. d.
Due on Bond	96043 0 0
Balance, due Leatham and Co.	4212 3 0
Total Debt of the late Corporation	£100255 3 0

Besides Annuities of £695. 10s. 0d. per annum.

EXCESS OF EXPENDITURE OVER INCOME.

	£. s. d.
In 1832	3403 9 9
1833	2641 14 11
1834	2231 6 9
1835	3966 7 11
	£12242 19 4

PARTICULARS OF DISBURSEMENTS.	1832. £. s. d.	1833. £. s. d.	1834. £. s. d.	1835. £. s. d.
Interest	3755 15 7	3897 16 7	3922 7 6	3922 6 9
Annuities	848 17 10	687 10 0	405 10 0	945 10 0
Salaries	1312 15 8	1194 4 2	1408 3 8	1350 8 2
Pensions	157 6 0	145 1 0	152 0 0	149 10 0
Assessments	393 5 5	312 8 3	325 12 2	284 8 1
Chief and other Rents	139 4 10	213 8 7	112 12 11	156 12 1
Tithes of Rossington	525 0 0	525 0 0	525 0 0	450 0 0
Drainage Tax	55 0 8	....	82 11 0	82 11 0
Insurance	14 5 0	14 5 0	14 5 0	14 5 0
Race Subscriptions	260 0 0	260 0 0	330 0 0	280 0 0
Training Grooms' Tickets	....	25 4 0	37 16 0	32 11 0
Police at Races	129 9 6	80 6 0	16 15 0	166 16 2
Charities and Donations	455 3 6	260 9 9	367 10 0	472 16 2
Jarratt's Charity	110 0 0	110 0 0	110 0 0	110 0 0
Tradesmen and Workmen's Bills and Repairs of Farm Houses, &c.	3248 19 10	3764 17 5	2741 1 8	4152 16 2
Mayor's Balls	315 0 0	315 0 0	*157 10 0	315 0 0
Balance paid to Mr. Nicholson (late Mayor)	....	....	....	*157 10 0
Street Lamps	469 0 0	477 15 0	477 15 0	488 5 0
Gas for Mansion-House and Jail	59 12 0	55 11 3	36 11 6	60 3 3
Streets Paving and Materials (exclusive of Flagging)	267 9 6	308 8 10	348 11 7	320 7 6
Repairs of Marsh Gate Road	155 13 4	113 13 2	105 8 8	89 6 0
Scavengers	187 4 0	187 4 0	187 4 0	187 4 0
Gravel for Foot Paths	30 10 0	14 18 4	....	....
Labourers' Wages on Estate, Plantations, &c.	454 19 0	445 8 1	435 16 4	517 14 4
Rent Day, Committee, and Sessions' Dinners	289 14 1	196 14 11	241 0 3	348 6 10
Law Expences, including the sum of £993. 13s. 6d. incurred (1835) in opposing the Municipal Act	599 0 8	....	....	1937 17 11
Honorary Grant to Town Clerk	....	....	105 0 0	....
Repairs of Sandal Road	86 17 6	71 4 0	80 2 0	79 5 0
Tenant Right	....	....	69 19 4	72 19 0
Tillage allowed to Tenants	130 0 0	193 17 2	271 10 10	525 15 10
Keep for Horses	58 15 8	66 15 6	72 4 7	90 7 7
Stamps	24 7 6	6 11 0	14 6 3	26 0 9
Vagrants	99 17 8	111 12 4	80 19 0	81 8 5
In exchange for Land, &c.	115 0 0	....	....	....
Constables at Sessions	11 0 0	19 17 0	15 4 0	....
Subscription to the Doncaster and Selby Road	....	1000 0 0	....	250 0 0
Killing Rabbits, &c.	....	10 1 4	10 10 0	33 13 0
Watchmen	....	....	....	24 0 0
Subscription to Church Organ and Bells	....	....	....	150 0 0
Purchase of Land in Cleveland Street	....	....	....	32 4 0
Additional Allowance to Mayor	....	....	....	105 0 0
Sundries	122 19 2	105 4 7	85 14 9	106 10 8
£	14882 3 11	15190 7 3	13346 13 0	18569 9 8

BY ORDER OF THE COUNCIL,

T. B. MASON,

TOWN CLERK.

COUNCIL CHAMBER, GUILD HALL, DONCASTER,
JANUARY 19, 1836.

Figure 4. Income and Expenditure of the Corporation of Doncaster, 1832-1835. *Doncaster Archives DZ ML 3/58/3*

committee, set up at the instigation of Alderman Hurst. [15] This had made a detailed survey of all Corporation property. Using some questionable methods, it had found that the value of this property had increased from £26,823 in 1730 to £312,428 in 1830. During the same period the Corporation's debt had increased from £3,622 to £94,835. (In 1833, the Corporation of York had debts of £21,500 and that of Lincoln, £29,242. Doncaster's debts were now comparable with those of Bristol. Only the Corporation of Exeter, which had taken up a costly scheme for improving the town's port facilities, was more deeply in debt than Doncaster.)[16]

Two features of the Corporation's handling of its financial affairs were strongly criticised at the 1833 public enquiry. The first was the custom whereby members of the Corporation were allowed to occupy 'allotments' of land at reduced rents. It was claimed on average each member was putting £11 a year in his pocket which would have gone to the Corporation. Another was the farming of the river tolls to George Robinson at the same rent of £100 a year as his father John had agreed to pay many years earlier. This was in spite of a great increase in traffic on the river. After the enquiry the rent was hastily raised to £250, but it was argued that if the lease had been fairly auctioned, some bidders would have offered as much as £350.

The passing of the *Municipal Corporations' Act* two years later was followed by the election of a new Town Council. Few members of the old Corporation were elected to this new body. Councillors learnt that receipts from all sources other than loans had amounted to £14,603 in 1835 and that expenditure other than repayment of loans had been nearly £4,000 greater, at £18,569 (Figure 4). Of this, the interest on debt was £3,922 and on annuities, £946.[17]

Early in 1838, when debts had risen to more than £100,000, councillors were warned that expenditure was likely to exceed income by £1,500 during the current year and that there would be an annual deficit of at least £1,000 thereafter.[18] Councillors decided that interest payments had to be cut and that this could only be done by reducing the debt itself. To finance this they decided to sell the Rossington estate (Figure 5). This realised £94,000 and that of the advowson, a further £4,500.[19] The Council was able to repay all but £5,000 of its debt. Strict control brought expenditure down to the level of receipts and the Council was even able to enjoy a small surplus from year to year.

Was the sale of the Rossington estate the outcome of extravagance or incompetence ? Contemporaries blamed Corporation expenditure on food and drink and a local historian writing some years later repeated the charge: 'Although their extravagances were [not] entirely attributable to the luxuries of the table...they gave splendid balls and entertainments...they often lived the life of princes!'.[20] By 1835 the Mayor's 'salary' had fallen to £315 but £348 was spent on 'rent day, committee and sessions' dinners'. On it own, this expenditure would not account for the £4,000 deficit, but the last recommendation of the Finance Committee on the very eve of the abolition of the old Corporation, that the steward should 'sell all the empty wine bottles and place the amount thereof to the credit of the Corporation' suggests that cuts in entertainment expenditure would have been possible.

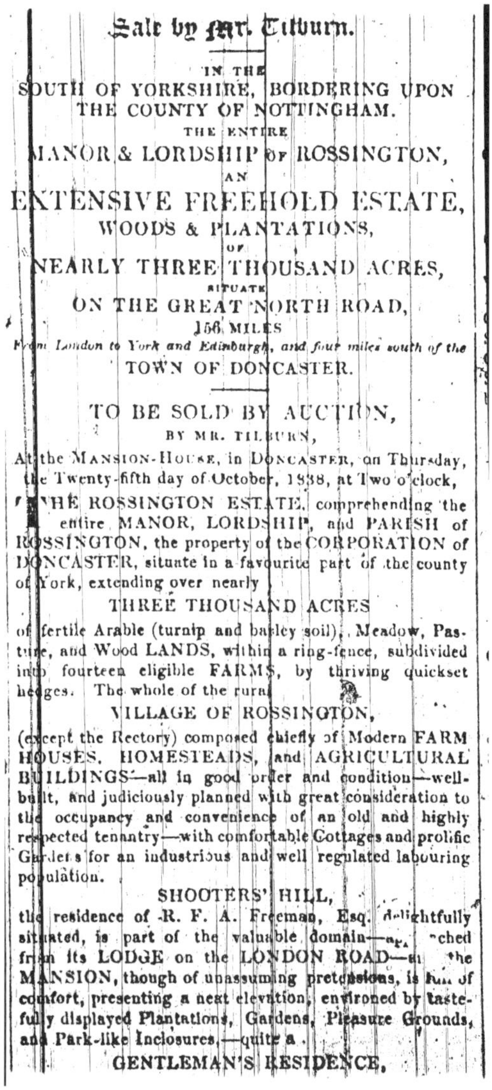
Sale by Mr. Tilburn.

IN THE
SOUTH OF YORKSHIRE, BORDERING UPON THE COUNTY OF NOTTINGHAM.
THE ENTIRE
MANOR & LORDSHIP OF ROSSINGTON,
AN
EXTENSIVE FREEHOLD ESTATE,
WOODS & PLANTATIONS,
OF
NEARLY THREE THOUSAND ACRES,
SITUATE
ON THE GREAT NORTH ROAD,
156 MILES
From London to York and Edinburgh, and four miles south of the
TOWN OF DONCASTER.

TO BE SOLD BY AUCTION,
BY MR. TILBURN,

At the Mansion-House, in Doncaster, on Thursday, the Twenty-fifth day of October, 1838, at Two o'clock,

THE ROSSINGTON ESTATE, comprehending the entire MANOR, LORDSHIP, and PARISH of ROSSINGTON, the property of the CORPORATION of DONCASTER, situate in a favourite part of the county of York, extending over nearly

THREE THOUSAND ACRES

of fertile Arable (turnip and barley soil), Meadow, Pasture, and Wood LANDS, within a ring-fence, subdivided into fourteen eligible FARMS, by thriving quickset hedges. The whole of the rural

VILLAGE OF ROSSINGTON,

(except the Rectory) composed chiefly of Modern FARM HOUSES, HOMESTEADS, and AGRICULTURAL BUILDINGS—all in good order and condition—well-built, and judiciously planned with great consideration to the occupancy and convenience of an old and highly respected tenantry—with comfortable Cottages and prolific Gardens for an industrious and well regulated labouring population.

SHOOTERS' HILL,

the residence of R. F. A. Freeman, Esq. delightfully situated, is part of the valuable domain—approached from its LODGE on the LONDON ROAD—the MANSION, though of unassuming pretensions, is full of comfort, presenting a neat elevation, environed by tastefully displayed Plantations, Gardens, Pleasure Grounds, and Park-like Inclosures,—quite a

GENTLEMAN'S RESIDENCE,

Figure 5. Part of the advertisement for the sale of the Manor of Rossington, to take place at the Mansion House on 25 October 1838.

Ventures such as the purchase of the town's waterworks in 1775, the redemption of the Land Tax and more especially the purchase of the tithes on Corporation property in Doncaster and nearby villages, largely financed by loans at 5 per cent, or annuities at 10 per cent, often yielded barely enough income to meet interest charges. A loan of £1,000 was made to the Doncaster-Thorne turnpike at 5 per cent, no more than the cost of borrowing, and by 1831 even this interest had not been paid for several years. The Corporation had purchased the *Dolphin Inn* for £840 but drew only £30 a year in rent; here, however, the principal motive may have been to gain possession of the inn yard in order to enlarge the market place.

Reports of the Finance Committees repeatedly drew attention to a problem that was never solved, that of arrears. Burks' 1805-6 rental shows that tenants began that year with arrears of £3,185, rising to £3,215 during the year. Some members of the Corporation were among the worst offenders. John Robinson, the farmer of the river tolls had paid no rents for this nor on his other tenancies since 1801 and his arrears alone were £924. These had risen to £2,574 by 1815, when total arrears were nearly £6,000. Many of those in arrears, however, including the late John Robinson, had counter-claims against the Corporation. Finance Committees' reports returned again and again to the 'manifest impropriety of permitting the accumulation of ...arrears'. One proposed that no member be elected alderman who was more than £75 in arrears, and others published the names of offenders, declaring that their 'conduct will be marked with just and becoming severity as being calculated to affect most deeply the respectability and independence of this ancient Corporation'.

A serious criticism of the Corporation is that it failed to do all it could to increase its receipts. It relied on its own slowly increasing rental income when the incomes of other townspeople were increasing as a result of the town's growing prosperity. Nobody proposed increasing receipts by imposing some form of rate or property tax to take advantage of this. Although borough corporations had no powers to levy such a rate, they could apply for a private act of parliament for a body of 'improvement commissioners' to be appointed. This would have the power to levy rates in order to meet the cost of lighting, paving and cleansing the streets and even of watching and policing them. By ensuring that some or all of the commissioners were members of the Corporation, the improvement commission could easily be controlled by the Corporation. In Leeds this had been done as early as 1754. In Doncaster the Corporation insisted on providing public services out of its own revenues. Street lighting alone cost £488 in 1835, paving £320 and scavengers (street cleaners) £187. Indeed, it became a source of pride that there were no rates: giving evidence to a House of Lords committee in 1835 the town clerk said that not only was there no borough rate but that 'there will never be any occasion whatsoever' for one. Later, the sale of the Rossington estate was defended on the grounds that this had allowed the Town Council to avoid imposing a rate. An unfortunate tradition was established of avoiding the levying of any rate, even when this meant going to extraordinary lengths to do so. This hampered the development of such municipal activities as the provision of elementary education in the borough, or improving the town's water supply during the remainder of the century.

Notes and References

All references unless otherwise stated are to documents in the Doncaster Borough Archives.

1.Report of the 'Stock Committee', 1831 AB 7/3/7/8; Titheable Lands schedule DK BAX 10/15.
2. Appendix to the *First Report of the Commissioners appointed to inquire into the Municipal Corporations of England and Wales,* Part III (1835): the Corporation of Leeds p 1623: the Corporation of Newcastle pp 1651-3.
3. Courtiers of the Corporation Vol III, AB 2/1/3, 24 July 1752.
4 Steward's Cash Ledger 1805-10, AB 6/1/7/4.
5. Steward's Rental Ledger 1796-1812, AB 7/1/166.
6. E M Sigsworth, 'Modern York' in *Victoria County History of York,* 1961, p 230; for Leeds, see *Appendix to First Report as above, p 1623.*
7. Steward's Cash Ledger 1805-10, AB 6/1/7/4.
8. Steward's Ledger 1797-1808, AB 6/1/9.
9. R A Church, *Economic and Social Change in a Midland Town. Victorian Nottingham 1815-1900,* 1966, p 180.
10. Steward's Cash Ledger 1805-10, AB 6/1/7/4.
11. Reports of the Finance Committees 1815-27, AB 2/2/19/1;Statement of the Income & Expenditure of the late Corporation 1832-5, DZ ML 3/58/3.
12.Disbursements 1629-30 AB 6/1/2/7: '24 May 1629 Consideration to Widow Picot for £40 for half year 33s.'
13. Reports of Finance Committee 1815-27, AB 2/2/19/1.
14. The *Doncaster, Lincoln and Nottingham Gazette,* 20 Dec 1833.
15. Report of the 'Stock Committee' 1831, AB 7/3/7/8.
16. E M Sigsworth, 'Modern York', in *VCH York,* 1961, p 264; JFW Hill, *Georgian Lincoln,* 1966, pp 249-50; G Bush, *Bristol and its Municipal Government 1820-51,* 1976, p 88; R Newton, *Eighteenth Century Exeter,* 1984, p 135.
17. Statement of the Income and Expenditure of the Late Corporation 1832-5, DZ ML 3/58/3.
18. Reports of the Finance Committees AB 2/2/19/3.
19. The *Doncaster, Lincoln and Nottingham Gazette,* 14 December 1838.
20. C W Hatfield, *Historical Notices of Doncaster,* 1865, Vol II, p 180.

Acknowledgements

I am grateful for the help given by Dr Brian Barber and his staff at the Doncaster Borough Archives in the preparation of this article, and to Mrs Rachel Homer and Mr Stuart Jackson who read earlier drafts and made a number of valuable comments.

7. The Doncaster Plant Churches: St James and St Judes

by Roger Glister

THE 'PLANT AND WORKSHOPS' of the Great Northern Railway very nearly did not come to Doncaster at all. For, despite plans being drawn up by the General Superintendent of the railway, Edward Bury, siting the works at Doncaster, Archibald Sturrock, the Locomotive Engineer favoured Peterborough and even sanctioned the purchase of some 28 acres of land to the north of the town upon which to build it. However, higher counsels prevailed and on 3 June 1851 a directive from the Board stated that the new permanent wagon and carriage repair shops would be built at Hexthorpe. In compensation, Peterborough acquired a large engine shed, a turntable and extensive additional sidings.

During the summer of 1851 a small wagon repair shop and mineral office were built at Hexthorpe whilst the detailed plans for the new workshops were drawn up. An estimate of £45,000 was arrived at and tenders were invited for the construction work. On 23 March 1852 A & G Holmes of Liverpool was awarded the contract and undertook to carry out the work at ten per cent below schedule. Sturrock was given a budget to equip the workshops with the necessary machinery and tools; most of these were supplied by J Naysmith & Co of Patricroft.

By May 1852, the engine erecting shop, the smithy and iron stores were completed and a new larger wagon repair shop was well under way. At the end of June, engines were brought in for repair and maintenance, and by the beginning of August the plant was in full use. Capacity was soon reached, for in 1855, further extensions were undertaken and two new fire engines stationed on site to deal with any emergencies. It was also in 1855 that Archibald Sturrock moved his headquarters from Peterborough to Doncaster at the behest of the directors.

The chairman of the Great Northern Railway Company was Edmund Beckett Denison, a native of Leeds and M P for the West Riding of Yorkshire. Denison, reputedly the richest citizen of Doncaster at the time, was concerned by the lack of education and worship facilities for his rapidly expanding workforce. By January

1854 almost one thousand workmen, with their wives and children, had been transferred from the former workshops at Boston. Denison put it to the Board and shareholders that, as the Great Northern Railway was responsible for the considerable growth of population in Doncaster, they should be willing to provide schools and a church. Whilst he got total backing for money to build the necessary school, it was a different matter altogether using company funds to found a church.

The school project got under way at once, the building contract being awarded to C Lister & Son of Doncaster to a design by Henry Goddard, and was opened in January 1855 admitting 246 boys and girls. By 1863 the roll had been increased by a further 240 infants. The Reverend J Campion, already offering spiritual guidance and welfare to the workforce and their families, was appointed headmaster. The cost to the Company was £1,212.

Despite the opposition of many shareholders to the building of a church with trading capital, Denison was determined to see his scheme through and opened a subscription list among sympathetic shareholders and friends. This move proved successful and by May 1857 the fund stood at £5,641, this sum was deemed sufficient to guarantee the project and so construction work was put in hand. The list was headed by Earl Fitzwilliam, chairman of the South Yorkshire Railway and an influential coalowner from Wentworth. This railway company was closely connected with the Great Northern Railway which had supported its development and welcomed the vast tonnage of coal that it brought to Doncaster from the South Yorkshire coalfield.

The Great Northern had provided land for building of the church and free conveyance of the building stone from Acaster in Lincolnshire. By October 1858 the church of St James, capable of seating a congregation of close on 700, was consecrated. In 1862 Edmund Denison headed a consortium that purchased, for £350, an organ from St George's, Doncaster. For thirty years St James' Church catered for the steadily increasing population of the parish, wherein the village of

Figure 1. The imposing structure of St James's Church.

Figure 2. St James's Church with Type 47 locomotive St Andrew. The car park occupies a large part of the former Plant Works sidings and carriage works.

Hexthorpe was being developed in proportion to the Plant Works expansion (Figures 1 & 2).

As early as 1874 accommodation for Anglican worship in Hexthorpe was provided by the building of a School Hall in Shadyside which was used extensively until, in 1890, it was realised that better facilities were needed and a permanent church was the answer. Three benefactors blessed the scheme with generous contributions. A Hexthorpe resident, Mr Pybus, gave a donation of £500 and a parcel of land at the junction of Shadyside and Sunnyside and Edmund Beckett Dennison, now Lord Grimthorpe, and his sister undertook to provide the rest of the cost of the new church. The plans were drawn up by Mr Herbert Athron of Dolphin Chambers, Doncaster from a preliminary sketch by Lord Grimthorpe and an estimate of £4,320, submitted by Mr W Anelay, was accepted with the work commencing in May 1893.

The building was constructed of selected Balby bricks with Acaster stone dressings in the Gothic style (Figures 3,4 & 5). The interior of the church is completely open, there being no pillars at all. The roof, of pitched pine, is supported integrally by iron tier struts and collars (Figure 6), as indicated by Lord Grimthorpe's original drawing. This ensures an

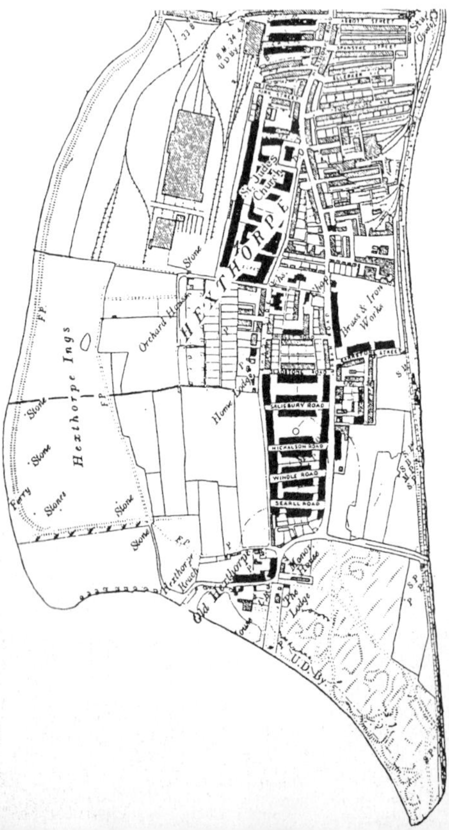

Figure 3. Parish of St Jude, Hexthorpe c 1900, showing Plant Works, sheds and sidings behind the church.

uninterrupted view of the choir and chancel is enjoyed by the whole congregation. The roof is covered with flat Bromley tiles which were supplied by Peake & Co from Tunstall, Staffordshire. Entrance to the building was provided by means of two doors in the west wall which proved unsatisfactory and, in 1910, they were bricked up and replaced by a doorway with porch at the west end of the south wall.

On Saturday 2 June 1894 the Bishop of Beverley, The Right Reverend R J Crosthwaite, performed the Ceremony of Dedication. The service took the form of a shortened version of the Evening Prayer and Lord Grimthorpe read the Lesson, an extract from the *Epistle to the Hebrews.* At the conclusion of the service the organist, Mrs College, accompanied the congregation in singing the hymn *The Church's One Foundation* and the collection totalled £12 8s.8d. The Consecration ceremony took place on 17 July 1900 with His Grace the Archbishop of York, Dr Maclagan, officiating. A good congregation, including many clergy from neighbouring parishes, were present to witness the solemn and impressive service appointed in the Diocese of York for the Consecration of Churches. On this occasion the collection amounted to £5 14s.0d.

Very little is known of St Jude, therefore it is a somewhat unusual dedication for a church. It is believed that St Jude was a brother of St James and the close ties between the two churches warranted the title. This St Jude was the apostle who, in the Gospel according to St John, once asked a question of our Lord. This is the sum total of our knowledge concerning the gentleman.

The organ (Figure 7), built by Abbott and Smith of Leeds for £235, was dedicated by the Bishop of Beverley on 10 January 1901. The instrument boasted 722 pipes and was blown by hand until October 1942 when an electric blower was purchased at a cost of £61 17s. 0d. Of this amount, £50 was in the form of an interest-free loan from the Fabric Fund and was repaid at the rate of £10 per annum.

In 1910, whilst the entrance was undergoing alteration, the chancel was also substantially enlarged. The original gas lighting was endured until February 1922 when electric light was installed for the

Figure 4. St Judes from the East end.

Figure 5. St Judes from the West end.

Figure 6. St Judes interior showing iron tie rods in the roof.

Figure 7. St Judes interior: organ and roof tie rods.

sum of £132. The last additions to the fabric of St Jude, completed in 1925, was the building of the two vestries at the north-east corner at a cost of £800, the builder being Messrs Mullins & Co.

The chief benefactor of the church, Lord Grimthorpe, died in 1905 and bequeathed a legacy of £3,000 to be invested and the interest therefrom used for the repair and maintenance of the fabric. This fund was to be controlled and administered at the discretion of the churchwardens.

From these early days to the present time, St James and St Jude have enriched the communities of their respective parishes with the help of all who attend and administer the wide variety of services and functions that make up the lifeblood of our parish churches.

Bibliography

Evans, Rev E J H, *A Short History of Saint Jude, Hexthorpe*, 1944.
The *Doncaster Gazette*, June 1894.

Acknowledgements

The writer would also like to thank Mrs Sue Warnes of Hexthorpe for her generous help with material for this article; also Reverend A J Gilbert, vicar of St Judes, for his kind permission to photograph the church interior.

8. Jigsaws of building History: Three Parish Churches in the Lower Don Valley

by Derek Holland

GUIDEBOOKS OFTEN TELL of Decorated churches here and Perpendicular churches there, when often the reality is far more complicated. Many parish churches are mixtures of styles and of work carried out at different times. This study looks at three such churches, which by their great visual variety can claim to be jigsaws of history. Much of their building history can be read in stone by those who try to disentangle the complexities of their development.

All three churches are situated well to the east of the magnesian limestone belt, in a lowland area where good building stone is not to be found. Yet these churches and their neighbours are all built of stone. Early church-building utilised glacial cobbles, ploughed and gathered from the local fields. This was probably the characteristic building material for churches in this locality (apart from timber) in Anglo-Saxon and early Norman times, and it is to be found in all three churches in differing quantities (Figure 1). However, some cut and carved blocks of magnesian limestone were being used here in late Norman times. The highly decorative south doorway at Fishlake,

Figure 1. St Oswald's, Kirk Sandall: glacial cobbles in south aisle walls, together with Norman window in east wall.

the nave arcades, corner-stones and splayed windows at Kirk Sandall, and the west doorway at Hatfield are of this material. A certain amount of limestone rubble of all shapes and sizes was also used here in the Norman period.

By the early thirteenth century high quality cut-and-shaped blocks were in more extensive use, as seen in the north and south arcades at both Fishlake and Hatfield. Aisle wall material at both Fishlake and Hatfield comprises a mixture of roughly-shaped blocks and thin rubble, the sort of material obtained from the upper layers of a magnesian limestone quarry. Certainly, from the early fourteenth century onwards there was ready access to the finest quality magnesian limestone, for the central-tower crossing piers and arches at Hatfield, the chancel walls at Fishlake, and the elaborate forms of Decorated window tracery and window surrounds in these churches. Without access to magnesian limestone of the highest quality, masons would have found it impossible to build the mid-fifteenth century west tower at Fishlake and the late-fifteenth century tower at Hatfield, together with the nave clerestories in both churches.

How did such huge quantities of magnesian limestone get to these and other churches in the eastern lowlands ? Long distance overland transport was clearly out of the question for such large amounts. The river Don, which flows through the limestone gorge at Sprotbrough and on through the lowlands to the east, would clearly be the answer. Stone is a heavy and bulky commodity which travelled best by water; Kirk Sandall and Fishlake are by the side of the river Don and Hatfield is just two miles from it. Scientific analysis of a wide variety of stones from work of different dates within these churches would be needed before anything approaching certainty could be expressed about the localised origins of stone from particular quarries. It seems, however, likely that much of it would come from the Levitt Hagg area of the Don gorge. A possible source for some of the fine quality carved work might be the medieval quarries at Marr, lying two-and-a-half miles NNW of the river at Sprotbrough.[1] A direct track joined the two villages.

Kirk Sandall (Figure 2)

The medieval Kirk Sandall parish stretched from the south bank of the river Don to the sandy heath around Armthorpe. Its settlements included Kirk Sandall itself, neighbouring Long Sandall and the villages of Armthorpe and Edenthorpe (Streetthorpe). A church already existed at Kirk Sandall at the time of Domesday Book (1086),[2] and the Scandinavian element 'Kirk' in the place-name

Figure 2. St Oswald's, Kirk Sandall: view from the south.

indicates the existence of a church here before the Norman Conquest of 1066. The earliest part of the fabric of Kirk Sandall church is the west wall, with its rubble construction and patches of herringbone masonry. It is certainly no later than the early years of the Norman era (c 1070-80) and is probably late Anglo-Saxon. The north and south aisles were added in the Norman period, witness the two-bay north and south arcades and the Norman splayed windows at the east and west ends of the south aisle. Straight joints mark the addition of the two aisles to the nave (Figure 3 & 4). The chancel was rebuilt at this time. Very little change took place in the fabric of this small church between the twelfth century and the early sixteenth century. But new windows were added in the fourteenth century, and these allowed more light into a previously dark building. The separation of Armthorpe from the old parish left it poorer in terms of income and serving only the small villages of Kirk Sandall and Long Sandall, and the hamlet of Edenthorpe. Much of the territory was sandy heath, and there was not the ingredient of marshy waste to encourage new settlement in the years before the Black Death of 1348-49. The substantially unaltered Norman church reflects lack of growth in settlement and population. There never was a west tower to this church, and originally doubtless a single bell hung in a little

Figure 3. St Oswald's, Kirk Sandall: west wall of south aisle, adjoining south-west corner of probable Anglo-Saxon nave.

bellcote over the western gable of the small building. Subsequently a low bell-tower was erected over the south aisle, and this remained until the 1920s.

However, in c1520 a major change came about in this church: the building of the chapel to the north of the chancel, an event due to the generosity of one man. William Rokeby had served as rector of Kirk Sandall (1487-1502) early in his career, the Rokeby family having owned the manor and the right to nominate the priest. The Reverend William Rokeby went on to become vicar of Halifax in 1502, at a time when its growing woollen cloth industry made it something of a boom town. From there he went to become Bishop of Meath in Ireland in 1507, and reached the pinnacle of his ecclesiastical career as Archbishop of Dublin in 1512. It was much easier for English clergy to move about the domains of the Roman Catholic church before Henry VIII's revolution. Having begun at Kirk Sandall, Rokeby remembered his native village and in his will (22 November 1521) directed:

> *That aftir my deth my body be emboweld, and my bowelles and herteto be buried in the church of Halifax Wytn.* [within] *the quere; and my body to be buried in the new chapell at Sandall.*[3]

In other words the chapel had been built and made ready before the end of 1521. The new chapel was bigger than the chancel and more magnificent than any other part of the church, being built of ashlar blocks of magnesian limestone in contrast to the rubble construction of the rest of the church. It must have been a great showpiece, with its late Perpendicular architecture, its Rokeby tomb, its contemporary stained glass, and Rokeby's coat of arms at the apex of the eastern gable. It remains the most exuberant piece of work from the 1520s in the Doncaster area (Figure 5). Simultaneously, a little restoration of the

Figure 5. St Oswald's, Kirk Sandall: the sixteenth century Rokeby Chapel from the north-east.

west wall of the north aisle was carried out in ashlar limestone. It was also in the early sixteenth century that a carved wooden screen was placed to divide the east end of the church from the nave and aisles.

In 1818 the upper part of the bell-tower was built of ashlar magnesian limestone, over the south aisle.[4] It may have replaced an earlier timber-framed bell-stage. Victorian alterations to the church included the following. A new nave roof was built at a higher level, open to the lofty timbers inside, and covered outside with flat red tiles. The new stone, towards the top of the nave east and west gables, can be clearly seen. Crosses were placed at the east and west apexes. The line of the old nave roof can still be discerned on the east wall of the nave, above the chancel. The aisle walls were heightened and new roofs built there. The south porch was erected, with cross on its south gable. J M Teale, a Doncaster architect, is recorded as working on a church restoration here in 1864.

Significant events in the recent structural history of the church centre around the 1930s, the 1960s, and 1980s. The south bell-tower was rebuilt for structural reasons in the early 1930s, in a vernacular style. This involved the removal of the 1818 stone bell-stage and its replacement by a timber-framed pyramid with triangular bell-openings. It remains a visual curiosity and rare example of church work of this period in the area. At the same time, the chancel walls

Figure 6. St Oswald's, Kirk Sandall: view from the west.

were heightened and the roof rebuilt. Also in the 1930s, a spacious new vestry was added at the north-west corner of the church. Canon Popham, the rector who so loved this church, probably saw this vestry as a means of grafting onto the church an office, for a work and a store room, and a space for the robing of priest and choir. Such space was simply not available in the old church. The new structure was built of Ketton limestone, a rare use in this area of this gritty oolitic limestone from Rutland (Figure 6). The old village declined after 1922, when Pilkingtons built their glassworks and new village. Properties were purchased and gradually the settlement was demolished, including farms, cottages, and the seventeenth century village grammar school. This process lasted until the 1970s.

In the mid-1960s, during the incumbency of the Reverend Taylor, plans were laid for the demolition of St Oswald's church, and the removal of the stones of part of it for rebuilding on a site amidst a housing estate on the borders of Kirk Sandall and Edenthorpe. This scheme, prepared by Diocesan architect George Pace, would have given an air of antiquity to the proposed new church, by placing transposed old work side-by-side with new design. But it would have resulted in the needless total destruction of a church which had stood on its river-side site since Anglo-Saxon times. Furthermore, only part of the old building was to be reused, namely the Rokeby Chapel.[5]

There was considerable local opposition to this scheme, despite the desire of the rector and a section of the Parochial Church Council to see it accomplished. Fortunately, from the point of view of conservation and antiquity, the proposals foundered through lack of money and real grass-roots support. The need of the parish for a church in the centre of population was satisfied by the building of a functional church and church hall. St Oswald's church was left for the future on its now-isolated site. In the 1980s it became a redundant church, in the care of the Redundant Churches Fund. It has been carefully conserved and the sixteenth century stained glass in the Rokeby Chapel has been restored. It remains as a superb example of a small parish church displaying the work and care of many generations, and as a historic marker for a now-vanished village.

Fishlake

Fishlake parish had originally been part of the large medieval parish of Hatfield, but achieved independence early. The village is situated at the extreme southern end of the parish, on the northern bank of the river Don, and at its centre is the medieval church. The parish stretched three- and-a-half miles to the north and included the later settlement of Sykehouse, first recorded in 1404.[6] Edmund Fitzwilliam Esquire had a private chapel in his house here in 1425.[7] In 1433 the people of Sykehouse made an agreement with the Prior and Convent of Durham to build a chapel here.[8] This building was abandoned and fell into ruin after the Reformation. Then in 1617 it was repaired and used again. A brick west tower was built in 1724, and survives as the earliest part of the present building. The nave and chancel were rebuilt in brick in 1867-68, to the designs of C Hodgson Fowler.[9] The extensive parish to the north of the original settlement and church is an indication of the large amount of waste land included in the medieval parish. There was a great wood to the north, and Sykehouse probably originated as a scattered settlement in this woodland. Parts of the parish were marshland. Both of these environments afforded great opportunities for expansion in the twelfth and thirteenth centuries.

Fishlake church is dedicated to St Cuthbert, a rare dedication in the area. A list of 1416 made by Prior Wessyngton of Durham Cathedral Priory names the resting-places of the bones of St Cuthbert, when in the ninth century the monks of Durham carried them around for seven years to escape the destruction of the Vikings. One of the Yorkshire resting-places listed there is 'Fysshlake'.[10] This

Figure 7. St Cuthbert's, Fishlake: glacial cobbles and Norman doorway in the chancel south wall.

is the only known instance of this place-name, and taken together with the dedication of Fishlake church, this fascinating piece of evidence takes us back to the Dark Ages. There is also a mention of 'Cuthbertehaven' in a lease agreement of 1438 between the Prior and Convent of Durham and Richard Wryghte of Fishlake; this land was part of the garden of Fishlake Rectory.[11]

Little remains of the Norman church, but on the south side of the chancel there is a small section of rubble walling (glacial cobbles) with a round-arched priest's door in it (Figure 7). This is probably all that is left of the original church of the early Norman period. [12] Somewhat later is the grand south doorway dating from c1150-60. This may imply other new work on the church in the mid-twelfth century, but no other evidence remains. It is a heavily-carved doorway with extensive imagery (Figure 8), fully described by Charles Keyser in the early years of this century.[13]

A major expansion came in the early years of the thirteenth century, when north and south arcades were built in the early Gothic (Early English) style. These comprise circular columns with circular capitals, together with double-chamfered pointed arches (Figure 9). There is also a probable stretch

Figure 8. St Cuthbert's, Fishlake: south doorway (detail). A variety of human and animal heads, stylized foliage, animals and Biblical scenes are depicted around this doorway.

Figure 9. St Cuthbert's, Fishlake: early thirteenth century north arcade.

of the original north aisle wall, comprised of thin pieces of magnesian limestone rubble. These arcades date from the very time in the early 1200s when expansion of settlement and population were taking place in many parts of England, where the existence of wasteland made this possible. Such a parish was Fishlake.

The chancel at Fishlake dates from the mid-fourteenth century, and the destroyed east window depicted the Reverend Richard Mauleverer, Rector of Fishlake from 1351 until 1368, kneeling in a blue gown accompanied by three greyhounds.[14] There would have been much hunting available to a rich clergyman in this locality in the fourteenth century. The flowing tracery of this east window represents the Decorated style at its peak, and in the English form which came nearest to the French Flamboyant style (Figure 10). It is also very close in style to the east window of Sutton-cum-Lound (Notts), twenty miles to the south over the flat lands, and both may be the work of the same master-mason. There was originally a chapel and vestry on the north side of the chancel, but this was demolished at the Reformation leaving only a blocked two-bay arcade. This extension was made in the time of the Reverend Richard Marshall, who died in 1505 and whose altar tomb now lies to the north side of the chancel. Part of the inscription tells us: 'Here lyeth Richard Marshall...The vi [th] vicar of this church...in whose tyme this chancell and vestry bildite was'.[15] He did not build the chancel, but extended it on the north side (the vestry), added the clerestory and altered the roof-line. The decorated font (at the west end of the nave) was probably made c1330-40, and is a superb example of carved magnesian limestone work of this

Figure 10. St Cuthbert's, Fishlake: mid-fourteenth century chancel, from the east.

Figure 11. St Cuthbert's, Fishlake: fifteenth century west tower, from the north-west.

time. Octagonal in plan and supported on a chalice stem, its carved saints are placed under nodding ogee arches.

Another glory of Fishlake church is the Perpendicular west tower, built in the time of Edward IV (1461-83), as shown by the carved heraldic devices of a falcon and fetterlock, and a rose surmounted by a crown, the badges of this king.[16] High on the exterior west wall of the tower is a statue of St Cuthbert holding St Oswald's head. Oswald was killed by Mercians at the Battle of Masserfeld in 642, and his recovered head was placed in Cuthbert's tomb in Durham.[17] Below is a huge window, which lets the late afternoon and evening light flood down the nave. Inside the church this window is matched by a lofty tower arch (Figure 11).

A Perpendicular clerestory was added above the nave, so letting more light flood in. In the years towards c1500 the north and south aisles were each extended eastwards by one bay. They have characteristically flattened (or four-centred) early Tudor arches, and because of extension embrace the western end of the chancel. These two extensions formed two chapels dedicated to the Holy Trinity on the south and the Blessed Virgin Mary on the north. The Reverend Thomas Fairburn had requested burial in the Holy Trinity chapel in 1496. [18]

Little else was added to Fishlake church until the Victorian era. It was carefully restored and repaired in the mid-nineteenth century. The chancel was restored in 1854-57 by the Dean and Chapter of Durham, patrons of the living. [19] By then the walls were beginning to collapse from the weight of the early Tudor clerestory and the addition on the north side. The buttresses and the east window tracery were badly buckled. The east window was completely remade, after drawings had been made of the existing design. The restoration was accurately executed under the Durham Cathedral master-mason. The Victorian restoration was inspired by the Reverend George Ornsby, vicar of Fishlake from 1850 until 1886. He also had the chancel tiled, new heating stoves installed, a new pulpit and lectern were obtained, new pews were made (to replace the old box pews), a new organ was installed (1856), and the tenor bell was recast.[20] A gas supply (presumably from Thorne gasworks, across the river Don) made new church-lighting possible. Two-thirds of the cost of these works was given by Canon Ornsby and his friends, and the rest raised in the parish. There was much local grumbling about the spending of £121 of locally-collected money for this work.[21] The gas fittings can still be seen on the nave piers.

Figure 12. St Lawrence's, Hatfield: view from the north-east.

Hatfield

Hatfield parish is very large now, but was even larger in the early Middle Ages, including Fishlake and Thorne. Thorne remained part of Hatfield parish until after the Reformation. The territory of this vast area was heathland and fen. It was on this heathland that the famous battle was fought in 633 AD, when the forces of Penda of Mercia routed the army of Edwin of Northumbria, and Edwin himself was slain.[22] Settlement was on islands of sand and gravel, and the heathland gave its name to Hatfield village. The dependent village of Stainforth was situated on the river-side so that the ford across the river Don shaped its place-name.

The church is cruciform in plan, perhaps an indication of its early importance (Figure 12). There is a strong likelihood of an Anglo-

Figure 13. St Lawrence's, Hatfield: south wall, showing glacial cobbles (below) and magnesian limestone (above), with windows of c1300 (right) and c1310 (left).

Figure 14. St Lawrence's, Hatfield: glacial cobbles and Norman doorway (c1120-30) in west front.

Saxon church having been built here, but no trace of it has yet been found. A church and priest are recorded in Domesday Book in 1086.[23] The early Norman church was built of rubble, including many glacial cobbles - such as survive in profusion on the west front and along the lower courses of the western end of the south wall (Figure 13). The evidence of the west front seems at first to suggest that the Norman church was as wide as the present church from north to south. The glacial cobbles stretch right across the west front, and there are Norman windows in the west walls of both aisles (Figures 14 & 15). However, the

glacial cobbles in the aisle west walls, together with the Norman windows, could be reused material from an early Norman aisle-less nave. Strength is lent to this idea by the north and south aisle arcades, which are identical and in the early Gothic (Early English) style of c1200. They have circular columns, square capitals, and double-chamfered pointed arches. Similarity with those at Fishlake is noted, though those of Hatfield are slightly earlier. If Norman arcades had been built it is unlikely that they would have needed rebuilding as early as c1200. The Early English font dates from the early 1200s and is made of magnesian limestone. The quatrefoil-shaped bowl is supported on a large central column with four slender columns supporting at the outer edges. The whole rests on a circular base.

Hatfield's central tower was begun in the first half of the fourteenth century, probably in the 1330s. Work proceeded to the full height of the four Decorated crossing-arches and several feet above, and then came to a halt. The likely explanation for this break is the catastrophic interruption caused by the Black Death in 1348-49. With somewhere between a third and a half of the population scythed off, there would be no chance of many building projects continuing. It seems likely that Hatfield's tower remained unfinished for over 100 years, and new work brought it to completion between c1480 and c1500. The Savage family heraldry carved on the inside and outside of the upper part of the tower relates to two of its members. Thomas Savage was created Archbishop of York by Henry

Figure 17. St Lawrence's, Hatfield: sixteenth century south chapel, from the south-east.

VII, and must often have stayed in the archbishop's palace at Scrooby, just across the border in Nottinghamshire. Sir Edward Savage was keeper of the royal chase at Hatfield under Henry VII.[24] Rich people have often given a boost to church-building and Savage patronage enabled the parishioners of Hatfield to finish their tower.

The nave was heightened with a Perpendicular clerestory, letting in more light, and this was accompanied by a new flatter roof (Figure 16). The transverse pointed arches and pillar buttresses in the north aisle, together with external buttresses at the same points, were added to provide strengthening needed after the building of the clerestory. The latter's downward thrust was considerable and the north wall's foundations may have been weaker, perhaps for reasons of surface geology rather than workmanship. At any rate such strengthening was not deemed necessary on the south side.

The north and south chantry chapels were added to the chancel (Figure 17). They were not part of an original scheme of rebuilding, as is evidenced by the straight joints to be seen on the outside. This work was done within the years c1500-30. The north chapel was dedicated to St Catherine and a boss formerly in its oak roof depicts St Catherine and her wheel.

The late Victorians added extra bells to the tower and modified the timberwork in the bell-chamber, which was lifted several feet. This eventually caused cracks to appear in the tower, and the damage had become serious by the mid-1960s. Hatfield's bells did not ring for a long time, because of this. Essential work on the tower has been carried out in the early 1990s, during the incumbency of the Reverend Canon John Sweed. This also involved replacing a certain amount of rotten timber.

The small amount of stained glass which Hatfield church possesses is mostly Victorian, including a window by Kempe in the south aisle.[25] The medieval stained glass vanished during the puritan iconoclasm of the seventeenth century. Much of the glass is now plain, which contributes to the light and airy atmosphere of this church. From the 1960s onwards several Modern windows have been added in the south chapel and the north aisle. The plain glass and the angular patterns of the leading form a fitting complement to Perpendicular architecture. These windows are in a style begun by George Pace and developed by his partner Ronald Simms. The vicar, John Sweed, has an exciting plan for a new window to celebrate the millennium, and this will show saints of the second millennium, together with events from local and national history.

One puzzle remains at Hatfield. At the south-west corner of the north aisle are the remains of a large staircase, which now leads nowhere. It is circular in form, with spiral stone steps. Now rising only a few feet, it does not relate to any surviving part of the church. One possibility is that it led to the now-vanished west gallery which was built in the church in the early nineteenth century. However, such a substantial stone staircase seems unlikely as access to a wooden gallery. Yet what else did it serve? There is no other evidence of a west tower ever having been planned. The structure remains a mystery at the moment.

All medieval churches need repairs and restoration from time to time, and these three are no exception. Whilst the burden falls on the parish communities in Fishlake and Hatfield, and on the Redundant Churches Fund in Kirk Sandall, the contributions of visitors and well-wishers are always welcome. Please visit these churches, enjoy and understand them, and respond appropriately in return. You will help to ensure that part of our heritage will be there for future generations yet unborn.

Acknowledgements

My thanks to successive incumbents of Kirk Sandall, Fishlake and Hatfield, for repeated opportunities to look round churches in their keeping. I am especially grateful to the late Canon Ted Greathead and Canon John Sweed, Vicars of Hatfield, for sharing thoughts with me about the history of their church. They are not, of course, to be blamed for any of the above! My thanks also to Rachel Holland, for typing the manuscript. My wife Enid took the photographs and helped in many other ways.

Notes and References

1. L F Salzman, Building in England down to 1540: *A Documentary,* History, Oxford, 1967, p 131, notes the use of Marr limestone at Westminster Hall in 1395 and stored for use on royal manors in 1444. Doncaster area limestone was used c1417 in the building of Sion Abbey.
2. M L Faull & M Stinson (eds), *Domesday Book: Yorkshire,* Part One, Chichester, 1986, 12w12, p 321b
3. Will quoted in J E Morris, *The West Riding of Yorkshire,* London, 1911, p 292.
4. Jim Pain first showed me photographs of the old tower at Kirk Sandall. He also, together with Mary Duckitt, pointed out that the Kirk Sandall tower pinnacles found a new home at the top of Kirk Bramwith church tower.
5. The plans for this scheme were circulated in the parish in an illustrated leaflet.
6. A H Smith, *The Place-Names of the West Riding of Yorkshire,* Part One, Cambridge, 1961, p16
7. K Arthur, *Historical Notes of Fishlake Church and Parish,* Doncaster, 1961, p 23.
8. Arthur, *ibid,* p24.
9. Arthur, *ibid,* p 26.
10. Arthur, *ibid,* p 8.
11. *ibid.* The Durham connection dates back to the fourteenth century. In 1351 the prior and convent of Lewes granted the advowson of Fishlake church (and others) to the king. Shortly afterwards, the king granted the advowson of Fishlake to Ralph Neville. Then in 1384 John Neville of Raby granted the advowson of Fishlake to the prior and convent of Durham, to help them establish Durham College (later Trinity) in Oxford. In 1387 Fishlake church was appropriated to the college. After the Dissolution, Fishlake church was granted to the Dean and Chapter of Durham. See A H Thompson & C T Clay (eds), *Fasti Parochiales,* vol 1, part I, Yorkshire Archaeological Society Record Series, vol LXXXV, Wakefield, 1933, pp 114-15.

12. Fishlake church was one of the group granted to Lewes priory (Sussex) by William, Second Earl Warenne, c1091-7. See Thompson & Clay (eds), *ibid* p 114.
13. C Keyser, 'The Norman Doorways of Yorkshire' in T M Fallow (ed), *Memorials of Old Yorkshire*, London, 1909.
14. Morris, *op cit,* p 190 and Yorkshire Archaeological Society Record Series, vol. XXXIV, *Roger Dodsworth's Yorkshire Church Notes,* p 75.
15. Morris, *op cit,* p 191.
16. Arthur, *op cit,* p 11.
17. A Jones, *Chambers' Guide to Saints,* Edinburgh, 1992, p 82 & p186; D Attwater & C R John, *Penguin Dictionary of Saints,* Harmondsworth, second edition, 1983, p 253.
18. Arthur, *op cit,* p 16.
19. Arthur, *op cit,* p 19.
20. Arthur, *op cit,* p 36.
21. Arthur, *op cit,* p 37.
22. Bede, *A History of the English Church and People,* ed by L Sherley-Price, & revised by R E Latham, Harmondsworth, 1968, p 138.
23. Faull & Stinson, *op cit,* 12W1, 321a.
24. D Holland (ed), *Hatfield in History,* Sheffield, 1970, pp 4-5: J Tomlinson, *The Level of Hatfield Chase,* Doncaster, 1882, pp 127-28.
25. N Pevsner, *The Buildings of England: Yorkshire, The West Riding,* Harmondsworth, 1959, p255

Glossary

Boss: An ornamental feature covering the intersection of stone ribs or timber beams in a roof.
Capitals: The decorative stone at the top of a column, on which the arch rests.
Clerestory: A range of windows in the upper stage of the main (especially nave) walls of a church.
Decorated: Gothic architecture in England c1290-1350. Some of the grander examples are typified by rich, naturalistic sculpture of foliage.
Early English: Early Gothic architecture in England c1200-1300. It is the first of the three phases of the Gothic style in England. In the grander examples it is typified by rib vaults, pointed arches, lancet windows, and flying buttresses.
Fetterlock: A shackle used to restrain a falcon or other bird of prey, and fastened to its leg.
French Flamboyant: The Late Gothic style in France. It produced window tracery with flowing lines, closely resembling the natural forms of plants, water etc. Occasionally, the mid-fourteenth century Decorated style in England reached these heights.
Gothic: The whole of English architecture from c1200 to c1530.
Herringbone masonry: Courses of diagonally-laid walling, with each layer placed in the opposite direction to that below. It sometimes occurs in decorative bands. It is especially characteristic of c1040-1080.
Norman: Romanesque forms of architecture introduced into England by the Normans after the Conquest of 1066. The style lasted until the introduction of the Gothic style. It is typified by thick walls, heavy rounded arches, splayed windows, and often highly-decorative doorways and sometimes chancel arches.
Ogee arch: A sharp double-S form used in arches, window lights, and doorways, characteristic of the Decorated style. In a nodding ogee arch the upper part leans forward.
Perpendicular: Late Gothic architecture in England c1350-1530. It is characterised by straight and slender verticals and horizontals in window tracery. The style is much plainer, and more mechanical, than the Decorated style.
Puritan iconiclasm: A mid-seventeenth century frame of mind, which encouraged a fundamental reappraisal of ecclesiastical furnishing and decoration. It led to the destruction of much medieval stained glass and sculpture.
Quatrefoil: A shape formed by four lobes or equal curves. It is used in windows, in the sectional shape of some columns and capitals, and for the bowls of fonts. It is typical of the later phase of Early English and of the Decorated style.

9. Rememberd Forever: Medieval Church Monuments in the Doncaster Area

by Simeon Bennett and Tony Dodsworth

MANY PARISHES IN ENGLAND have at their heart an ancient church where generations of village inhabitants have worshipped. The church building and many of its fittings reflect the community in which it is situated and by careful study can help to bring that community alive even over a period of several hundred years. Some individuals within that community, usually those with most influence, are particularly easy to make contact with because their memorials can still be seen inside the church. These monumental memorials may date back as much as nine hundred years and some allow the visitor to see the type of costume and even the hairstyle prevalent in a time long past. These memorials come in a great variety and up to the early years of the sixteenth century can be largely classified into slabs, brasses and table tombs with or without effigies. The Doncaster area is particularly fortunate in that a good representation of church monuments has survived from the Middle Ages. The monuments that feature in this chapter can still be seen in the following churches, St Peter's, Conisbrough, St Peter's, Barnburgh, St Mary's, Sprotbrough, St Katherine's, Loversall, St John the Baptist, Wadworth and St Mary's, Tickhill (see Figure 1).

To be buried inside a church in medieval times you had to have exceptional status locally; the vast majority of people in a community were consigned to an unmarked grave in the churchyard. To those of the greatest status went the 'best' locations within the church, close to the main altar or in the chancel. As these locations became crowded the idea of building chantry chapels in the aisles close to the chancel became more common. A record of the establishment of a chantry chapel, especially in the fourteenth and fifteenth centuries, can often be found in documentary evidence even if their location within a church today may be difficult to pin down. The developing belief in the necessity of prayer for the dead partly accounts for the growth of chantries at this time. The rich and powerful (usually the lord and lady of the manor) left money in their wills for the construction of the chapels and for payment of priests to specifically say masses and prayers in the chantry for their salvation from purgatory. Another

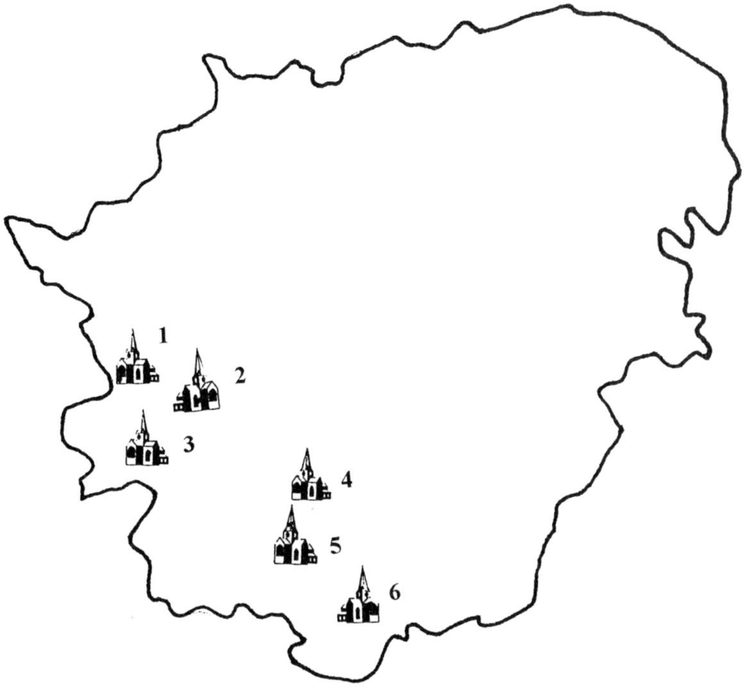

1. St Peter's, Barnburgh. 2. St Mary's, Sprotbrough. 3. St Peter's, Conisbrough. 4. St Katherine's, Loversall. 5. St John the Baptist, Wadworth. 6. St Mary's Tickhill.

Figure 1. Churches with monuments in the Doncaster Area mentioned in this chapter.

aspect of the development of a chantry chapel dedicated to a particular local family would seem to have been the desire to establish their link with that place in as substantial and long-standing a way as possible and to emphasise their dynastic continuity. The Cresacre Chapel in the North Aisle of St Peter's, Barnburgh is an excellent example of this. Similarly it is believed the Fitzwilliams set up the Chantry Chapel of St Thomas the Martyr in St Mary's, Sprotbrough.

One of the earliest and most interesting church monuments to be found in the Doncaster area can be seen at St Peter's, Conisbrough. Joseph Hunter writing in the 1820s tells us that a stone probably of Saxon antiquity could be seen in the church. He adds the information that this stone had formerly lain in the churchyard. In more recent times this has been described by P F Ryder as 'the elaborate Romanesque tomb-chest' and as such is more likely dated about 1150. The whole chest is richly carved (Figure 2) with coped lid decorated with medallions enclosing signs of the zodiac, mounted knights

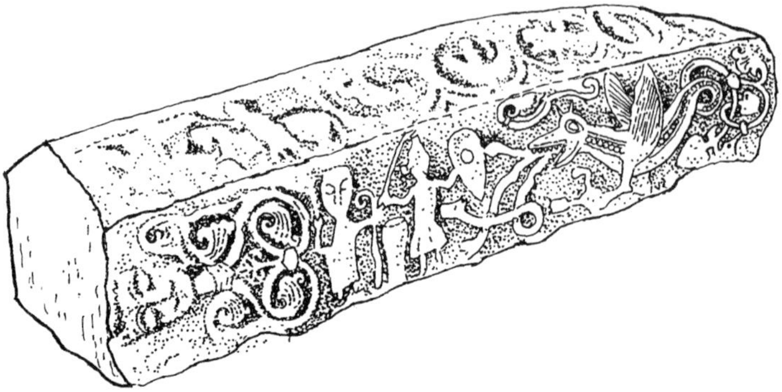

Figure 2. The tomb chest in St Peter's, Conisbrough. Based on a drawing in Peter Ryder's *Saxon Churches in South Yorkshire.*

and winged beasts. One side is decorated with palm leaves while the other shows a knight with a sword and shield challenging a fiercesome-looking dragon. Standing behind the knight is an ecclesiastical figure, presumably a bishop as he holds a crozier. Hunter is keen to link this image with the story of St George but it is very unlikely.

Church monuments as early as this one at Conisbrough nearly always took the form of a decorated lid over a stone coffin and did not represent in any way the person interred. The exceptional nature of this tomb lies in the amount of detailed decoration used, more normally a very simple cross sufficed. At this time it would have been rare to have any burials inside the church.

As the thirteenth century progressed so did the fashion of actually representing the deceased person. Initially a figure was carved in low relief on a slab of rock but later in the century, as carving skills developed, more undercutting of the figures took place with the effigy increasingly becoming free of the underlying slab. Even so only individuals of real standing in the community such as a local magnate, church founder or benefactor would possibly have been represented in this way.

A veritable treasure-house of features of historical interest can be found at St Mary's, Sprotbrough and, in the context of this chapter, pride of place must go to the freestone effigies of a knight and lady and a later brass also depicting a knight and lady. All those represented are believed to be members of the Fitzwilliam family who share their heraldic arms with an earlier helmed knight at Blyth just beyond the Doncaster area. The church underwent a number of changes between 1300 and 1350 and was significantly enlarged. The construction of a chantry chapel in the south aisle seems to have been directly linked to

Figure 3a. The Fitzwilliam Knight effigy in St Mary's, Sprotbrough. *Tony Dodsworth*

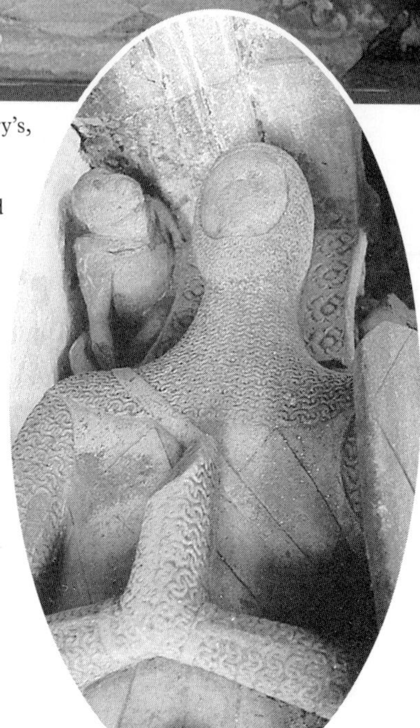

Figure 3b. Detail of the Fitzwilliam Knight - head and upper body. *Tony Dodsworth*

Figure 3c. Detail of the Fitzwilliam Knight - feet resting on on a lion. *Tony Dodsworth*

Figure 3d. Drawing of the Fitzwilliam Knight in the 1660s. From Henry Johnston's notebook at the Bodleian, Top. Yorks c13-14 f237.

Figure 4a. The effigy of Isobel Deincourt in St Mary's, Sprotbrough. *Tony Dodsworth.*

Figure 4b. Detail of the monument to Isobel Deincourt - head showing pleated wimple and attendant angels. *Tony Dodsworth.*

the desire of this Fitzwilliam family to be associated with Sprotbrough and its church, the family being extensive landowners in the local area. A chantry chapel containing effigies of the Fitzwilliams achieved that purpose. The survival of the two effigies in the chapel in such excellent condition is far from common, both apparently being fortunate in escaping the worst ravages of the Reformation and the iconoclastic storm that followed it in the mid-sixteenth and seventeenth centuries.

The effigy of the knight (Figure 3) lies in a niche in the south wall of the chapel under a finely decorated ogee arch. The Fitzwilliam arms are clearly seen on the figure's surcoat and shield but doubts remain as to who precisely is represented. Some believe it to be Sir Edmund Fitzwilliam who was executed in 1322 following the Battle of Boroughbridge but others think it more likely represents Sir William Fitzwilliam who died at some time between 1338 and 1342 and was the husband of the lady represented by the second effigy. The effigies attracted the attention of Joseph Hunter in the 1820s who believed they possibly represented

Figure 4c. Detail of the monument to Isobel Deincourt - finely carved hair and feathered wings of one attendant angel. *Tony Dodsworth.*

Sir William and his wife Isobel.

The knight is covered in mail from head to foot and was examined by I'Anson earlier this century and linked with others in Yorkshire. Strangely he states that the shield bears 'no carved charge' when the Fitzwilliam arms are obvious on it today and were clearly described by Hunter last century. Considering its suggested date of the 1330s-1340s it is a very unusual military effigy in that the legs are straight when most knights of this time are shown with crossed legs. His feet rest on an eccentrically-styled lion and at his head one battered angel has survived (the foot and hand of the other one can still be made out). Carved angels were a particular target of the church reformers in the reign of Edward VI. Uniquely his head rests on a very flat cushion with curved edges decorated over all its visible surface with a flower motif. So many elements of this monument are unusual that some doubts exist as to whether it is genuinely of its proposed date, it may be a later replacement of an original figure although still very old. What definitely can be stated is that when drawn by Johnson in the 1660s its appearance was very similar to today.

There seems to be no doubts about the authenticity of the female effigy reputedly representing Isobel Deincourt, the wife of Sir William (Figure 4). She is shown wearing a finely pleated wimple that normally would be a sign that the person represented was a widow (as indeed Isobel was for the last few years of her life). The

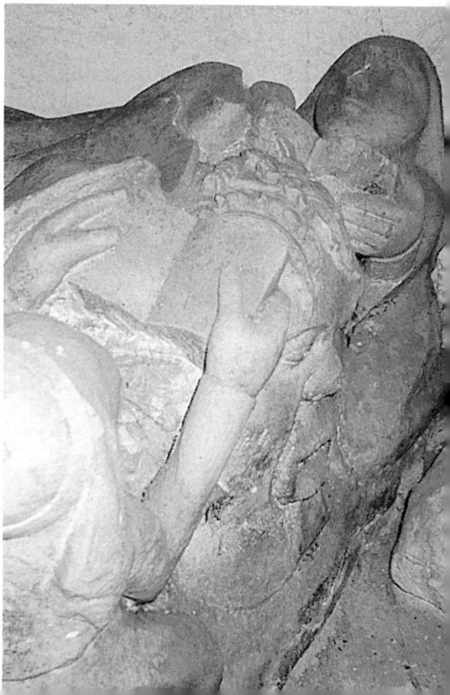

Figure 4d. Detail of the monument to Isobel Deincourt - angels reading at the feet resting on a Green Man. *Tony Dodsworth.*

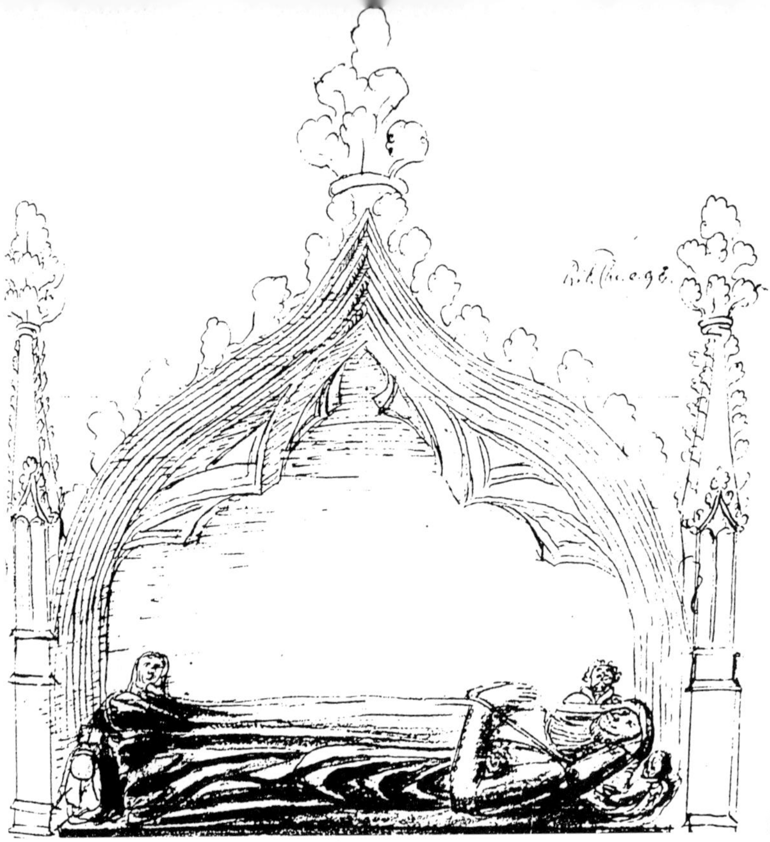

Figure 5. Drawing of the monument to Isobel Deincourt in the 1660s. Note at this time the female figure lies under the carved ogee arch where today the male figure is found. From Henry Johnston's notebook at the Bodleian, Top.Yorks c13-14 f237.

effigy is in a remarkably good state of preservation with the angels at the head and feet all undamaged. The carving of the drapery on the figure is of great quality and examination of the attendant angels at the head reveals the most beautifully produced curls of hair as well as delicately feathered wings. These angels wear a collar of diamonds which is likely to represent the Fitzwilliam heraldry; such a representation on attendant angels would be extremely rare. Equally unusual the lady's feet rest on the head of a Green Man, a figure which surprisingly is found quite often in medieval churches but rarely on effigies. The grotesque face is hard to see as it lies close to the eastern end of the quite recently constructed niche but a careful inspection reveals that the top of the Green Man's head is decorated with exquisite stone carving of curling oak leaves and acorns.

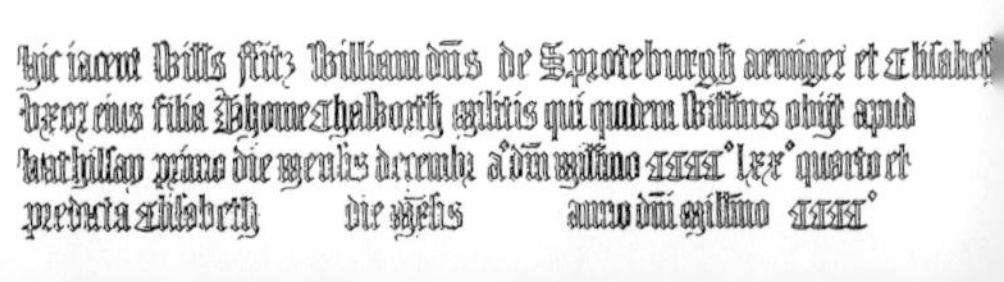

Figure 6. Drawing of the brass of William Fitwilliam (died 1474) and his wife Elizabeth. By William Cowen from Joseph Hunter's *South Yorkshire*.

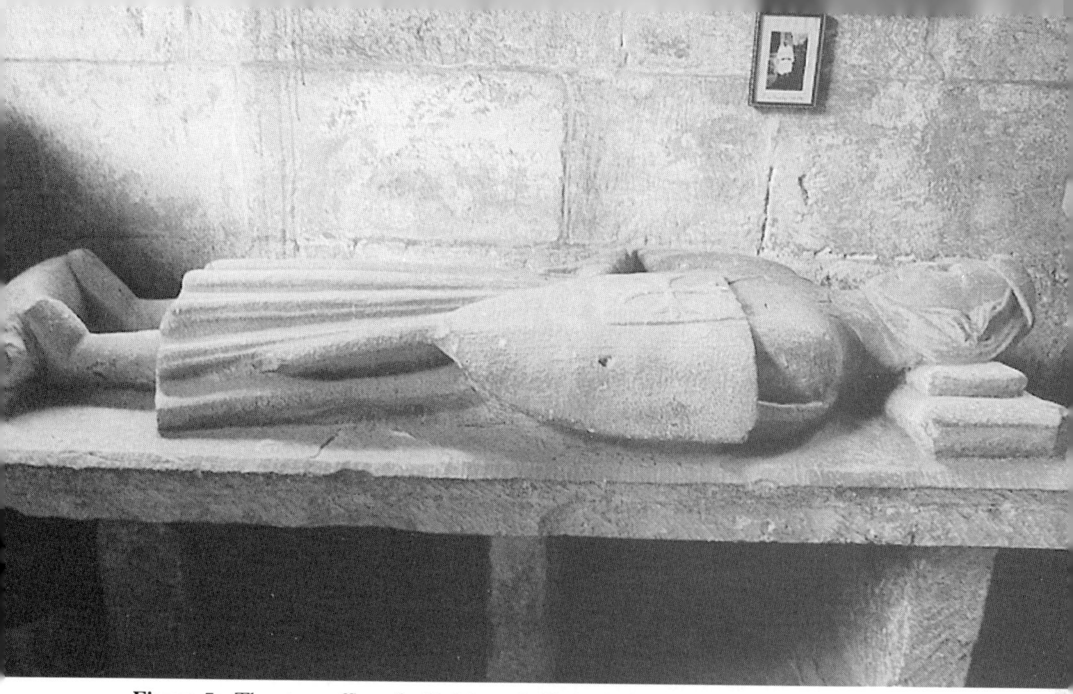

Figure 7a. The stone effigy of a Knight at St Katherine's, Loversall. *Tony Dodsworth.*

Two small figures wearing head-cloths are carved on either side of the Green Man resting their books on his head. Even the nails of these splendid figures can be seen carved delicately on their fingers. This is certainly a female effigy that stands comparison with some of the finest in Yorkshire and might be compared with the ladies of broadly similar date at Felixkirk and Church Fenton, both found to the north of the Doncaster area. Close inspection of this figure will certainly be a rewarding experience (Figure 5).

Also in the church at Sprotbrough, but this time set into the floor of the chancel, is the recently restored brass of a later William Fitzwilliam and his wife Elizabeth, daughter of Thomas Chaworth (Figure 6). Brass was a memorial medium used less often in Yorkshire than in some areas further south (like Essex) where good quality stone was in short supply. This brass has an inscription and so the figures shown are easy to identify. This William Fitzwilliam died in 1474.

Lying not far to the south-east of Sprotbrough is the small and relatively isolated church of St Katherine's, Loversall. To some extent the church is dominated by its gabled south chapel, built by the Wirralls, which now includes the effigy of a

Figure 7b. Drawing of the effigy at Loversall. From M H Bloxam, *On Certain Sepulchral Effigies and Monuments in South Yorkshire.*

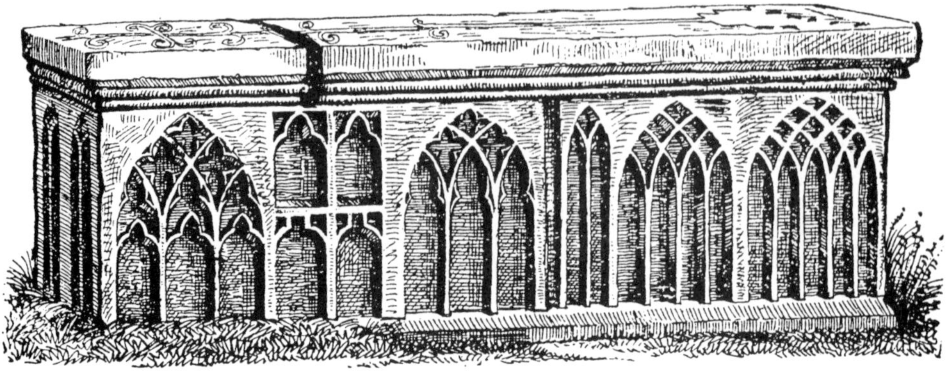

Figure 8. Drawing of the Fourteenth Century tomb chest in the churchyard of St Katherine's, Loversall. Based on a drawing in Frederick Burgess, *English Churchyard Memorials.*

robed figure believed to represent a fourteenth century knight (Figure 7). This monument was possibly removed from the nave during the Overton restoration of the late eighteenth century. The figure is represented with his right hand presumably on the hilt of his sword but it is obscured by the shield on his left arm. Unusually no mail is shown on the figure, neither on the body nor on the head. He appears to wear a type of folded cowl over his wavy hair and his feet rest on presumably a damaged lion, the legs being represented in an uncrossed position. His head rests on two elongated rectangular pillows. The Knights of the Military Order of St John of Jerusalem held property in Loversall at one time and this fact linked with the patonce cross shown on one quarter of the shield has led some to believe the figure represents a knight of that order. This seems to ignore the evidence that the de Middletons, ancient landowners in Loversall, bore just such a patonce cross in a quarter of their arms. They had apparently died out before the date of this effigy but it is possible that the de Ripers family that succeeded the de Middletons adopted the same arms. The flat overall appearance of this effigy suggests a relatively thin

Figure 9a. The wooden effigy of Sir Thomas Cresacre (died c1346) in St Peter's Church, Barnburgh. *Tony Dodsworth.*

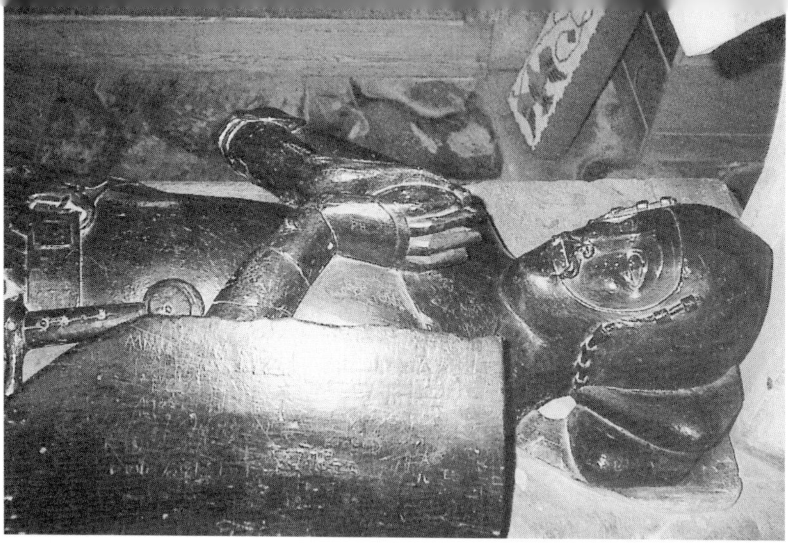

Figure 9b. Detail of the effigy of Sir Thomas Cresacre - view of the head. *Tony Dodsworth.*

block of stone was used by the mason.

An even more unusual monument survives outside in the churchyard at Loversall where an early fourteenth century tomb chest is found (Figure 8). This early tomb chest is as Frederick Burgess describes it in English Churchyard Memorials, 'unique for the various patterns of window tracery carved upon its sides, which would seem to be taken from some master mason's pattern book'. This chest was obviously highly regarded by Pevsner, certainly much more so than Hunter who described its sides as 'rudely decorated with arch-work in various device'! On the lid of the chest a foliated cross has been carved.

At St Peter's Church, Barnburgh is found one of the really outstanding church monuments in this part of Yorkshire. This is an effigy of Sir Thomas Cresacre who is believed to have died about the middle of the 1340s (Figure 9). Unusually he has been carved out of oak and is described by Pevsner as being of 'outstanding quality, gentle in the attitude and execution'. He lies on top of a tomb chest erected for one of his descendants, Percival Cresacre (died c1477), and beneath the closely cusped arch of the same tomb. The Cresacre family was associated with the Barnbugh area from

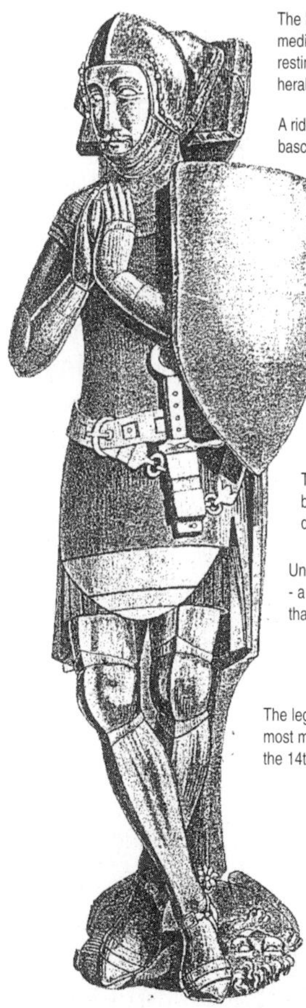

Figure 9c. Labelled drawing of the effigy of Sir Thomas Cresacre. Based on a drawing in M H Bloxham, *On Certain Sepulchral Effigies and Monuments in South Yorkshire.*

the late thirteenth century; this ended when the heiress, Ann Cresacre (born 1510) married John More. She, herself, is of considerable note for her husband was none other than the son of Sir Thomas More, who was Henry VIII's Chancellor before falling out of favour and being executed. As a result of this link a wonderful drawing of Anne by Hans Holbein, the court painter, has survived. It is the real thrill of history to imagine this Anne, linked to so many famous events in the early days of the Reformation, gazing out across the Dearne Valley from the churchyard of St Peter's.

Earlier this century Alfred Fryer wrote the definitive account of Wooden Monumental Effigies in England and Wales and in this he gives a detailed description of the wooden Cresacre monument. He also draws attention to 'its high artistic conception' and speculates that it might even be a true likeness of Sir Thomas (in general it is believed this would have been unusual at this date). The effigy is of considerable interest because of the way the defensive equipment of the day is represented on the figure. The ridged bascinet he wears on his head is clearly shown as well as a variety of other types of protection on his shoulders, elbows, knees and feet. He is particularly special because he is shown wearing an unusual military garment called a cyclas. This garment, apparently unique to England, seems to have been in fashion between about 1321 and 1346. A cyclas is perhaps best described as a surcoat but with the front cut away to the middle of the thighs and slit up the sides to the hips. It is thought it was less restrictive for fighting than a surcoat. Fryer informs us that 'vast numbers of Yorkshire people annually visit the effigy of Sir Thomas Cresacre', an interesting insight into leisure activities before the days of television! These crowds were particularly attracted by the legend attached to the figure that Sir Thomas had been attacked by a wild cat in a wood near Barnburgh village and after a running fight both died in the porch of the church. Some red-coloured stones in the floor of the porch were believed to have been permanently stained by blood from this encounter. Many such legends are associated with ancient church monuments across the country. Sir Thomas is represented holding his heart in his hands, a not uncommon style in medieval monuments, and this perhaps indicates that his heart was actually preserved in the church or for some devotional purpose the significance of which is not recognised

Figure 10a. Drawing of the stone effigy of a knight/forester at St John the Baptist, Wadworth. Note the hunting horn and 'buckler'-type shield. From M H Bloxam, *On Certain Sepulchral Effigies and Monuments in South Yorkshire.*

Figure 10b. Detail of the effigy of the knight at Wadworth - view of the bearded face. *Tony Dodsworth.*

today. The effigy was removed to London for a short time in the late 1980s to 'star' in a museum exhibition on 'The Age of Chivalry'.

A fine collection of medieval monuments in varying states of preservation can be found in the church of St John the Baptist in Wadworth. These monuments have been moved around considerably over the years and three can now be found propped up under the west tower. One of these is an unusual figure showing the head and feet of a male figure but with most of the body in between obscured by a flat section of stone rather like a blanket. The figure is as Pevsner described 'modelled by scooping out a hollow area around it' and probably dates to the first half of the fourteenth century. The technique was possibly employed when the slab of rock to be used was too thin to produce a more conventional effigy. Certainly less skill would have been required to produce such a monument and so perhaps it was cheaper to buy.

Close by can be found another unusual monument, this time in a more traditional pose but with some special 'extras'. This monument, carved in a darker yellowy-brown rock than normally seen locally, is believed to represent a bearded male of the fourteenth century whose undefended head rests on two cushions (Figure 10). It was seen by Hunter in the 1820s when it was apparently 'almost buried in a heap of rubbish'. The figure is unusual in showing no mail or armour but wearing a sword with a small shield (called a buckler) plus a hunting horn. The horn is a rare feature on an effigy (an earlier example can be seen on a knight in Pershore Abbey, Worcestershire) and is believed to show that the person represented had responsibility for hunting in the area. The figure is straight-legged with the feet resting on the damaged remnant of possibly a lion. This is no expert piece of effi-

Figure 11. Drawing of the tomb chest of Edmund Fitzwilliam (died 1421) and his wife Maud at Wadworth. By William Cowan from Joseph Hunter's *South Yorkshire.*

Figure 12a. Tomb chest of Edmund Fitzwilliam (died 1421) and his wife Maud at Wadworth. *Tony Dodsworth.*

gial carving but the hands joined in prayer allow the carver to represent a line of round buttons running down from the wrist along each sleeve.

The outstanding monument in Wadworth church represents Edmund Fitzwilliam (died 1421) and his wife, Maud, daughter of Sir John Hotham of Holderness (Figure 11). The material used for this monument is alabaster and by this date in the fifteenth century a widespread trade in such effigial tombs had developed based in the North Midlands (close to the source of the alabaster). By this date the effigies had become far more standardised but this should not stop us from appreciating their quality (Figure 12a). The effigies were usually represented lying on a decorated tomb chest. Alabaster was particularly suited to the carving of intricate detail and this can be clearly seen on the tomb of Edmund and his wife despite deliberate mutilation and centuries of graffiti (not apparently just a modern curse!). By this time the knight is shown with his head resting on his helm; he is encased in plate armour from head to toe with just his

Figure 12b. Detail of Maud Fitzwilliam from the tomb chest at Wadworth showing her elaborate hair decoration precisely represented in alabaster. *Tony Dodsworth.*

Figure 13a. Tomb chest and effigies of Sir Richard Fitzwilliam (died 1497) and his wife, Lady Lucy Neville in St Mary's, Tickhill. *Tony Dodsworth.*

face showing. The traces of the drooping moustache that remain are entirely characteristic of a figure of this date. The SS collar round his neck is again a common feature most notably associated later on with allegiance to the Lancastrian cause in the Wars of the Roses. His bascinet (helmet) is ringed by a decorated band called an orle and he

Figure 13b. Detail of Sir Richard Fitzwilliam and his wife. Note Sir Richard's elaborate SS collar. *Tony Dodsworth.*

also wears a decorated belt. A comparison with the Fitzwilliam knight at Sprotbrough shows just how far armour had developed in the hundred years up to the 1430s.

His wife lies on his right with her head on two cushions; these were once supported by two attendant angels but only their lower halves remain (Figure 12b). Her hair is still beautifully decorated and her feet are covered by a long kirtle. Somewhat unusually there is no dog shown at her feet. The tomb chest she lies on with her husband has five angels carrying shields on the north side but only two survive completely on the south side. In 1465 Edmund's son, Edmund, was buried close by but he lies under a plain altar tomb with heraldic shields and a clear inscription.

Finally to complete the sequence we move to the church of St Mary the Virgin, Tickhill. Here lies the tomb of Sir Roger Fitzwilliam and his wife, Lady Lucy Neville, which is dated after the accepted end of the medieval period in 1485 but shares sufficient characteristics with others in the Doncaster area to be considered in this chapter (Figure 13a). Richard died about 1497 but his widow married again before her death in about 1534. Roger Dodsworth saw this tomb in 1620 in the 'south quire' but certainly by 1828 it was in its present position close to the north door for Hunter records it as such. It is surprising to discover how often effigies and tomb chests have been moved

Figure 13c. Tomb chest and effigies of Sir Anthony Browne and his wife in Battle Abbey, Sussex. *Tony Dodsworth.*

around their churches over the centuries. The tomb is not well preserved; it is a pity the iron railings that now protect it were not in position a few hundred years earlier! The tomb chest is best seen on its south and west sides. The south side consists of three compartments separated by columns and each containing a shield beneath a shell-shaped and fluted canopy. Acanthus leaves decorate parts of the chest and highlight that a new era in the artistic design of tombs had arrived for they represent the Renaissance style and as such are 'one of the earliest examples in England of that style' (according to Pauline Routh in her book *Medieval Effigial Tombs in Yorkshire*). Originally it is believed that the tomb was sited in the House of the Austin Friars in Tickhill but it was presumably removed to St Mary's at some time following the suppression of monasteries in 1537.

The effigy of St Thomas is badly damaged being split by a large diagonal crack across the body and with the hands, right elbow and right leg missing (Figure 13b). Despite this it is easy to see he wears a tabard decorated with the Fitzwilliam lozenges and around his neck is fastened a really stylish SS collar. His hair is uncovered, as was normal in effigies of this time, and worn long. His wife lies to his left with her hands missing and her face badly mutilated (as is her husband's). Despite the damage the alabaster figure of Lucy shows plenty of interesting detail of the clothes then worn and especially a heavy chain necklace with probably a fish pendant. The fish is believed to be a pike then known as a 'lucye' and so is a conceit linked to her name. The design of the tomb chest may be closely compared to one in Battle Abbey where Lucy's son by her second marriage to Sir Anthony Browne (Figure 13c) is buried. This son died in 1548. The Battle Abbey tomb has been repainted in bright colours and reminds us that this would have been the case originally in Tickhill, indeed Hunter mentioned the tomb 'painted in gorgeous manner' when he examined it in 1828.

In some respects this chapter has been dominated by descriptions of the effigies of the various branches of the Fitzwilliam family for examples are found in Sprotbrough, Wadworth and Tickhill. These clearly display their heraldry the Fitzwilliam lozenges either on shields, surcoats or tabards and this should remind us of one purpose of such ostentatious display of status in death. As mentioned earlier families of some standing were keen to establish their links with specific places and a family chantry chapel with effigies in the local church was one clear way of doing so. The religious beliefs of those represented were also important for they took seriously the torments of purgatory and wished to be prayed for as much as possible after their deaths. Whatever their purpose, we can only be grateful that at least some of these fine monuments have survived to allow us to wonder at the artistry of their creators and to put us so firmly in touch with people who lived more than five hundred years ago. The fact that this 'church art' is still largely in the buildings and in the places it was originally produced for should heighten our interest in it and our appreciation of it.

Bibliography

Beastall, T W, *Portrait of an English Parish Church - St Mary the Virgin, Tickhill, Yorkshire,* nd (1989).
Bloxam, M H, *On Certain Sepulchral Effigies and Monuments in South Yorkshire,* Yorkshire Architectural Society, York, 1850.
Burgess, Frederick, *English Churchyard Memorials,* SPCK, 1979.
Fryer, Alfred, *Wooden Monumental Effigies in England and Wales,* Elliott Stock, 1910.
Hunter, Joseph, *South Yorkshire* (Vol1), London, 1828-1831.
I'Anson, W M, 'Some Yorkshire Effigies', *Yorkshire Archaeological Journal,* Vol XXVII, 1923.
I'Anson, W M, 'The Medieval Military Effigies of Yorkshire (Part 2)', *Yorkshire Archaeological Journal,* Vol XXIX, 1927.
Kemp, Brian, *Church Monuments,* Shire Publications Ltd, 1985.
Kemp, Brian, *English Church Monuments,* B T Batsford, 1980.
Markus, Mary, 'An Attempt to Discriminate the Styles' - the sculptors of the Harrington Tomb, Cartmel, *Church Monuments,* Vol XI, 1996.
Parker, W J, *The Cresacre Treasure.*
Pevsner, Nicholas (revised by Enid Ratcliffe), *The Buildings of England - Yorkshire, The West Riding,* Penguin Books, 1967.
Routh, Pauline, *Medieval Effigial Alabaster Tombs in Yorkshire,* Ipswich, 1976.
Ryder, P F, *Saxon Churches in South Yorkshire,* South Yorkshire County Council, 1980.

Acknowledgements

We are indebted to Brian Elliott for his encouragement and advice while completing this chapter. We would also like to acknowledge the co-operation of Reverend Canon S J Matthews of St Mary's, Sprotbrough and of Reverend R W Ivell of St John the Baptist, Wadworth. Extra help with regard to the history of St Mary's, Sprotbrough has been provided by Bill Cavill and we thank him for it. The staff of the Local History Section at Doncaster Central Library also offered expert help. Specialist information and advice with regard to medieval church monuments have been provided by Brian and Moira Gittos, Mary Markus as well as Richard Knowles. The Bodleian Library, University of Oxford, has kindly allowed the reproduction of Henry Johnston's drawings. Finally thanks to Jane for all the hard work of checking and word processing.

Further detailed information about church monuments may be obtained from the Church Monuments Society (contact c/o The Society of Antiquaries, Burlington House, Piccadilly, London, W1V OHS). Members of the Society receive two detailed newsletters each year plus a high quality illustrated journal.

10. Denaby Main: The Development of a South Yorkshire Mining Village

by Melvyn Jones

COLLIERY SETTLEMENTS HAVE BEEN a characteristic feature of South Yorkshire for at least 200 years. Some, particularly those associated with the exploitation of the concealed coalfield on or to the east of the Magnesian Limestone escarpment in the first two or three decades of the twentieth century, may last for at least another century in their present form. Others have disappeared completely within a century of their creation. Yet others still remain, but most of the original buildings have been replaced.

In terms of their **physical morphology,** that is their size, shape and internal design, South Yorkshire's colliery settlements are of five basic types.

1. Small colliery settlements, often in the form of a single or small number of terraced rows, often next to the pit gates, for example, Long Row, Carlton, near Barnsley, and Westwood Rows at Thorncliffe, near Sheffield, now both gone. Colliery rows were typical of small-scale mining developments or the early stages of large colliery developments on the exposed coalfield in the nineteenth century. They were sometimes distinct units within larger settlements but were also often built away from existing villages, in the case of the Long Row at Carlton for convenience next to the pit, and in the case of Westwood Rows away from other miners' cottages because they were erected for blackleg miners during a lockout in 1869-70. The miners' rows at Elsecar (Old Row, Station Row, Reform Row) come into this category. Elsecar was a very small hamlet around a green before mining development.

2. Medium-sized colliery villages, again of nineteenth century origin, largely unplanned, away from existing villages. Worsbrough Bridge, developed next to a branch of the Dearne and Dove Canal and the South Yorkshire Railway is a good example of this type of pit village.

3. Large colliery settlements, in the form of small towns, with no overall plan developed over a long period in the nineteenth and twentieth centuries around the cores of pre-existing villages, for example, Mexborough, Wath, Wombwell.

4. Large colliery settlements that grew up over a long period in the nineteenth century, often with no overall plan, and built away from pre-existing villages. Parkgate, near Rotherham, a combined iron and steel making/colliery settlement, eventually outgrowing its pre-existing neighbour Rawmarsh, is one of the best-known examples.

Writing about types 2, 3 and 4, Coates and Lewis in 1966, described them as 'unplanned, untidy, colourless and for the most part treeless.' They went on to say:

> *These are untidy and dirty landscapes. Domestic and industrial smoke, smells from coal-preparation plants, dilapidated pre-mining buildings, decaying terrace-houses, smoke-blackened buildings, garish colour schemes, unkempt gardens and allotments, prefabricated or improvised garages and acres of sheer dereliction and waste cannot fail to have an impact on the observer, shocking the sensitive, disgusting the idealist and fascinating the inquisitive stranger.*[1]

Needless to say, there has been considerable improvement since 1966. Now there are no collieries whatsoever on the exposed coalfield west of the Magnesian Limestone escarpment where these settlements developed in the nineteenth century. The colliery buildings have been demolished, spoil heaps have been landscaped and planted upon, and the housing has undergone considerable improvement or been demolished and redeveloped.

5. Large planned colliery villages, all on the concealed coalfield, all of early twentieth century origin, either engulfing pre-existing villages (e.g. Maltby) or growing up alongside but separate from a pre-existing village (New Edlington next to Old Edlington, New Rossington next to Rossington, New Bentley next to Bentley, Woodlands next to Adwick le Street). These are planned villages and often incorporate well laid out estates of geometrical design. They housed miners at widely spaced collieries (shafts were much deeper and much more expensive to sink on the concealed coalfield so the pits were designed to work much larger areas underground than their counterparts on the exposed coalfield) and so another characteristic of many of these villages is that they are separated from each other by large tracts of countryside, unlike types 1 (where they survive), 2, 3 and 4 on the exposed coalfield which merge into each other as in the Dearne Valley between Wombwell and Conisbrough.

Not all colliery settlements fit into these five basic types, and in a number of cases on the exposed coalfield west of Rotherham, some colliery settlements, are very complex, having engulfed pre-existing settlements, spread in all directions and incorporated other colliery settlements into their built up area. In addition, some of the older colliery settlements on the exposed coalfield later acquired geometrically laid out estates (type 5) like the new colliery settlements in the Doncaster area.

Denaby Main is a typical example of the fourth type of colliery settlement described above. It is characterised by its one company origin, its location away from pre-existing settlements and the way in which the pre-mining administrative, property and field boundaries determined to a great extent the details of its original layout. It is also an example of what Dr J. D. Marshall has called an *industrial colony:* 'a settlement that has been 'planted' by an employer at a point where he can gather a labour force for the immediate use of a local industry.'[2]

Four distinct phases in the physical development of the village of Denaby Main can be identified.

Phase 1: Sinking and opening out the colliery and the creation of an 'embryonic' industrial colony

Before 1864, and the beginning of the sinking of Denaby Main Colliery, the land on which the colliery village was to be developed was low-lying farmland to the south of the meandering River Don (Figure 1). The nearest villages were about a mile away: Mexborough to the west, Old Denaby to the south-west and Conisbrough to the east.

The site of Denaby Main Colliery was determined by a combination of local geology and transport considerations. At the time of its opening for commercial production in the late 1860s Denaby Main Colliery was the most easterly coal mine on the South

Figure 1. The Denaby Main area before colliery development in the 1860s. Note the Denaby / Conisbrough boundary, field boundaries, Doncaster Road and the railway, all of which were to be major influences on the layout of the mining village.

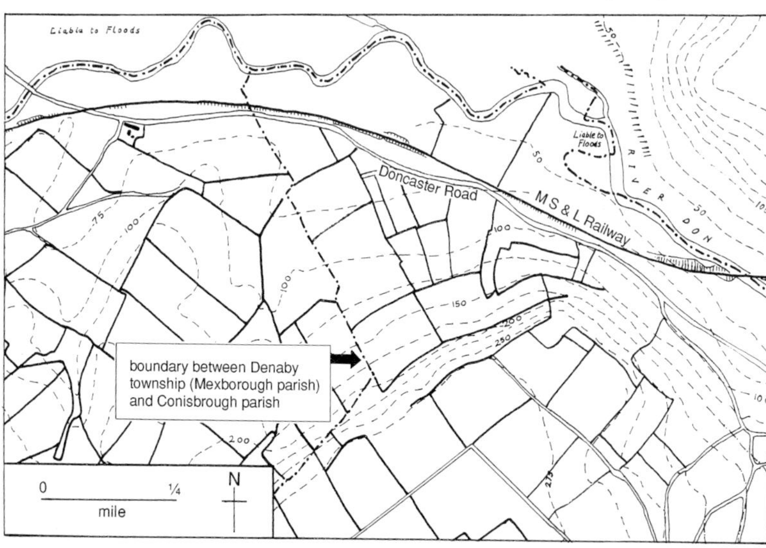

Yorkshire coalfield[3] and also the deepest. It was to retain these two distinctions for another 30 years.

Any saving in sinking the shaft was valuable hence a site at one of the lowest points in the area on the flood plain of the River Don was inevitable. The fact that this was where the Manchester, Sheffield and Lincolnshire Railway (later Great Central Railway and then London & North Eastern Railway), the navigable Don and the Don Navigation (canal) were located was also crucial. The site chosen for the colliery consisted of fourteen acres of land in Lower Crane Close, Spittleholm and Broomcroft belonging to the Fullerton estate at Thrybergh Park.

An attempt to sink a mine in Denaby township (which was part of Mexborough parish) beside the River Don had met with failure in the 1850s because of the volume of water encountered and the expense of combatting this problem.[4] The coal-owners who leased land at Denaby in 1863 must have been fully aware that they faced large initial expense in sinking a very deep shaft and in overcoming the water problem. The initial capital outlay was £30,000 provided by five shareholders who by 1867 were: John Buckingham Pope and Richard Pope (West Yorkshire coal-owners), Richard Pearson (also a West Yorkshire coal-owner), Edward Baines Senior (a Leeds newspaper owner and Liberal MP), Joseph Crossley (of Halifax, carpet manufacturer) and Joseph Huntriss (of Doncaster).

The *Doncaster Gazette* reported on 16 December 1864 that the sinking of the colliery had begun:

> *DENABY MAIN COLLIERY COMPANY - This company last week got fairly to work in sinking their shaft to the Barnsley Bed. The machinery and engines are of first-class character, and fully equal to the great depth to which the shaft will have to be sunk.*[5]

They immediately encountered water and were to do so for the first hundred yards. By August 1866 the sinkers had reached a depth of 150 yards and had overcome the water problem,[6] and by February 1867 the shaft was 200 yards deep and progress was 'favourable'.[7] Eventually the Barnsley seam was reached at a depth of 448 yards in the late summer of 1867.[8] It was nine feet and eight inches thick.

It is not absolutely clear when the colliery started commercial production. An NCB handout (not dated) seen at Cadeby Colliery in 1969 stated that 'the first coal was drawn in 1865. The Barnsley seam was worked continuously from that date'. In view of the fact that the Barnsley Bed was not reached until more than two years later suggests that the NCB date is out by several years. The fact that, as we shall see, there was a major dispute at the pit from March to September

1869 when about 250 colliers were employed, suggests that commercial production began in late 1867 or in 1868.

Just as the start of commercial coal production at Denaby Main Colliery cannot be pinpointed exactly, so are the details of the size and layout of the early mining village at Denaby Main. In his *From Doncaster to Hallamshire*, published in 1879, John Tomlinson wrote a detailed description of the early village:

> *... Speaking from personal observation, extending over the last dozen years, I can truly assert that the surface plant at Denaby Main have grown. Not very long ago the 'pit-hollow' presented a few unsightly excrescences, or spoil banks, with an engine house, rough 'head-gear' and a number of small one-storied human dwellings not inaptly termed 'sparrow-barracks'.*
>
> *... the aspect and associations of Denaby have greatly changed ... Here, right in one's path, looms a gigantic colliery, with its tall chimneys, elevated head-gear, huge spoil-banks, tramways, work shops, offices and long rows of cottages - a thickly populated village, all in a lump.*
>
> *... I noticed a little school-room in a hollow place, under the shadow of that pit-hill - a not very eligible site, although young lungs breathe freely. I observed also a dissenting Chapel, and a plain, unromantic church, half-warehouse and half cottage, with a very wooden porch and arched belfry, in the latest Gothic style.*[9]

Tomlinson's Sparrow Barracks were over Grey's Bridge, half a mile to the west of the colliery in Mexborough opposite the *Miners' Arms.* The rest of the early village (Tomlinson's 'long row of cottages') seems to have consisted of cottages, more than 80 in all, standing adjacent to the colliery along the northern side of Doncaster Road. It is also likely that a substantial number of the cottages on the south side of Doncaster Road, on the south side of Annerley Street and the north side of Cliff View date from this period of development (Figure 2). The OS Six-Inch map of 1903 shows a school in the backyard of the cottages on the north side of Doncaster Road - presumably the one referred to by Tomlinson. There was also a bye-law application for a Wesleyan Chapel at Denaby Main in 1870. At this stage both the colliery and the colliery village were in Denaby township (part of Mexborough parish) near the boundary with Conisbrough parish.

In 1864 while the colliery was being sunk, another development was taking place. In that year a glassworks (the Providence Glassworks) was opened at Denaby Main by Kilner Brothers of Thornhill Lees, Dewsbury, manufacturers of the famous 'Kilner jar'. The glassworks and its associated residential colony were located over half a mile to

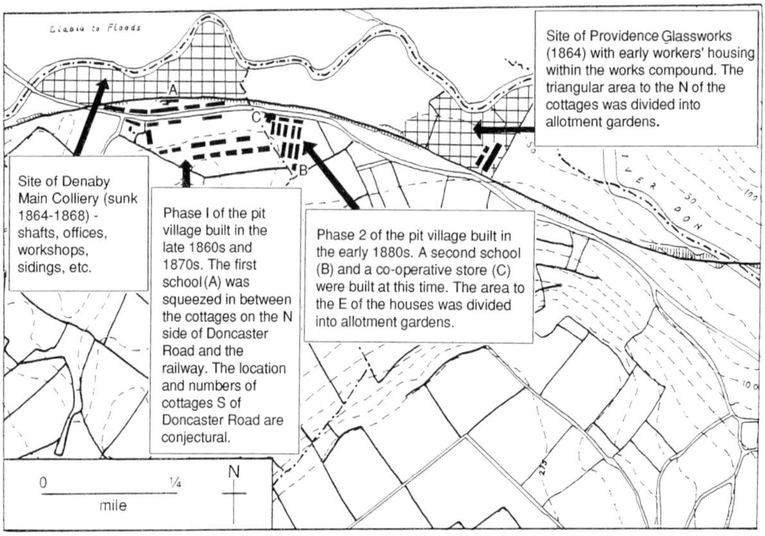

Figure 2. Denaby Main by the early 1880s showing phases 1 and 2 of the development of the pit village and Kilners' Glassworks and its associated housing.

the east of Denaby Main Colliery on low land to the north of the Doncaster Road in Conisbrough parish. In 1879 about 200 men, women and boys were employed there, many of them living in 'two rows of comfortable cottages, numbering upwards of 40 in all, attached to the works.'[10] Some of these cottages are located on Figure 2 and shown in Figure 8.

Phase 2: Expansion of Denaby Main in the early 1880s

On 1 November 1880 the Denaby Main Colliery Company leased six acres in Underhill Field in Conisbrough parish from Andrew Montagu of Melton Hall and the second phase of the development of Denaby Main began. On this land they laid out Rossington Street, Tickhill Street, Melton Street and Melton View and built about 100 houses. They also built part of the Co-operative stores in Melton View.[11] This important but relatively small extension to the village is shown in Figure 2.

Phase 3: The sinking of Cadeby Main Colliery and the large-scale expansion of Denaby Main

In January 1889 an agreement was made between Denaby Main Colliery Company and Dame Georgina Copley of Sprotbrough for the exploitation of the Barnsley seam under the Magnesian Limestone outcrop to the east of Denaby Main under Dame Georgina's Sprotbrough, Cadeby, Scawsby and Marr Grange estates.[12] By March

1889 a local newspaper was able to report that work on the new colliery - Cadeby Main Colliery - had begun.[13] It was opened in 1893.

In anticipation of the expansion of their mining operations the Company set about acquiring more land on which to extend their colliery village and this ushered in a decade of substantial village expansion. In December 1889 they leased more land in Underhill Field in Conisbrough parish from Andrew Montagu of Melton Hall and bye-law applications to build houses were made in 1891 and 1893 resulting in the development of Marr Street, Sprotbrough Street, Edlington Street, Clifton Street and Firbeck Street.[14] Altogether 348 dwellings were erected together with three shops (in Wood View on Doncaster Road). To match this residential development another school was built at the top of Rossington Street (opened in 1893).[15] These developments are shown in Figure 3.

Even further expansion was foreshadowed in 1893 when a further ten acres were leased from Andrew Montagu immediately to the east of the plot leased in 1889. The company then proceeded to lay out and build upon six more streets: Balby, Blythe, Loversall, Scawsby, Cusworth and Wadworth. Altogether they built 307 four-roomed houses and 96 six-roomed houses on this plot.[16] They also built a public house (Denaby Main Hotel - *'The Drum'* as it is more popularly known). A little later (1897) a bye-law application was made to

Figure 3. The opening of Cadeby Main (1893) and further extensions (Phase 3) to Denaby Main village in the 1890s and the first years of the twentieth century.

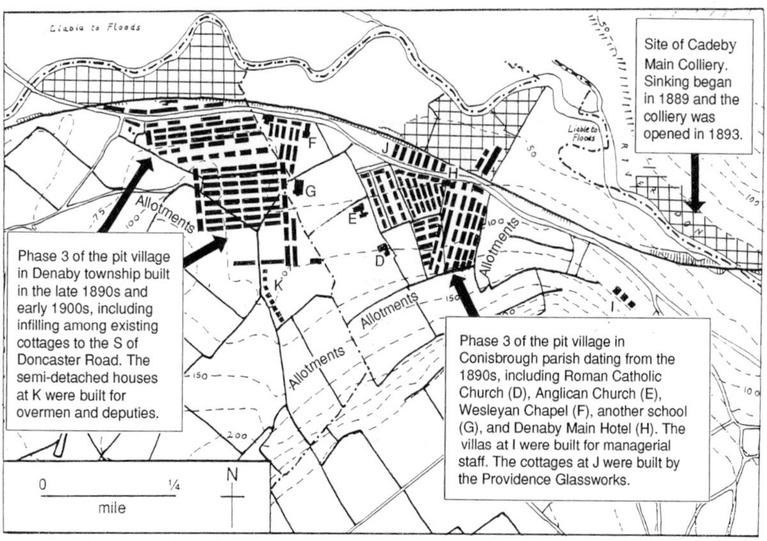

Figure 4. St Alban's Roman Catholic church, 1898, *Chris Sharpe, 'Old Barnsley'*

build St Alban's Roman Catholic Church which was completed in 1898. See Figure 3 for the location of these developments.

During this phase of the development of the colliery village, Kilners' made plans to enlarge the housing provision for their workers. An application was made in 1892 to build 150 houses on the narrow strip of land south of their works between the then Sheffield, Manchester and Lincolnshire Railway and Doncaster Road. They eventually built

60 houses on four short streets - named John, William, George and Thornhill running at right angles to the road and the railway (See Figure 3 and Figure 8).

The turn of the century saw another surge of building which was to more or less round off the development of the colliery village. This was in Denaby township, the scene of the earliest village development 30 years earlier. A bye-law application was made in March 1898 to build 233 houses on Adwick Street, Annerley Street, Barnbrough [*sic*] Street and Doncaster Road, among pre-existing housing. Another application was made in November 1901 to build a further 552 houses in Annerley Street, Cliff View, Warmsworth Street, Braithwell Street, Maltby Street, Ravensfield Street, Bolton Street and Tickhill Street. Land was conveyed to the Colliery Company for these two develop-

Figure 5. The park at Denaby Main. On the right can be seen the market place. The large building beyond the park is the cinema. Through the gap to the right of the cinema can be seen Wood View running down to Doncaster Road. Across Doncaster Road can be seen John Street, one of the rows of houses built by Kilners' Glassworks. The chimneys of the Glassworks rise behind John Street. In the background on the extreme right can be seen the headgear of Cadeby Main Colliery. *Chris Sharpe, 'Old Barnsley'*

ments in March 1899.[17] Separate bye-law applications were made for smaller adjoining developments in Tickhill Street (31 houses) and Tickhill Square (16 houses).[18] The houses in Tickhill Square were semi-detached, with front and back gardens and WCs. They were allocated to pit deputies and overmen.[19] All these developments are located on Figure 3.

At this time two other developments took place at the other (eastern) end of the village. All Saints' Church was built in 1900[20] and six superior semi-detached villas - Haydon House, Dunragit House,

Rockland House, Ashlea House, Goodnestone House and Albany House were built in Buckingham Road for managerial and other professional company staff.[21]

By the beginning of the twentieth century Denaby Main village was virtually complete and provided accommodation for about 2,500 employees at the two collieries. Its morphology was relatively simple. To the north of the main railway line lay Denaby Main Colliery, Cadeby Main Colliery and their spoil heaps and a complex network of mineral railways and sidings. This area also included Kilners'

Figure 6. Doncaster Road, Denaby Main about 90 years ago. This was the commercial artery of the village. In this view there is a butchers' shop, a chemists', and, in the far distance, the three balls of a pawn shop can just be made out. *Chris Sharpe, ' Old Barnsley'*

Figure 7. Vertical aerial photograph showing Denaby Main in 1959. *Crown Copyright reserved*

Glassworks and some of their early housing. To the south of the main railway, and predominantly south of Doncaster Road lay Denaby Main village, containing about 1,500 houses. The housing was in two large blocks, one in Denaby township, the other in Conisbrough parish. Between the two main blocks of residential development lay a wedge of non-residential land containing schools, an Anglican church, a Roman Catholic church (Figure 4), a cricket ground and a football ground. By 1930 this area also contained the Fullerton Hospital, the Miners' Welfare Institute, a cemetery and, at the Doncaster Road end, a park, a market place and a cinema (Figure 5). Doncaster Road contained both housing and a ribbon of commercial development (Figure 6). Lastly, surrounding the village on the west, south and east were extensive allotment gardens. By 1900, although the toilets were still earth closets (middens), facilities in the miners' houses had improved in two respects: gas lighting had replaced candles and paraffin lamps and a reservoir had been built on the North Cliff to the south of the village which was filled with water pumped from Cadeby Main Colliery and then supplied to the village by stand pipes. Figure 7, a vertical aerial photograph taken in 1959, shows the 'completed' village, which outwardly changed little in the first 65 years of the twentieth century.

One of the main characteristics of the 'completed' mining village was the uniformity of it all. Every street was straight, and within each block of development the streets were laid out in parallel rows of red brick houses separated in large parts of the village by wide communal yards with blocks of brick-built outside lavatories (see Figure 8). Even the pavements were of red brick. This uniformity was carried through in minutest detail: almost all the buildings erected in the fifteen year period from about 1890 - colliers' houses, the villas built for the managerial staff, and the colliery offices - were characterised by a horizontal decorative brick band in the walls (Figure 9) and by a triangular tile decoration along the roof ridge. The absence of trees and shrubs in almost all the residential areas emphasised the unrelieved uniformity of the place. The uniformity was even carried through into the street names which, with just a few exceptions, were named after local villages.

It is interesting to record two opposing evaluations of the village within a few years of each other on either side of the year 1900. Mr Eldon Bankes, KC, speaking on behalf of Denaby and Cadeby Collieries in 1904, at a hearing held in connection with the 'bag-muck strike' of 1902-03, said:

At the time when the strike occurred they owned I think some 1,400

Figure 8 (a). Oblique aerial photograph of part of Denaby Main village taken in the mid-1920s. It mainly shows housing from the early 1890s. In the right foreground at right angles to Doncaster Road and the railway are the barrack-like Loversall, Blythe and Balby Streets. The lavatory blocks in the wide communal backyards of these three streets had recently been demolished and individual outside toilets built on to each house. In the left foreground nearest the camera are Cusworth Street and Wadworth Street. Beyond these at right angles to Doncaster Road area Marr Street, Sprotbro' Street and Edlington Street still with lavatory blocks in their communal backyards. Beyond the railway lies the Providence Glassworks. On the extreme right of the works complex is one of the firm's original rows of cottages built in the mid-1860s, and beyond that a small area of allotments. In the left middleground between the railway and Doncaster Road are Thornhill Street and George Street, two of the four streets built by Kilners' in the 1890s. *Aerofilms*

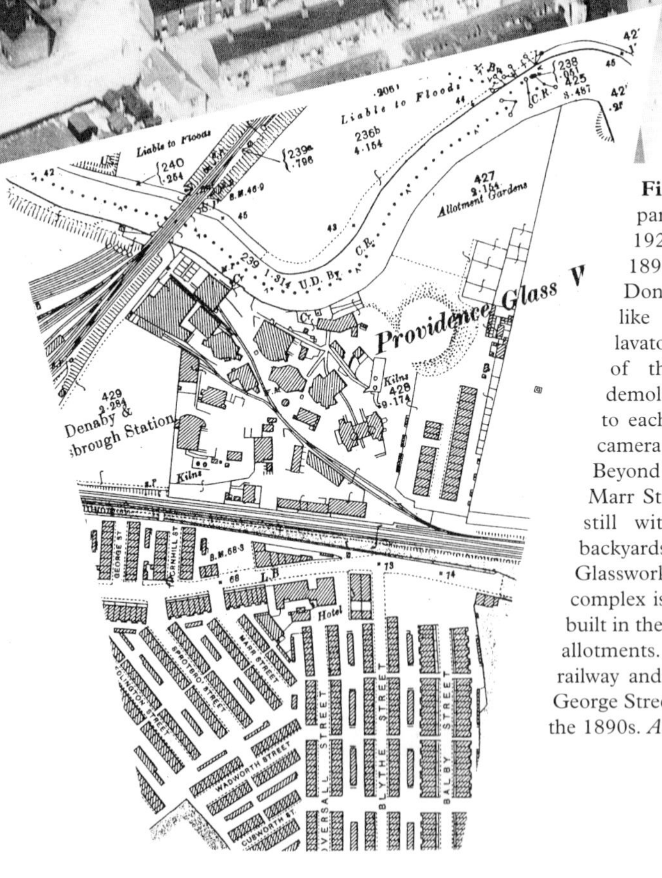

Figure 8 (b). Map of area shown on **Figure 8 (a).** *Ordnance Survey, Six Inch sheet 284.10, surveyed 1901, published in 1902*

Figure 9. Detail of the decorative brick band found on the walls of buildings throughout the village built during phase 3 (c. 1890-1905). *The Author*

houses. They were congregated together close to the Denaby Pit, and they formed the village of Denaby Main. The company had all along taken the greatest pains and succeeded in their efforts in making these houses as sanitary and as comfortable as possible; and, in addition, they had taken great pains to introduce into that village anything that occurred to them to be for the welfare of the men in the way of reading rooms, and recreation rooms and matters of that kind; and I do not think it can be disputed that the village, as owned and managed by this Company was in itself what might be called something equivalent to a model mining village.[22]

In complete contrast, a reporter writing in the *Christian Budget* on 8 November, 1899 under the heading 'THE WORST VILLAGE IN ENGLAND?' said:

I am sitting down to write this article in numb despair, for the mining community I have to describe is so repulsive that many who have never been near it will refuse to credit the story.[23]

The truth lay somewhere between these two extremes. Conditions must indeed have been squalid in the oldest, smallest and most crowded parts of the village. In these areas there were no private gardens or yards and toilet facilities and water supplies were shared. The proximity of the village to the pits could not be avoided. At least the prevailing south-westerly winds blew smoke and dust away from the village. Some of the housing built for overmen and deputies in Wheatley Street, Tickhill Street and Tickhill Square were very sound and survive today. And in their prime, the villas in Buckingham Road (Figure 10) would not have been out of place in the most affluent Victorian and Edwardian suburbs anywhere in the country.

Whether the houses of the colliery village were soundly built or not, or well appointed or not, was secondary to the fact that they were owned by the colliery company. As the late Jim MacFarlane has pointed out in his articles on the village[24], this meant that the loss of accommodation became as much an issue as the loss of wages whenever there was a dispute or whenever a miner was dismissed for whatever reason. There were very few locals among the original 'colonists' in Denaby Main village and no well developed local traditions and allegiances. And like the working men, the colliery proprietors at Denaby Main were not local; they were determined, experienced, risk-taking entrepreneurs, largely from West Yorkshire.

Figure 10. Colliery company villas in Buckingham Road, 1998. *The Author*

They were determined to make their venture work - and on their terms. These unique circumstances meant that everyone employed by the company tended to fall into one of two camps - they were either union men or company men. The result of this situation was that every time there was a major dispute between the Miners' Union and the colliery company, the families of the men involved living in company property were made homeless. This happened in 1869, 1877, 1885 and 1902-03. Moreover, as the nineteenth century progressed the village became larger and larger and more and more employees at the two collieries were housed in company property. During disputes large parts of the village had to be evacuated and the population dispersed to be temporarily housed in churches and chapels in the surrounding area, in the houses of family and friends not in company property and even in tents and in the surrounding countryside, only to return in most cases (and only once, in 1869, in triumph) to the village - but not necessarily to the same house - once the dispute was resolved. The village was therefore not only a convenient place of residence for the mining population, but also a means of social control for the mining company during the years of heaviest investment during the last forty years of the nineteenth century.

Phase 4: Phoenix from the ashes: the redevelopment of the village

In the mid 1960s it was decided that the village, the oldest parts of which were almost 100 years old, was obsolete, and a redevelopment programme was embarked on that would take almost two decades, but which would see Denaby Main rise from the dust as a moden community with the most up-to-date housing and community facilities based on the latest planning principles and ideas of housing design. Ironically by the time the redevelopment of the village was complete, it was no longer a mining village, Denaby Main Colliery having closed in 1968 and Cadeby Main Colliery in 1986.

Relatively little of the physical fabric of the original mining village remains. The entrance to the site of Denaby Main Colliery is marked by a colliery winding wheel and much of the surface operational area of Cadeby Main Colliery is

Figure 11. The village school built in the early 1890s, now empty and boarded up *The Author*

Figure 12. Tickhill Street with some of the few original colliery village houses still surviving. Note the decorative band halfway up the walls. *The Author*

Figure 13. Semi-detached villas in Tickhill Square, looking towards terraced houses in Wheatley Street, survivors from phase 3 of the development of the colliery village. Note the decorative band on the walls, and the characteristic porches as in Tickhill Street. *The Author*

Figure 14. A silent tribute to the more than 200 miners who lost their lives at Denaby Main Colliery and Cadeby Main Colliery. A miner struggles amidst fallen debris beside a grieving wife. The sculpture by Graham Ibbeson, unveiled in 1987, the year after the closure of Cadeby Main Colliery, stands beside the library in the centre of Conisbrough. *The Author*

being developed as the Earth Centre. Much of the rest of the sites of the two collieries has been landscaped. In the village itself the Roman Catholic church still stands as an imposing landmark, but the large school built in the 1890s stands empty (Figure 11) and the large Wesleyan chapel and the later cinema, although still standing, are used as a body building and fitness centre and a photographic laboratory respectively. A few streets of houses built in the late 1890s also survive among the modern housing. On Wheatley Street and Tickhill Street (Figure 12) there are substantial terrace houses and in Tickhill Square semi-detached houses (Figure 13), their origins betrayed by the tell-tale decorative band of brick work.

Conclusion

Colliery villages are an important element of the South Yorkshire landscape, but during the last 40 years, as collieries have closed and the miners' cottages and other important buildings have become outdated or redundant, they have sometimes been wholly or partly swept away. Even when colliery housing has survived, its origins have sometimes been almost forgotten.[25]

It is important to record both the physical and social development of colliery settlements. In the case of Denaby Main, the village has been well served by the late Jim MacFarlane, the social historian. Using a combination of documentary, cartographic, photographic and field evidence, the present study has attempted to record in detail its parallel physical development.

Notes and References

1. B. E. Coates and G. M. Lewis, *The Doncaster Area, British Landscapes Through Maps 8*, Geographical Association, 1966, pp. 34-35.
2. J. D. Marshall, 'Industrial Colonies and the Local Historian', *The Local Historian,* volume 23, No 3, 1993, p. 146.
3. J. MacFarlane, 'Counter-Offensive for a South Yorkshire Mining Community' in R. Harrison (ed.) *Independent Collier: The Coal Miner as Archetypal Proletarian Reconsidered,* The Harvester Press, 1978, pp. 180-200.
4. J. Tomlinson, *From Doncaster into Hallamshire,* 1879, p.144.
5. *Doncaster Gazette,* 16 December, 1864, p. 6.
6. Tomlinson, *From Doncaster into Hallamshire.*
7. *Doncaster Gazette,* 2 February, 1867, p. 6.
8. Tomlinson, *From Doncaster into Hallamshire.*
9. Tomlinson, *From Doncaster into Hallamshire,* pp. 149-50.
10. Tomlinson, *From Doncaster into Hallamshire,* p. 140.
11. Company trust deed dated 22 November, 1923 and copy of mortgage dated 6 May, 1896 which refer to the original indenture of lease dated 1 November 1880. Both documents were consulted in 1969 in box files containing records of the Amalgamated Denaby Collieries in the NCB Reference Archives, at that time housed in the disused Denaby Main pithead baths building.
12. Indenture securing debenture dated 23 February, 1889, Amalgamated Denaby Collieries box files, NCB Reference Archives.
13. *Doncaster Gazette,* 8 March, 1889, p. 7.
14. Company trust deed 1923, Amalgamated Denaby Collieries box files, NCB Reference Archives.
15. *White's Directory* 1896-96, Volume 2.
16. Company trust deed 1923; indenture and plans of new houses at Denaby Main, 15 November, 1895; both in Amalgamated Denaby Collieries box files, NCB Reference Archives.
17. Bye-law applications dated 22 March, 1898 and 16 November, 1901. Amalgamated Denaby Collieries box files, NCB Reference Archives.
18. Bye-law applications 9 January, 1901 (Tickhill Street) and 31 May, 1902 (Tickhill Square), Amalgamated Denaby Collieries box files, NCB Reference Archives.
19. A. J. Booth, *A Railway History of Denaby and Cadeby Collieries,* Industrial Railway Society, Bridlington, 1990, p. 11.
20. *White's Directory,* 1905.
21. Bye-law applications 1899 (land conveyed to Company 22 February 1899); trust deed 1923, both in Amalgamated Denaby Collieries box files, NCB Reference Archives.
22. Transcript of Denaby and Cadeby Collieries Ltd. v. The Yorkshire Miners' Association, 1904, p. 6.
23. Quoted by MacFarlane in 'Counter-Offensive for a South Yorkshire Mining Community', p. 180.
24. See for example 'Essay in Oral History - Denaby Main - a South Yorkshire Mining Village', *Bulletin of the Society of Labour History,* Volumes 25 and 26, pp. 82-100 and pp. 39-42 respectively, 1972; 'Counter-Offensive for a South Yorkshire Mining Community', 1978 (for full details see note 3); *The Bag Muck Strike 1902-03,* Doncaster Library Service, 1987; *Coalminers, Glassworkers and Potters: a profile of the Denaby Area 1801-1871,* Doncaster Library Service, no date.
25. For an example of the study of the physical and social development of an almost forgotten South Yorkshire coal mining community see M. Jones, 'A Welsh Diaspora and a Yorkshire Colony: the establishment of a Welsh community in Carlton and Smithies' in B. Elliott (ed) *Aspects of Barnsley 2,* Wharncliffe Publishing Ltd.,1994, pp. 49-72.

11. Music in Doncaster During the Napoleonic Wars, 1793-1815

by Philip L Scowcroft

WHEN WAR WITH FRANCE broke out in February 1793 Doncaster's musical entertainment had barely entered the age of sophistication, there being indeed very little of it in a public sense. There were the Corporation 'waits', which had existed for centuries as professionals playing out of doors or for special occasions. There were usually three or four of them at any one time and some had long careers - on 13 December 1808 Joseph Hatfield, a wait for 44 years, died aged 64. There was the Parish Church, equipped since 1740 with a fine Harris organ and since 1756 with an Organist, Edward Miller (Figure 1), who was a musician of national reputation and energetic in teaching, composition and organising concerts.[1] To the waits and the Church had been added in 1776 a third musical 'strand', the Theatre Royal in the Market Place,[2] whose enormously long programmes included music, either incidental to plays or as song and dance interludes, or, quite frequently, as operas, by composers like Charles Dibdin, Thomas Arne and Stephen Storace. The Theatre was open usually for about a month every year, its season beginning during or just after the St Leger race meeting (which then took place in late, rather than as now, early, September) and concluding at the end of October or beginning of November. The company presumably had its own orchestra; we do not know its size but it must have been small as both stage and orchestra pit were very restricted in size.

Musical stage pieces, or 'operas', during the 1793 season included *Fontainebleau* (music mainly by William Shield), *Rosina* (Shield), *No Song No Supper* (Storace), *The Woodman* (Shield), *Hartford Bridge* (Shield), *The Haunted Tower* (Storace) and the 'Grand Pantomimical Operatical Spectacle', *The Surrender of Valenciennes* with 'New Scenery, Machinery, Music etc'. (composer[s] unknown). Several hundred 'operatic' performances took place in Doncaster during our chosen period, but many of these 'operas' we might call 'plays with music': 'musicals' and light in touch and entertaining.

Concert activity for the year 1793 was rather above average: divertimentos on the 'guittar' (sic) by the Polish midget Count Boralowsky

Figure 1. Edward Miller (1735-1807), Organist, Musician and Local Historian.

(16 May, Mansion House); a Mansion House concert in Race Week (27 September), starting at 12 noon to allow listeners to go on to the races afterwards and including 'a Solo Concerto on the Violin and a Sonata on the Grand Pianoforte, by Mr Miller, junior'; and, in Tickhill Parish Church on 22 August, a performance of Handel's *Messiah* by 'a very numerous band of Vocal and Instrumental performers selected from the Musical Societies in Yorkshire...the Grand Choruses...supported with Kettle Drums, Trumpets, French Horns, Double Bass &c'.

Enthusiasm for private musicmaking was certainly growing in Doncaster at this period. On several occasions either side of 1800 the local press carried advertisements for musical partworks like the *New*

Musical Magazine (January 1794), *The Monthly Banquet* (November 1795) and *The Piano-Forte Magazine* (20 August 1796), all of which could be obtained locally. Dr Edward Miller, as he now was, published many works in the fourteen years prior to his death on 12 September 1807: *Sixteen Easy Voluntaries* for organ (1797), *Twelve Canzonets* (1800), *The New Flute Instructor* (1800), Dr Watts' *Psalms and Hymns* (two editions, 1800 and 1806, the second part of the second edition including ten pieces for the 'Practise of Societies of Singers' and an appendix, available separately, containing 'twenty favourite AIRS AND DUETS for domestic use on a Sunday Evening at the Piano-Forte'), *A Musical Primer* (July 1807) and a number of separate topical songs, such as *Britons Ever Shall be Free*, *The Little French Emigre* and *The Negro Boy* (agitation for the abolition of the slave trade was beginning).[3] Many of Miller's earlier publications were still available and his son, William Edward, wrote a song about the naval victory of The Glorious First of June in 1794 (Figure 2). Music was taught in several of the town's private schools; Miller himself taught at Mr Falconer's in Hall Gate between about 1801 and 1805 and in other schools. Other teachers, like Edward Wilson of Frenchgate and Mrs Brown (late Miss Correy 'of the London and Edinburgh concerts') in the Market Place, advertised their services. Instruments were offered for sale, often by Sheardown, the *Doncaster Gazette* publisher, who had Broadwood and Rolfe pianos, flutes, clarinets, 'hautboys', flageolets, etc in 1801; Isaac Brailsford advertised a Snetzler organ in 1808 'in perfect repair and (possessing) in an eminent

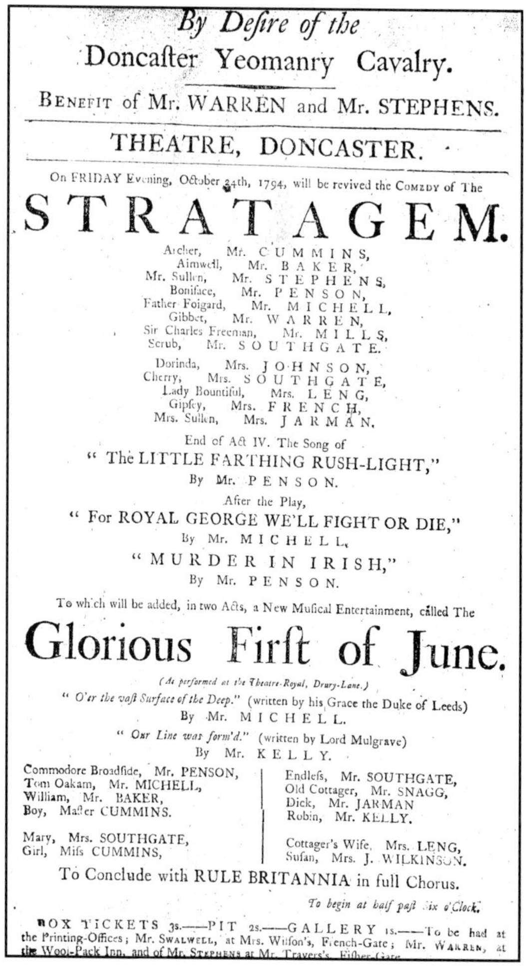

By Desire of the
Doncaster Yeomanry Cavalry.

BENEFIT of Mr. WARREN and Mr. STEPHENS.

THEATRE, DONCASTER.

On FRIDAY Evening, October 24th, 1794, will be revived the COMEDY of The

STRATAGEM.

Archer, Mr. CUMMINS,
Aimwell, Mr. BAKER,
Mr. Sullen, Mr. STEPHENS,
Boniface, Mr. PENSON,
Father Foigard, Mr. MICHELL,
Gibbet, Mr. WARREN,
Sir Charles Freeman, Mr. MILLS,
Scrub, Mr. SOUTHGATE.
Dorinda, Mrs. JOHNSON,
Cherry, Mrs. SOUTHGATE,
Lady Bountiful, Mrs. LENG,
Gipsey, Mrs. FRENCH,
Mrs. Sullen, Mrs. JARMAN.

End of Act IV. The Song of
" The LITTLE FARTHING RUSH-LIGHT,"
By Mr. PENSON.
After the Play,
" For ROYAL GEORGE WE'LL FIGHT OR DIE,"
By Mr. MICHELL,
" MURDER IN IRISH,"
By Mr. PENSON.

To which will be added, in two Acts, a New Musical Entertainment, called The

Glorious First of June.

(As performed at the Theatre-Royal, Drury-Lane.)
" *O'er the vast Surface of the Deep.*" (written by his Grace the Duke of Leeds)
By Mr. MICHELL.
" *Our Line was form'd.*" (written by Lord Mulgrave)
By Mr. KELLY.

Commodore Broadside, Mr. PENSON,
Tom Oakam, Mr. MICHELL,
William, Mr. BAKER,
Boy, Master CUMMINS.
Mary, Mrs. SOUTHGATE,
Girl, Miss CUMMINS,

Endless, Mr. SOUTHGATE,
Old Cottager, Mr. SNAGG,
Dick, Mr. JARMAN
Robin, Mr. KELLY.
Cottager's Wife, Mrs. LENG,
Susan, Mrs. J. WILKINSON.

To Conclude with RULE BRITANNIA in full Chorus.

To begin at half past Six o'Clock.

BOX TICKETS 3s.——PIT 2s.——GALLERY 1s.——To be had at the Printing-Offices; Mr. SWALWELL, at Mrs. Wilson's, French-Gate; Mr. WARREN, at the Wool-Pack Inn, and of Mr. STEPHENS at Mr. Travers's, Fisher-Gate.

Figure 2. Doncaster theatre playbill, 1794. Notice that the entertainment is 'By Desire of the Doncaster Yeomanry Cavalry'. The Glorious First of June was a British naval victory of 1794; this musical version was first performed in London on 2 July (almost incredibly), three months before it arrived in Doncaster. *Doncaster Museum and Art Gallery Collection*

Degree the rich mellow tone peculiar to Snetzler's organs'. Clearly much private musicmaking went on.

Of course there was a war to be fought and a threatened French invasion to be guarded against but in a way this situation stimulated music. From time to time regular, militia and volunteer regiments were quartered in the town, sometimes for weeks and months at a stretch: the Sussex Fencible Cavalry, Dumfriesshire Fencibles, North York Militia, Lancashire Militia, Royal Lancashire Fencibles, Prince of Wales' Dragoon Guards, the 21st and 46th Foot, the 7th Light Dragoons, the 3rd Dragoon Guards, the Loyal Nottinghamshire Fencibles and Irish Fencibles were only a few of the visiting military in these years. Many of these regiments had bands which doubtless provided diversion for the townspeople. In a parade of the Yorkshire West Riding Yeomanry Cavalry in front of the (old) *Angel Inn* (in Frenchgate) on 12 September 1794 the Rotherham troop was preceded by three trumpeters. In November 1794 the band of the Sheffield Volunteers played in Doncaster when the standards of the 1st Yorkshire West Riding Yeomanry Cavalry had been consecrated; ten years later, in April 1804, when the Volunteers themselves were stationed in the town for fifteen days, they had with them a 'full band of music'. On 8 November 1794 an advertisement appeared in the *Doncaster Gazette* for musical recruits, two French horn players, two clarinets, two fifes and two drummers. The local volunteer infantry regiments which had been mustered in Doncaster and Bawtry formed bands. In March 1804 we read of the Bawtry Volunteers being 'preceded by the band', which band later that year was deemed to be good enough to be fetched in post-chaises from Thorne where the regiment was then stationed, to play at a Mayoral dinner at the Mansion House. It had been formed late in 1803 'at the sole expence (sic) of Lord Gallway'; in January 1805 it was advertising in the *Gazette* for a drummer. On 11 May 1804 the band of the Doncaster Volunteers was praised for its exertions in enabling it 'after but a few days to play in so respectable a manner'. When the Volunteers were given the option of transferring into the local militia in 1808 four drummers from the band did so. The band of the 3rd West York, then the local militia regiment, is mentioned as parading the streets when news of the Treaty of Amiens, to be a shortlived peace in the event, came through in 1802 and it played excellently at a Mansion House dinner celebrating the next 'peace' in 1814. A military band, playing 'by permission of Dr Miller', even invaded the Theatre in 1796 and this 'novelty' earned approval (This may have been the local militia band; whatever band it was, it was apparently its first public appearance).

Occasionally these troop movements produced more formal musicmaking as when the East Norfolk Militia was stationed in the town during the summer of 1800. On 8 September the Bandmaster, one T Wright, junior, directed a concert at the Mansion House including a Haydn 'Overture' (almost certainly a Symphony), a Pleyel Quartet, glees by Callcott and Harrington, a Stamitz Symphony and a Clarinet Concerto, a Quartet, the *Bugle Horn Concertante* and a 'Grand Military Piece with Drums &c.', all composed by Wright himself. A month earlier Wright had contributed a Clarinet Concerto, probably that same one, to a Mansion House concert in honour of the Prince of Wales' Birthday which included more Haydn and Pleyel, together with songs and an unspecified violin concerto. The previous year (24 April) Dr Miller directed a so-called 'Military Concert' whose programme is worth listing in full: Grand March from *Judas Maccabeus* (Handel): Air from *Bluebeard* (Thomas Attwood); Glee, We Be Three Poor Mariners (Thomas Ravenscroft); Air, The Soldier Tir'd of War's Alarms, from *Artaxerxes* (Thomas Arne); Air from *The Castle Spectre* (Joseph Mazzinghi); *March of the 5th West York* (Miller); *Britons Strike Home* (Purcell); See the Conquering Hero from *Judas Maccabeus*; Glee, *I'll live no more Single* (Miller);[4] Song and Chorus, *Britons Ever Shall be Free* (Miller); and God Save the King, 'with variations and full chorus'. A shortish concert for that period; but tickets were only 3/6d (available from Sheardown's and from the *Angel* and *Red Lion* inns) as against the more usual 5/- for a concert,

LAST WEEK.

BY DESIRE OF

The Officers of the 31ſt Regiment of Foot.

Benefit of Mr. and Mrs. J. Wilkinſon.

THEATRE, DONCASTER.

On MONDAY Evening, October 30th, 1797, will be preſented a favourite COMIC OPERA, called The

Siege of Belgrade.

(Muſic by Storace.)

WITH ADDITIONAL SCENERY.

Seraſkier, Mr. WOOD,
Colonel Cohenbergh, Mr. CUMMINS,
Uſeph, Mr EMERY,
Iſmael, Mr. MILLS,
Leopold, Mr. PENSON,
Peter, Mr. CRISP,
Anſelm, Mr. MICHELL,
Michael, Mr. HOPE, Auſtrian Soldier, Mr. JARMAN.
Catharine, Mrs. J. WILKINSON,
Lilla, Miſs DUNCAN,
Chita, Mrs. SOUTHGATE,
Fatima, Mrs. CUMMINS.

END OF THE PLAY,

A Minuet and New Gavotte,

By Mr. J. WILKINSON, and Mrs. MILLS.

To which will be added, (never performed here,) a New Opera, in One Act, called

BANTRY BAY;

Or, The French Invaſion in Ireland.

Mc. Loughlan, Mr. GRIST, Phelim, Mr. WILLIAMS,
Patrick, Mr. MILLS, Captain of Volunteers, Mr. DUNN,
Billy O'Ronke, Mr. EMERY, Donnybrook, Mr. MICHELL,
Fiſhermen, Mr. WOOD, &c. &c. | Peaſants, Mr. HOPE, Mr. JARMAN, &c.
Fanny, Mrs. J. WILKINSON.

To conclude with a New Dramatic Entertainment of DANCING in Parts, called The

Caledonian Lovers;

Or, BLIND-MAN's BUFF.

Patie, Mr. J. WILKINSON, Old Darby, Mr. EMERY,
Old Joan, Mr. MICHELL, Boy, Miſs CUMMINS,
Villagers, Mr. MILLS, Mr. JARMAN, Mr. HOPE, Mrs. CUMMINS, Mrs. PENSON, and Mrs. FRENCH,
Bonny Laſſie, Mrs. MILLS,

In which ſhe will introduce a Scotch Hornpipe.

BOX TICKETS, 3s.—PIT, 2s.—GALLERY 1s.——To be had at the Theatre, from Eleven till One, at the Printing Offices, and of Mr. Swalwell, at Mr. Townrow's, Hall Gate, and of Mr. and Mrs. J. WILKINSON, at Mrs. Roebuck's, Far St. Sepulchre-Gate.

Figure 3. Doncaster theatre playbill, 1797. Notice the topical features: the French had attempted an invasion of Ireland, and was to do again; and the performances were 'By Desire of the the Officers of the 31st Regiment of Foot', then garrisoned in Doncaster. *Doncaster Museum and Art Gallery Collection*

and a ball did follow the music, as it usually did at the Mansion House at that period. A concert of vocal and instrumental music arranged by Mr Andrew Ashe, a visiting professional flautist, including a flute concerto played by himself and several 'favourite airs' sung by his wife and featuring 'Several Gentlemen Amateurs who have politely

Figure 4. Doncaster theatre playbill, 1811. Mr Incledon was a frequent visitor to the theatre; the music of both The Quaker and The Lock and Key was mainly by William Shield. *Doncaster Museum and Art Gallery Collection*

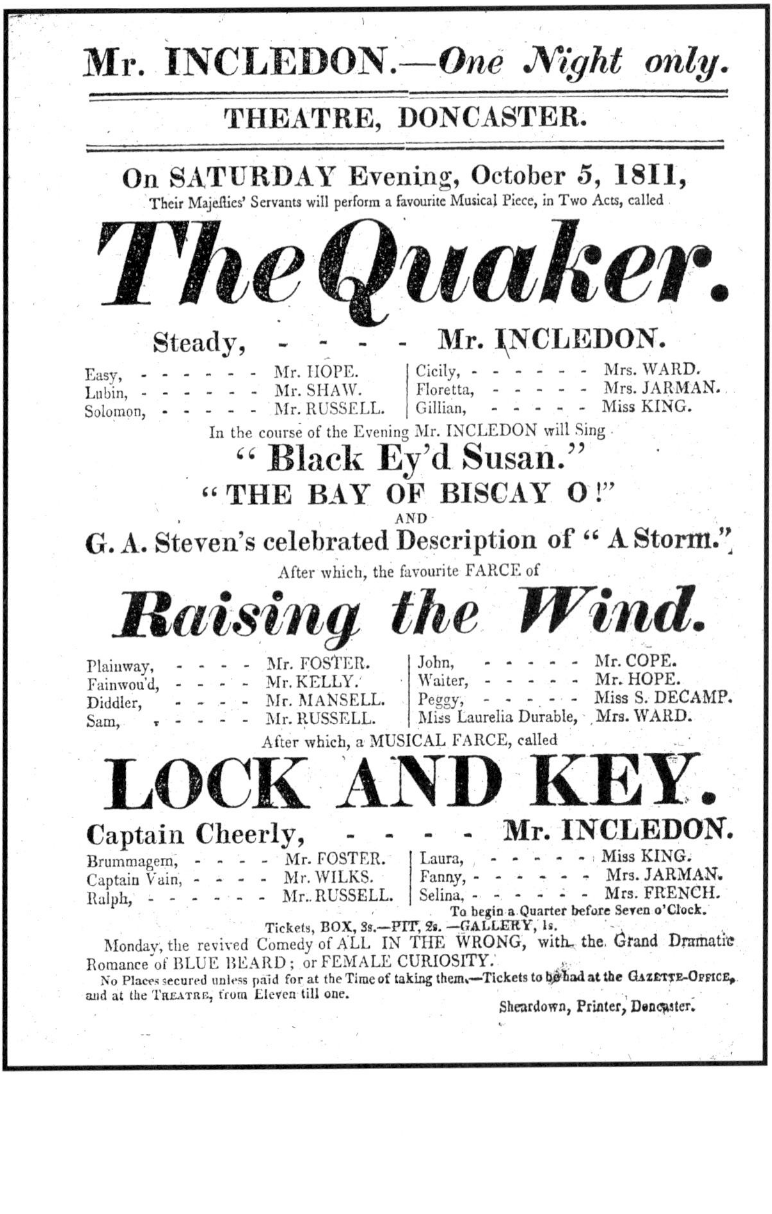

Mr. INCLEDON.—*One Night only.*

THEATRE, DONCASTER.

On SATURDAY Evening, October 5, 1811,

Their Majesties' Servants will perform a favourite Musical Piece, in Two Acts, called

The Quaker.

Steady, - - - -	Mr. INCLEDON.		
Easy, - - - - - -	Mr. HOPE.	Cicily, - - - - - -	Mrs. WARD.
Lubin, - - - - - -	Mr. SHAW.	Floretta, - - - - -	Mrs. JARMAN.
Solomon, - - - - -	Mr. RUSSELL.	Gillian, - - - - -	Miss KING.

In the course of the Evening Mr. INCLEDON will Sing

" Black Ey'd Susan."

" THE BAY OF BISCAY O!"

AND

G. A. Steven's celebrated Description of " A Storm."

After which, the favourite FARCE of

Raising the Wind.

Plainway, - - - -	Mr. FOSTER.	John, - - - - -	Mr. COPE.
Fainwou'd, - - - -	Mr. KELLY.	Waiter, - - - - -	Mr. HOPE.
Diddler, - - - -	Mr. MANSELL.	Peggy, - - - - -	Miss S. DECAMP.
Sam, - - - - -	Mr. RUSSELL.	Miss Laurelia Durable,	Mrs. WARD.

After which, a MUSICAL FARCE, called

LOCK AND KEY.

Captain Cheerly, - - - - -	Mr. INCLEDON.		
Brummagem, - - - -	Mr. FOSTER.	Laura, - - - - -	Miss KING.
Captain Vain, - - - -	Mr. WILKS.	Fanny, - - - - - -	Mrs. JARMAN.
Ralph, - - - - - - -	Mr. RUSSELL.	Selina, - - - - - -	Mrs. FRENCH.

To begin a Quarter before Seven o'Clock.

Tickets, BOX, 3s.—PIT, 2s. —GALLERY, 1s.

Monday, the revived Comedy of ALL IN THE WRONG, with the Grand Dramatic Romance of BLUE BEARD; or FEMALE CURIOSITY.

No Places secured unless paid for at the Time of taking them.—Tickets to be had at the GAZETTE-OFFICE, and at the THEATRE, from Eleven till one.

Sheardown, Printer, Doncaster.

consented to give their assistance' was possibly in aid of the Volunteer movement, as Lord Eardley, who was responsible for the concert, subscribed 100 guineas (£105) to the Doncaster Volunteers about that time.

Programmes at the Theatre also reflected the fact that there was a war on. Operas or semi-operas like *The Recruiting Sergeant* (music by Dibdin), *The Soldier's Return* (James Hook), *The Poor Soldier* (Shield), *The Rival Soldiers* (Shield), *The English Fleet in 1342* (John Braham) and *Bantry Bay*, or *The French Invasion in Ireland* (Figure 3) must have struck responsive chords in their audiences.[5] On 26 October 1798 a song, *Nelson for Ever*, was interpolated into a play, together with a tableau of the Thanksgiving Procession to St Paul's marking Nelson's striking victory at the Battle of the Nile two months before. A year earlier (23 October 1797) the evening's performances concluded with the National Anthem and *Rule Britannia* which had an additional verse written on the 'Occasion of Admiral Duncan's late Glorious Victory over the Dutch' (i.e. at the Battle of Camperdown on 12 October 1797). I have discovered no similar local celebration of the Battle of Trafalgar (21 October 1805), probably because the Theatre season was over before the news came through. Sometimes, however, the war could be forgotten, as when M Giroux's ballet dancers came for a season in 1811, or on 20 October 1800 when the New Musical Farce, *St David's Day*, was put on - 'a pretty Pastoral Piece, illustrative of the manners and customs of the Welch [sic]. The Overture is a compilation of simply and justly admired Welch tunes and the whole of the music is beautiful and peculiarly characteristic'. It was followed by a country dance, *Sir Watkin William Wynne's Delight.*

Public concerts were relatively scarce before 1808. We have already noted some of those that took place. There were few others in the fifteen years 1793-1807. The *Gazette* mentioned Dr Miller's 'First Concert' at the Mansion House at 11 am on 24 September 1795, the last of the three race days, which was 'attended by those of the first fashion in town, and the musical Amateurs appear'd much pleased with their entertainment'. Although it was described as a 'first' concert, I have not discovered any others that season. On 24 August 1804 a 'Band' of Silver Miners from Bohemia gave a vocal and instrumental programme at the Town Hall (in the Market Place) wearing 'working clothes as worn in mines'. The following 6 February 1805, back at the Mansion House, a concert of vocal and instrumental music featured Madame Amati and Master Bradbury, who both sang 'charmingly', Mr Mather from Sheffield, on cello, who arranged the concert, and Mr Ellis on flute. Two days before that, at the *Crown Inn,*

Bawtry, a concert for the benefit of Edward Wilson of Frenchgate, teacher of violin, cello and wind instruments, tuner of pianos, harpsichords and spinets and coach to the Volunteer Bands of both Bawtry and Doncaster, brought together singers and an orchestra to play Corelli, Haydn and Pleyel and accompany violin and piano concertos, the solo in the latter performed by Mr Simpson, Organist of St John's, Wakefield.

From time to time a touring actor-musician stopped off at the Theatre to give an 'entertainment'. On 8 July 1802 Mr Incledon of the Theatre Royal, Covent Garden, presented *Variety, or Something New,* a mixture of recitations and of songs especially written for him by composers like Shield, John Davy (who accompanied him on the piano), William Reeve, Carter and Joseph Mazzinghi. As Incledon had served in the Royal Navy it is hardly surprising that some of the songs bore titles like *The Sailor's Glory, The Post Captain* and *The Sea Fright.* Incledon returned several times to Doncaster (Figure 4): on 16 July 1806 he brought a fresh entertainment entitled *Hospitality, or The Harvest Home,* which included fourteen new songs by Thomas Attwood (notably *Nelson's Tomb*), Shield, Davy and C E Horn, who was the accompanist and who also played 'several select Airs and Rondos'; on 9 August 1809 he came with *A Voyage to India,* a similar mixture of spoken and sung words (the songs were by Mazzinghi, Davy, Henry Bishop, Stevenson and Shield) and 'select airs and rondos played on the Grand Pianoforte' by one Mr Kellner, junior. On 7 July 1804 Mrs Mountain, of the Theatre Royal, Drury Lane, presented 'an entirely nouvelle Species of Entertainment comprising an interesting and continued detail of Domestic Events, comic, serious and affecting, interspersed with Fifteen New Songs composed by Shield, Callcott, Webbe, Davy, Hook, Ross of Aberdeen, Mr Lanza, junior and Carolan'. Lanza himself accompanied and Mr Mountain played the violin in vocal and instrumental items. Four years later (16 April 1808) Mr and Mrs Matthews from Drury Lane brought their entertainment, *The Mail Coach, or Rambles into Yorkshire,* which included songs, recitations, ventriloquism and imitations; the Volunteer Band offered its services as an additional feature for this. Two entertainments during 1809 brought a Mr Bannister in July and a Mr Melvin in September. Bannister, accompanied by Mr Bond of Drury Lane, offered songs mostly composed by Reeve. A Mr Bond, probably the same one but now said to be of the Theatre Royal, Covent Garden, came with Matthews and Incledon on 13 December 1811 and 8 January 1812 with a doubtless similar entertainment entitled *Travellers,* or *Mail Coach Adventures.* Most eminent among these performers was however Charles Dibdin, who appeared on 14 July 1799 with his 'celebrated' entertainment *The Sphinx*; he returned for two nights in March 1803 with entertainments entitled *Sans Souci* and *The Cakehouse*. Noted artistes came to the Theatre during the autumn season also. In November 1809 a Miss Feron, described as 'the English Catalani', was engaged for three nights to sing many separate songs and to take part in the operas billed for those evenings.

We can perhaps read into the relative scarcity of local concerts in 1793-1807 period Dr Miller's advancing years (he died on 12 September 1807 aged 71) and his preoccupation with tasks like bringing out many of his published compositions and the *History of Doncaster* which appeared in 1804. Certainly his natural son, and successor as Organist at St George's, Isaac Brailsford, formerly an organist at Mansfield and Bradford and before that a chorister at the Chapel Royal, who was elected Parish Church Organist on 2 October 1807, showed considerable energy in promoting local music. He lost no time in pushing himself as a teacher of piano, violin and singing, as the *Gazette* carried an advertisement to that effect only one week later. He also set about reviving, or rather developing, the town's musical life. A series of Subscription Concerts at the Mansion House was announced for the 1808 winter season, the four dates being 26 January, 16 February, 7 March and 4 April. One singer, a Miss Jacobs, was engaged as principal soloist for all four concerts and the leader, Mr White, played a violin concerto in each concert, Brailsford a piano sonata in most concerts and a Mr Erskine an oboe concerto in the last of them. Handel's overtures to *Samson, The Occasional Oratorio, Il Pastor Fido, Ariadne* and *Ottone,* concertos by Avison and Corelli - the latter composer so popular for so long with English provincial orchestral societies - symphonies or overtures by Vanhal, Haydn, Jommelli, Martini and Gyrowetz,[6] a Quartet and a *Concertante* by Pleyel and glees by Shield, Callcott and William Horsley made up the musical diet. Miss Jacobs was 'in fine voice', especially in arias by Handel, and the concerts generally received 'liberal support' from the 'principal families of the town and neighbourhood'. Subscribers' tickets were a guinea (£1.05) which covered three concerts (they paid 2/6d for the fourth); non-subscribers paid 5/- per concert, presumably for inferior seats, but this was still a high price.

On 28 October 1808 the *Gazette* reported that the concerts would recommence in December 'provided an adequate subscription is obtained'. This must have been the case as three concerts were given on 31 January, 28 February and 10 April 1809, not to mention a further concert, outside the main series, for Mr Mather's benefit, on

24 April 1809, featuring vocalist Mrs Salmon and the gentlemen of the Sheffield Harmonic Society. The principal singer in the three Subscription Concerts was a Mrs Margerum; Mr White remained as leader with the task of playing a violin concerto in each concert and Mr Erskine returned to play the oboe in concerted items. Brailsford played a piano concerto in the second concert, Mr Mather another in the third. The mixture was much as before, the Handel overtures being *Berenice* and *Esther,* the symphonies being by Haydn, Kozeluch and Jommelli. Again the subscription was a guinea. The size of the orchestra is unknown, though we may hazard a guess at around thirty players with amateurs rubbing shoulders with professionals, as was common at that time in provincial England.

A further series of three Subscription Concerts took place in 1810, again with Mrs Salmon as principal vocalist. We have fewer details of the programmes; a bassoon concerto, played by a Mr Clifford, figured once and repertoire generally seems to have been similar to that of previous years. There was a hint that the subscription was insufficient, as subscribers had to pay 3/- to obtain admission to the last concert. There were no Subscription Concerts in 1811 or in immediately subsequent years, but Brailsford remained active in local concert life both before and after 1815. On 25 September 1809 he had arranged a single concert at the Mansion House as a Race Week attraction, bringing to Doncaster Miss Travis and Mr Lees as the principal vocalists and also calling on Mr Ellis (flute) and Mr Mather (cello). He himself led the orchestra and also played Steibelt's celebrated Rondo on the piano. Haydn was represented twice in the programme, which also included 'overtures' (presumably symphonies) by Gyrowetz and Kozeluch, glees by Spofforth and Calecott and numerous solo vocal items. A benefit concert for Brailsford was put on at the Mansion House on 28 November 1811 with two major singers, Mrs Salmon and Mr Bradbury, though a Mr Suett, later to be the first Organist of Christ Church Doncaster, also took part, with the cellist Mr Ashley and the indefatigable Mr White as leader. Handel - the overture to Ptolemy and various arias - Corelli, Haydn, Gyrowetz and a Piano Concerto by one Griffin, played by Brailsford, were the principal ingredients.

Brailsford's major achievement prior to 1815 was however his Grand Musical Festival of 1812: four concerts, two in church, two at the Theatre, on 19 and 20 August. *Messiah,* with an organ concerto, probably one of Handel's own, played by Brailsford, and preceding Part III, opened proceedings on the morning (11 am) of the first day. The next morning a miscellaneous sacred selection from *Athaliah,*

Joshua, Jephtha, Theodora, Judas Maccabeus and *Zadok the Priest* (all by Handel), *The Creation* (Haydn), plus liturgical works by Pergolesi, Galliard, Marcello, Mozart and William Boyce were put on. On each evening (7 30 pm) a 'grand miscellaneous concert' at the Theatre included secular items like 'Symphonies, Songs, Solos, Concertos and some of the newest and most popular Glees'. Mrs Salmon was again the principal vocalist and her 'unaffected and elegant singing' was much admired, but there were half a dozen other singers, at least three of whom earned critical acclaim. Messrs Brailsford, White (leader), Erskine (oboe), Hyde (trumpet) and Ashley (cello), all 'exerted themselves with the happiest effect'; the choruses, given by an ad *hoc* choir drawn from far and wide, were 'particularly grand and impressive'. Though many of the nobility and gentry were there, unfavourable weather prevented more people from coming - perhaps the 7/- cost of tickets for the centre aisle and galleries (side aisle seats were 3/6d) put people off as well - but the Theatre was well attended each evening (there, boxes cost 7/-, Pit seats 3/6d, Gallery 2/-). We do not know if this Festival, Doncaster's first since 1787, was a financial success, but it seems to have been the first of a series in Yorkshire, the others being in Barnsley and Leeds (1812), Rawmarsh (1813) and Snaith/Selby (1814).

The year 1812 was noteworthy musically, for on 11 May a Mansion House concert (and Ball, as usual) had been mounted for the benefit of the 'Musicians in the Service of the Corporation (i.e. the waits)'. Mrs Salmon and Mr Bradbury, two vocalists later to participate in the Festival, figured - concertos for flute and cello, two Haydn symphonies (the *Roxelane,* now known as No. 63, and one other) and others by Jommelli and Davaux were also in the programme. But there was little else on the concert front in the remaining years up to the Battle of Waterloo. We can briefly dismiss the concert of vocal and instrumental music by Signor Rovalla at the *Reindeer Inn* (13 June 1814)[7], when he sang and played six, seven or eight instruments at once (panpipies, Spanish guitar, bell harmonica, triangle, tabor, cymbals, bass drum, etc) as a gimmick, likewise a programme at the Town Hall in April 1815 by the 'celebrated Musical Phenomena, the Master and Miss Smith'. Signor Sampieri sang Italian songs at the Mansion House on 11 January 1814 but we can more fittingly close this survey with an account of Mr Wragg's Grand Concert and Ball at the Mansion House on 26 April 1814. This included vocal items from Miss Russell and Master Clarkson; the leader, Mr Morini, junior, the oboist, the ubiquitous Mr Erskine, and the cellist, Mr Wragg, all played concertos, Mr Morini's being 'much applauded'.

News of peace with France had just come through - Napoleon was to escape from Elba and force a replay at Waterloo the following year but at that moment everybody thought the long struggle was over. It was a time for rejoicing and perhaps a little one-up-manship. A verse was added to the National Anthem on this occasion:

George's Illustrious Name
Britain's proud deeds of fame
Europe shall sing;
France sees her Tyrant hurl'd
Waves her White Flag unfurl'd
Peace comes to bless the World
God save the King.

Whether at the Theatre or the Church or the concert room, music in Doncaster did well during the Napoleonic Wars.[8] It was to do so again in a much later conflict, in 1939-45; but that is another story.

Notes and References

1. For a full account of Miller's life and work, see Frederick Fowler, *Edward Miller: Organist of Doncaster, His Life and Times,* DMBC, 1979. The Harris organ of course perished in the fire of February 1853.
2. I am not aware when exactly the Theatre acquired the suffix 'Royal'.
3. *The Negro Boy* has been revived in Doncaster during the past generation.
4. Miller's glee has been sung on the Doncaster concert platform in modern times.
5. I have traced the performances of 101 different 'operas' (or plays with plenty of music) at the Theatre between 1793 and 1814. Most of these will have been played several times*; William Shield (16), Samuel Arnold and Michael Kelly (12 each), Stephen Storace (8), and Charles Dibdin (7) were the composers with most individual pieces staged. A majority of English operas of the time were 'pasticcios' to which several contributed music with one 'lead' composer putting each piece together. The 16 operas by Shield mentioned above, for example, were ones in which he was the 'lead' composer. See my article 'The Pasticcio Experience' in *British Opera in Retrospect* (British Music Society, 1985), pp 50-52, at p 51.
6. Sometimes spelt Jirovec (he was a Bohemian) but the German version of his name appeared in contemporary Doncaster advertisements and reports and was then common.
7. The *Reindeer* (or Rein Deer as it once described) Inn, demolished in the 1960s, was at the corner of Cleveland Street and Hall Gate. It was a major coaching inn.
8. The basic primary source of this article is the Doncaster Central Library's files of the *Doncaster Journal* and its successor organ, the *Doncaster Gazette;* all quotations are derived from those files. I also found useful Doncaster Museum & Art Gallery's extensive collection of play bills for Doncaster's Theatre (Royal).

* because by my count at least 293 'operatic' performances took place in Doncaster during that period: surely a Golden Age of musical theatre in the town.

12. Some Women in Austerfield Wills and Inventories 1658-1721

by Alice Rodgers

AUSTERFIELD IS NOW FIRMLY on the tourist route as the birthplace of William Bradford, Mayflower Pilgrim, but it was a significant place long before the seventeenth century (Figures 1 &2). Important enough to be the venue of a major church synod in 702, it is mentioned in Domesday Book as a dependency of the Manor of Hexthorpe. The planned twelfth century town and port of Bawtry is presumed to have been established in Austerfield's waste and in the thirteenth century a considerable grant of Austerfield's manorial land was made to the Knights Templar. According to Hunter, it was this holding which evolved into the 'inferior' Manor of Austerfield whose seventeenth century court rolls and papers are considered below.[1]

Austerfield manorial court and the proving of wills

Surviving rolls demonstrate that the prime purpose of the Austerfield Court was the transfer of copyhold land.[2] To this function was added that of probate (the proving of wills) where executors brought to the court a will and inventory (a room by room valuation of personal estate). In cases where people had died intestate, letters of administration were sought by family members or creditors and an inventory of the deceased's personal estate was presented to the court.

Austerfield Manorial Court was relatively unusual in concerning itself with probate as most people in the seventeenth century were required to prove wills in one of a number of church courts. During the Commonwealth (1653-60), all English and Welsh wills were dealt with at Canterbury so it is interesting to find records of a number of wills being brought before the Austerfield Court between 1658 and 1660.

Who left wills?

In the sixteenth and seventeenth century, wills are thought to have been made by between one quarter and one third of the adult male population, the proportion for women being very much lower.

Figure 1. Church of St Helena, Austerfield. Many makers of Asuterfield wills specified their desire to be buried in this churchyard: *Brian Elliott*

Figure 2. Monument to William Bradford in Austerfield churchyard. *The Author*

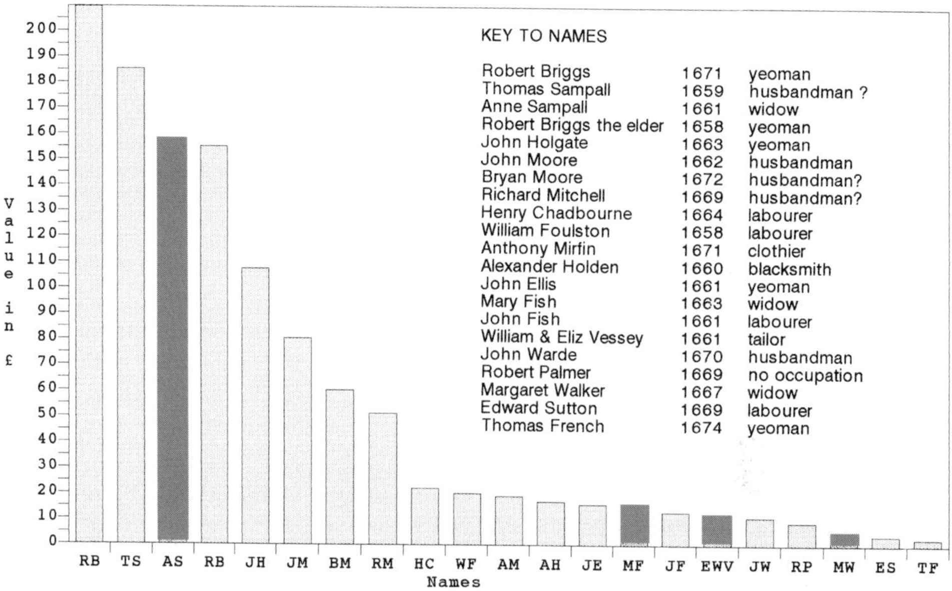

Figure 3. Values of Austerfield inventories 1658-1674 (female values in heavy shading).

Amongst the Austerfield Court records, the wills and/or inventories of a total of forty-one people survive for the period 1658 to 1721. Nine of these were women, all widows, of whom five left wills. The inventories of women show a cross section of values fairly evenly distributed amongst those of men (Figure 3). Where the record is most complete, between 1658 and 1674, a remarkable number of small estates are dealt with by the court.

Seventeenth Century Austerfield

Thomas Jeffery's map of 1772 shows Austerfield as a small linear settlement set astride the road from Finningley to Bawtry Carr. Later maps show that there were long narrow plots, containing orchards and crofts, set behind the row of, what must have been timber-framed and thatched houses on the eastern side of the road. The Austerfield Hearth Tax returns of Ladyday 1672 show no exceptionally large houses as befits a place without a resident lord. Only one property (possibly an inn) has five hearths, two houses have three, ten have two and twenty-one have one. Interestingly one of the three-hearth houses is occupied by a woman, Judith Hall, a likely relative of Mr Hall and Thomas Hall, substantial copyholders in 1669 and 1670. The other three-hearth, most of the two-hearth and some of the single-hearth houses are occupied by members of a core group of much intermarried yeoman /husbandman families, whose names are frequently recorded in court rolls, wills and inventories.

The community revealed by the court rolls and papers is one where almost everyone tilled at least some land and almost all kept livestock and where individual copyholdings were widely dispersed between six identifiable common fields (Figure 4). Rye (for breadmaking), barley (to be malted for brewing), *pease* and oats (for human and animal consumption) are the crops most frequently mentioned and small quantities of wheat are also present. Two commons provided grazing but meadow was at a premium, being evident in the low and outlying settlement of Brancroft to the north and in the recently drained West Field of the neighbouring Nottinghamshire/Lincolnshire parish of Misson. Both *steres* (oxen) and horses were used for husbandry and draught work and these, together with flocks of sheep represent the highest valued items in individual inventories. *Kine* or *cowes, swine* or *pigges, geese* and *pullen* (ducks and hens) are frequently observed and *stockes* (colonies) of *bees* are not infrequent.

As well as yeomen and husbandmen, an unexceptional range of rural trades is evident from preambles to wills or via inventories. Blacksmith, tailor, clothier, wheelwright and weaver are noted as distinct occupations and thatching, malting, carting and brick-making appear to have been carried out on a part-time basis. A watermill is named as a landmark. Female occupations can readily be assumed but are less specifically evidenced. Women bear and raise the children and use the abundantly available tools to prepare and preserve food, brew ale, care for poultry, milk cows, make butter and cheese, card and spin wool,

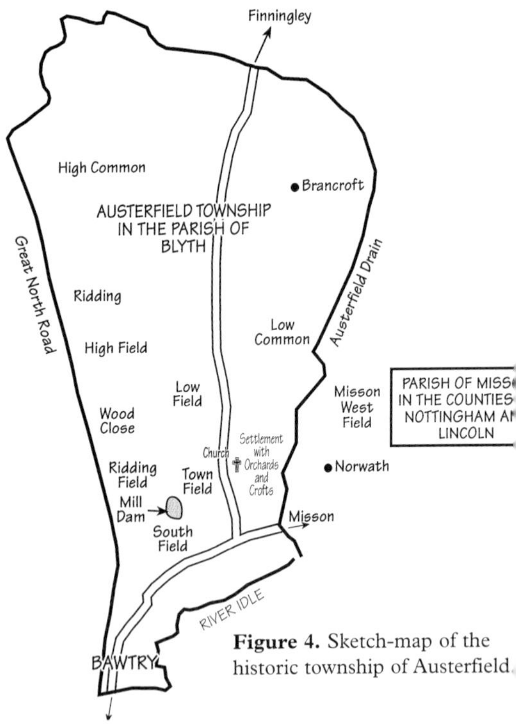

Figure 4. Sketch-map of the historic township of Austerfield.

linen and tow, make and launder clothes and furnishings, care for the sick and take produce to market.

Women recorded in male wills

A remarkably large amount of information about women can be gleaned from the wills of men. Then, as now, wives were frequently made executor but rarely were they given such clear brief as that proffered by Henry Chadbourne (1664):

> *I make and ordaine Jane Chadbourne my wife my whole and Sole Executor and give her alle my whole Estate and at her decease to Dispose of it as she pleaseth.*

John Moore (1662) gives his wife and executor Anne extremely clear instructions regarding a female relative, probably his sister, apparently pursuant of an earlier family will:

> *First whereas Joice Moore was by agreement to have her Table with the said John Moore for her life and cloathes and other necessaries if she would continue with him now the said John Moore did Declare his mynde to be that Anne Moore his wife shall finde and allowe to the said Joice Moore for her Life meate Drinke apparell and all other necessaries at the Charge of the said Anne if the said Joice will remaine with her. And further that the said Joice Moore shall have power at her Death to Dispose of ten poundes to whom shee pleased And that the said Anne Moore shall pay the same accordingly And if the said Joice Moore shall not remaine with the said Anne Moore to be mayntained by her That then the said Anne Moore shall pay unto the said Joice Ten poundes out of the personall Estate of the said John Moore upon the said Joices departure from her*

Care of his young daughter was an important feature of the will of widower John Holgate (1663). He had three children: John, who was of age, William, who was not yet twenty, and Mary, a child. John was to be his executor and a total of £20 was left to William. Mary, however, was to receive £40 'when she shall come to the age of fifteen yeares' and her father later adds that his son John is

> *to mayntaine and keep my Daughter Mary with meate drinke and apparill washing and lodging sufficient for such a Childe untill shee shall come to the age of fifteen yeares But if the said John my son refuse for to mayntaine my daughter Mary Then my son shall pay to my daughter Mary fower pounds yearly and every yeare untill shee shall come to the age of fifteen years.*

Thomas Sampall (1659) and Robert Briggs, the elder (1658) both leave meadow to daughters. The former gives his daughter Elizabeth

> *all my meadowe ground lying within the west feild of Misson one headland lying in the Slancs fower swath and a halfe within the Lowe of the new Ing and ten swath and a half lying in the Shorte of the New Ing.*

His other daughter receives twenty pounds. Robert Briggs, having left his daughter Anne

> *one Cupboard now standing in the howse and one Land Iron and all the furniture belonging to the fire stead in the howse,*

later adds to this

> *nyne Swath of meadow Lyinge and being in the feild of Missen in a place called the Lowe of the New Ing and Eight Swath of meadow at a place called the Hag butting upon the Eay And one Quarter of an Oxgange and one halfe Tofte in the new and one other halfe Tofte in the old...*

He later bequeaths to his son Robert 'one peeice of meadow lyinge within the west feild of Misson comonly called Norwath' but adds

> *But if the said Robert Brige the younger shall lett or hinder the said Anne Brige my Daughter of the Messuage or tenemt and halfe Oxgange of land which the said Robert Brige hath given this my Daughter Anne by surrender according to the custome of the manner That my daughter shall enter and enjoy the saide peeice of meadow* [lying] *and being in the west feild of Misson commonly called Norworth*

Interestingly the will of the younger Robert (1671) uses Norwith meadow in a similar way to ensure that his son, Robert (the third), pays money to his daughter when she comes of age. It must have been quite a prize!

'Partible inheritance' (where all children receive a share of an estate) was, clearly, the custom of Austerfield manor but small sums were left in wills to avoid those who had already been granted their share (perhaps as dowry), calling upon this custom to challenge a will. Thus Robert Briggs the elder leaves his oldest daughter 'toe shillings in satisfaction of her Childe part' and Margaret Brigges, daughter of John Ellis (1661), receives 'Twelve pence as the last and compleat payment of her fillial porcon'.

Unmarried daughters and sisters may have been a financial liability

Figure 5. A wain.

but they were essential to the well being of the community. Provision made by their fathers and brothers meant that they were unlikely to become a charge on the parish but it also ensured that kinship bonds were reinforced. Meadow could be let to provide income but it also represented a desirable dowry. The perpetuation of a system of husbandry based on the dispersal and re-formation of large landholdings depended on women of appropriate social standing and skill, marrying within the core group of families.

In a situation where marriage was certainly arranged by circumstance, and doubtless more formally, there were 'safety valves' at least for men. There is limited but uneequivocal evidence of fathers' wills acknowledging their illegitimate children. Jane Briggs, wife and executor of Robert the elder, can hardly have enjoyed fulfilling his wish:

I give unto my Sonne John Swales his children one Ewe and a Lambe.

Not all women women were left in secure financial circumstances. 'Widd.' Palmer who is recorded as 'poore' in the 1672 Hearth Tax return was almost certainly the wife of Robert Palmer for whom there is an inventory of 1669. His personal estate was valued at £8.18s.8d. and his dwelling had only parlour and 'howse' (living room). The simple furnishings included 'one bedstead, one chaffebed one blanket, one cufferlid (bed cover), one sheete' and 'one paire of curtens'. There were a few pots and pans, a candlestick, items associated with the hearth and a 'woole (spinning) wheele'. The bulk of his wealth was represented by 'one cow and one qui (heiffer), one stocke of bees, three roodes of rye in the ground and manure' together with 'gees and hens'.

Judith, the wife of Thomas French, whose inventory is dated 1674, was left poorer still. Despite being described as a yeoman, Thomas's personal estate was worth only £3.9s.1d. He had 'one wayne (Figure 5)' but no land or stock. Thomas French must have met a sudden, unexpected death because his estate accounts (detailed below his inventory), record payments to the 'Corroner, to the messenger for goinge for him', to the jury, 'the charges for searching for him' and 'for watchinge the Corpse when found' and 'to two women for layinge him in the coffin.' In total £3.17s.6d. was expended directly as a result of his death. Poor Judith inherited a debt of eight shillings.

The wills and inventories of widows

The study of any seventeenth century parish register will reveal ample evidence of early remarriage following the death of a husband or wife. All the Austerfield women who left wills and/or inventories were and remained widows so they are unlikely to be typical of women in general. Still they cast a fascinating light on a group possessed of considerable independence.

Five inventories survive for widows with personal estates valued at more than £70. Of these, four can be paired with wills and inventories of those who were certainly or very probably their husbands.[3] These, together with their dates and values, are those of Anne Sampall (1661, £155.14s.0d.) widow of Thomas Sampall (1659, £183.12s.4d.), Anne Moore (1684/5, £137.18s.10d.) widow of John Moore (1662, £80.0s.4d.), Martha Holdgate (1696, £77.8s.8d.) widow of William Houlgate (1693/4, £86.19s.4d.)[4] and Alice Chapman (1699/70, £164.18s.4d.) widow of William Chapman (1690, £115.5s.6d.). It is interesting to observe that the estates of those longest widowed, that is Alice Chapman and Anne Moore, were worth considerably more than those of their husbands despite bequests having been made out of the former. All four are the widows of yeomen or husbandmen and their main wealth is represented by farm implements, crops, horses, cattle and, most notably, flocks of sheep.

The inventory of Alice Chapman (Figure 6)

Alice Chapman was daughter of William Vessey, a member of one of the most important yeomen families. Neither her will nor that of her husband make reference to children and, after some small bequests and payments of nominal sums to people who seem likely to make a claim on her estate, the residue goes to her brothers. This demonstrates the role of women members in ensuring land was

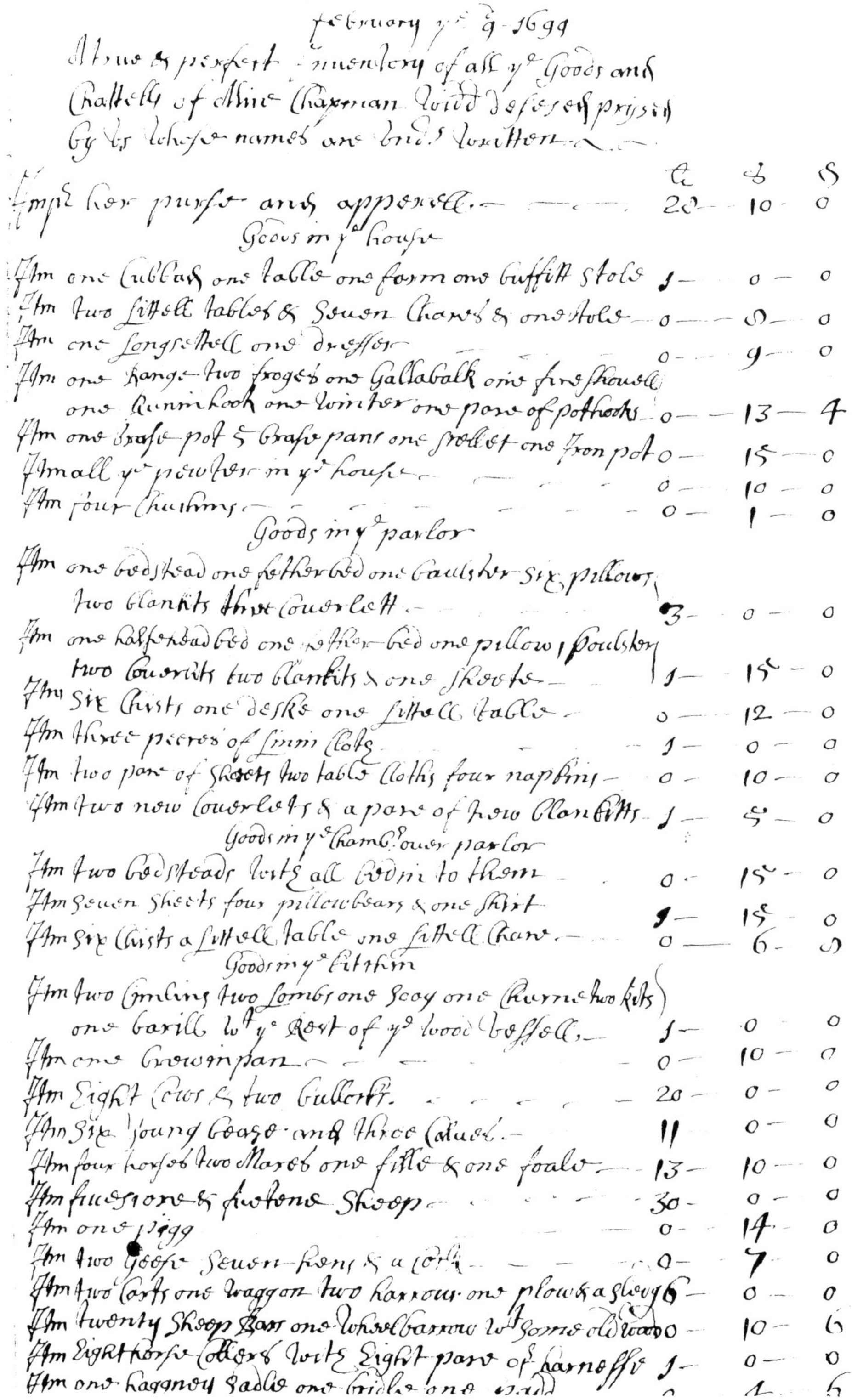

february ye 9 1699
A true & perfect Inventory of all ye Goods and
Chattells of Alice Chapman widd deseased prysed
by us whose names are under written

	li	s	d
Imps her purse and apparell	20	10	0
Goods in ye house			
Itm one Cubbard one table one form one buffitt stole	1	0	0
Itm two Littell tables & seven Chares & one stole	0	8	0
Itm one Longsettell one dresser	0	9	0
Itm one Range two froges one Gallabalk one fire shovell one Runnihook one winter one pare of pothooks	0	13	4
Itm one brase pot & brase pans one skellet one Iron pot	0	15	0
Itm all ye pewter in ye house	0	10	0
Itm four Chushins	0	1	0
Goods in ye parlor			
Itm one bedstead one fether bed one boulster six pillows two blankits three Couerlett	3	0	0
Itm one halfe headbed one fether bed one pillow 1 boulster two Couerlits two blankits & one sheete	1	15	0
Itm six Chists one deske one Littell table	0	12	0
Itm three peeces of Linin Cloth	1	0	0
Itm two pare of sheets two table Cloths four napkins	0	10	0
Itm two new Couerlets & a pare of new blankitts	1	5	0
Goods in ye Chamb. over parlor			
Itm two bedsteads with all beding to them	0	15	0
Itm seven sheets four pillowbears & one shirt	1	15	0
Itm six Chists a Littell table one Littell Chare	0	6	0
Goods in ye kitchin			
Itm two Gimlins two Lombs one Scoy one Churne two kits one barill wth ye Rest of ye wood vessell	1	0	0
Itm one brewinpan	0	10	0
Itm Eight Cows & two bullokt	20	0	0
Itm six young beasts and three Calves	11	0	0
Itm four horses two Mares one fille & one foale	13	10	0
Itm fivescore & twelve sheep	30	0	0
Itm one pigg	0	14	0
Itm two geese seven hens & a cock	0	7	0
Itm two Carts one waggon two harrows one plow & a sledg	6	0	0
Itm twenty sheep stees one wheelbarrow wth some old wood	0	10	6
Itm Eight horse Collers with Eight pare of harnesse	1	0	0
Itm one haggney sadle one bridle one [illegible]	0	4	6

Figure 6. Part of the probate inventory of Alice Chapman, 1699. *Lumley Archive. Reproduced with permission.*

brought into the core group of families. Alice Chapman has an unusually large sum listed under 'purse and apperrell [sic]' and this suggests recent sales, perhaps of sheep or wool, rather than wealth resulting from the practical support, during her lifetime, of those who were likely to inherit her estate. Her wealth seems to be the product of her own acumen.

The inventory of Alice Chapman
February the 9th 1699

A true and perfect Inventory of all the Goods and Chattels of Alice Chapman Widd deceased prised by us whose names are under written.

	£	s	d
Imprimis her purse and apperell	28	10	0
Goods in the house			
Itm one Cubbard one table one form one buffitt stole	1	0	0
Itm two Littell tables & seven Chaires & one stole	0	8	0
Itm one Longsettell one dresser	0	9	0
Itm one Range two froges one Gallabalk one fire shovell one Runinhook one winter one pare of pothooks	0	13	4
Itm one brass pot 5 brass pans one scellet one iron pot	0	15	0
Itm all the pewter in the house	0	10	0
Itm four Cushins	0	1	0
Goods in the parlor			
Itm one bedstead one fetherbed one boulster six pillows two blankits three coverlett	3	0	0
Itm one halfhead bed one fether bed one pillow one boulster two coverlits two blankits & one sheete	1	15	0
Itm six Chists one deske one littell table	0	12	0
Itm three peeces of Linn Cloth	1	0	0
Itm two pare of sheets two table Cloths four napkins	0	10	0
Itm two new Couverlets & a pare of new blankitts	1	5	0
Good in the chamber over the parlor			
Itm two bedsteads with all bedin to them	0	15	0
Itm seven sheets four pillowbears & one shirt	1	15	0
Itm six Chists a Littell table one littell Chare	0	6	8
Goods in the kitchin			
Itm two Cimlins two Lombs one sooy one Churne two kits one barrill with the Rest of the wood vessell	1	0	0
Itm one brewin pan	0	10	0
Itm Eight Cows & two bullocks	20	0	0
Itm six young bees[t]e and three Calves	11	0	0
Itm four horses two Mares one fille & one foale	13	10	0

Itm fivescore and fiveteen Sheep	*30*	*0*	*0*
Itm one pigg	*0*	*14*	*0*
Itm two Geese seven hens & a Cock	*0*	*7*	*0*
Itm two carts one waggon two harrows one plow & a sledg	*6*	*0*	*0*
Itm twenty sheep bars one wheelbarrow with some old wood	*0*	*10*	*6*
Itm Eight horse Collers with Eight pare of harnesse	*1*	*0*	*0*
Itm one haggney sadle one bridle one padd	*0*	*4*	*6*
Itm Rye in barn & rye in Chambers	*6*	*5*	*8*
Itm barley in the barne	*12*	*0*	*0*
Itm pease in the barne to thrash	*1*	*10*	*0*
Itm hay in the barne	*5*	*10*	*0*
Itm coales	*0*	*10*	*0*
Itm six acres of Rye Growing in the highfield	*9*	*0*	*0*
Itm acres of barley Ground on the Ringiflatt	*0*	*5*	*0*
Itm hang beef & bacon with some Cheeses	*1*	*10*	*0*
Itm in butery all earthen Vessells with all huselment in all the places before mentioned	*0*	*13*	*4*
	164	*18*	*4*

Debts Owing to the testator by bond	7	0	0
Lagacies Left by the Testator deceased	12	17	6

Joseph Hoyland
Wm Ellis
Robt Briggs Jun
Robt Briggs Senior
his mark

Martha Houlgate

Martha Houlgate illustrates the plight of the widow of a substantial member of one of the core families shortly to die leaving young children.

Abstract of Martha Houlgate's will sealed 25th April 1696

> *I give unto William Holdgate my eldest son three pounds to be paid unto him at or before Martinmas next by Dorothy Coates my mother in whose hands I leave it for him to be raised or paid out of my goods Item I give unto the said Dorothy Coates my mother Twenty pounds for the bring up of my Son Joshua Holdgate & Hanna Holdgate untill he coms to the age of thirteen years (& thin to be put to a Trade) and untill she be of the age of fourteen yeares, and what remaines of my goods and chattels after my debts and legacies be paid I give & bequeath unto my said Sonn Joshua & Hanna equally to*

be devided betwixt them and I desire my said mother Dorothy Coates to take care that it be put out for their best advantage. I give & bequeath unto my said son William all in interest in the house and land and also one Dresser in the house and if it shall happen that the said Joshua my son dye before my said daughter Hanna then my mind & Will is that she shall have what I leave to him, & if she dye before him then that her part fall to him.

Martha Holdgate's inventory reveals that roughly half of her personal estate was in the form of sheep and wool. With it is filed an undated account of money received and expected to be received for the sale of her goods and chattels together with details of disbursements and a bill from John Moore. These show £4.10s.0d. funeral charges for Martha and Joshua Houlgate, so her younger son cannot long have survived her. There is a payment of £2.0s.2d. 'for Hannah Houlgate apparell' and £5.4s.8d. is expended 'for puttin Willm Houlgate apprentice & for His apparell'. John Moores bill includes a charge of one shilling 'for Goeing with Willm Houlgate to Tickhill when bound appentice' and 2s.10d. 'Laid downe for a hatt for Willm Houlgate att Bawtry fayre.'

A less affluent group of widows consists of Margaret Walker (1667, £5.6s.0d.), Elizabeth Vessey (1661, £12.10s.0d.)[5], Mary Fish (1663, £15.13s.0d.) and Sarah Broomhead (1708, £29.10s.0d.). Both wills and inventories of all but Elizabeth Vessey survive and indicate that they had little by way of crops and farmstock.

Mary Fish, a widow without heirs divides her estate amongst her relatives, friends and their daughters. Her relationship to her legatees Thomas Vessey and George Skinner is not detailed. The bequests to women of clothing, bedding and lengths of cloth point to her personal investment of time and skill in spinning and sewing. Her inventory includes 'One Paire of Towe cards (devices for straightening out coarse fibres of flax or hemp prior to spinning), one Paire of wooll cardes and wooll' as well as 'hempe and yarne' but interestingly there is neither a wool wheel nor a tow wheel. She occupies two, well furnished rooms, has a considerable amount of stored food and keeps two cows, a goose, hens and a ewe hog, so she is by no means poor.

Abstract of the will of Mary Fish sealed 6th November 1663

Item I give to Thomas Grindall my cozen one Great Cheist with a Plate Locke on it and one Coverlid which was his fathers. Item I give to Mary Grindall my Cosin my best Red Peticoate and one Cubert in the howse and two Pewter Dishes and one Cufferlid and one Seeld Cheist and five yardes of Causey [or Kersey, coarse narrow

> woollen fabric]. *Item I Give unto Three Girles of George Basendales of Misterton Three Cufferlids and I give them one Carsey Blanket*

After small bequests of money she continues

> *Item I give unto Anne Geninge Two Cufferlids and three Pillowes.*

Margaret Walker is the poorest person to leave a will in the entire Austerfield series and represents a group about whom it is often impossible to find detailed documentary evidence. Although she apparently occupies only one room, has debts and leaves little, her personal needs are well catered for. The low value of her estate may be indicative of family wealth being passed on to children at an earlier stage rather than of her outright poverty. The preamble to her will, like many others in Austerfield, shows Calvinist overtones.

The will and inventory of Margaret Walker

> *In the name of God Amen the sixth day of July 1667. I Margaret Walker of Austerfield in the County of yorke widd beinge weake in body but of Good and perfect memory thanks be give to all mighty god for it doe make and ordaine This my last will and Testament in manner and forme followinge First I give and bequeath my soule into the hands of all mighty God my maker and Redeemer and my body to the Earth and my worldly Goods which the Lord hath been pleased for to bestow of me I Give and bequeath as followeth Imprimis I Give and bequeath unto Thomas Walker my sonne one little bras pot and one pewter dish one fether pillow one lininge pillow beare* [case] *after my deicese Item I give and bequeath unto Edmund Walker my sonne one little Brass pot and one dish one fether pillow one linninge pillow Beare after my dicease Item I make and ordaine Isabell Walker my daughter my whole and sole Executor and I give her all the rest of my Goods undisposed of for to enter to after my deicese In witness whereof I have here unto set my hand and Seale the day and yeare first above written Margaret Walker (her mke) witness William Chapman (mark) Richard Mitchell Jnr*

A true and perfecte Inventory of all the Goods and Chattels of Margaret Walker of Austerfield diceased prized the six and Twentieth day of September 1667 [by] *William Hall William Chapman Richard Mitchell and Edward Sutton.*

Imprimis her purse and apparrill	1	0	0
In the howse one bed Steade one fether Bed two covelds			

Two hardin [coarse] *sheets Two pillows*	1	0	0
Three lininge Sheets one longe Towell one pillowe beare	0	13	4
Three pewter dishes Two Salts one pewter candle Sticke one brass candle sticke	0	3	0
Fower bras pans one pot one skellit Fower yards of white carsey Cloth	0	8	0
One table one Buffete forme one Buffit stoole Three Chists one Cubert one Chaire	0	13	4
One woole whele one Tow whele one fryinge pan Two Spits one Land Iron one paire of Tongs and Roikin hooks	0	5	0
Two Barrils one Ciff Three Earthen pots with all other uefull Things in the howse	0	3	4
Suma Totalis	5	6	0
Debts owinge by the diceased	1	10	0

A note on Sources

The Austerfield Court Rolls and related papers 1633-1721, which form the basis of this article, are located in the Lumley Archive at Sandbeck Park. They date from the period of the Saunderson (Viscounts Castleton) tenure of the manor and predate its sale, probably in the 1760s, by their successors in title the Lumley family (Earls of Scarbrough) to the Listers of Bawtry. The wills and inventories are found in three distinct groups. Those covering the period 1658 to 1674 are copies forming an integral part of the court roll MCR/AU/1, those covering 1684-1721 are originals filed in the series MTW/B1/1-30 and a mixture of originals and copies for the Holgate family 1692-1717 are found at MTW/3. In addition Lumley MR/SA/1 and MAC/5 cast light on the date of the Saunderson and Lumley tenure of Austerfield Manor and Lumley EMA/4 supplies lists of copyholders for 1669 and 1670.

Notes and References

1. See 'South Yorkshire', vol I, p.79.
2. The term 'Austerfield Court' has been adopted as a convenient name for its courts baron and courts leet whose proceedings were not sufficiently distinguished in the seventeenth century to require separate rolls.
3. Details of wills, where available and of inventories have been matched as well as names.
4. This is possibly the William mentioned in the will of John Holgate above.
5. Her estate and that of her husband were valued as one as they died at about the same time.

Acknowledgement

I am indebted to the Earl of Scarbrough for permission to study and publish transcripts of documents in the Lumley Archive.

13. Bawtry: History in the Townscape

By Derek Holland

THE COMMUNITY HISTORY of Bawtry, as with other places, can be read in its streets and buildings. These, along with sheaves of documents, memories, and old photographs, are striking evidence of the town's past. Dominating everything is the Market Place, centre-piece of a town plan dating from Bawtry's origins as a market town and river port in the years around 1200 AD.[1] Its medieval lords laid out their small 'new town' at the junction of the Great North Road and the river Idle, on land at the frontier of Yorkshire and Nottinghamshire. The land was probably sandy waste in the northern part of Blyth parish. The plan, with its little grid of streets,

Figure 1. Leigh House, 4, Wharf Street. A large brick house of c1800-10, part of Bawtry's late Georgian rebuilding.

dates from the Middle Ages, but the buildings here and in other streets are much later - the results of successive rebuildings.

Most of Bawtry's buildings, in the old town centre, were put up between about 1770 and 1850, the great days of turnpike roads and long-distance coaching services. The little town stood at the junction of a major road (London-Edinburgh) with east-west routes to Sheffield, Gainsborough, and places beyond. Coaching inns like the *Crown* and the *Angel,* large houses (eg Leigh House in Wharf Street, Walker's on the corner of Church Walk and Market Place, and the houses in South Parade), and several cottages in Church Street and elsewhere, are all examples of the prosperity of these years translated into building projects.[2] So thorough was this Georgian and early Victorian rebuilding of Bawtry - and so savage the impact of the railways on long-distance coaching and its dependent trades - that very little further building took place in the town until the twentieth century.

Yet underlying this 1770-1850 rebuilding, and still in evidence in some parts of Bawtry, was an earlier one, which owed its impetus to the river trade on the Idle.[3] As the head of navigation on the river, Bawtry had become by the early eighteenth century - in the words of Daniel Defoe:

> *the chief center* [sic] *of exportation of this part of the country, especially for heavy goods, which they bring down hither from the adjacent counties, such as lead, from the lead-mines and smelting-houses of Derbyshire, wrought-iron and edge tools of all sorts from the forges of Sheffield, and from the country call'd Hallamshire.*[4]

Figure 2. 2 Church Street. The Dutch House at the corner of Church Street and Wharf Street. Built of brick with Dutch gables c 1690, it was refronted along Church Street in the Georgian era.

Figure 3. 1 Wharf Street. Grove House was built in the seventeenth century and refronted c1800-10.

Other important items of trade were millstones from Derbyshire (some going across the North Sea to Holland) and oak timber from Sherwood Forest (bound for the naval dockyards). Among the incoming goods were London groceries and Scandinavian fir timber.[5]

This river trade dissolved with the improvement of the navigation of the river Don (as far west as Tinsley by 1751) and the construction of the Chesterfield Canal (completed in 1777) from north Derbyshire to the river Trent at West Stockwith. Thenceforth, the Derbyshire and Hallamshire goods (and imports back) travelled more quickly and cheaply by these more direct routes, which cut out the need for lengthy, difficult and expensive overland carriage by packhorses and waggons to Bawtry.[6] The Don Navigation and the Chesterfield Canal penetrated right into the industrial heartlands of South Yorkshire and north Derbyshire.

Figure 4. Barton's Garage, Market Place. This opulent brick merchant's house was built by the Dawson family in 1691.

The era of river port prosperity in Bawtry has left us the Dutch House, its core of c1690 with a Georgian refronting along Church Street (Figure 2). Dutch gables are characteristic of areas in eastern England, which had trading contact with Holland; this one in Bawtry is one of the westernmost examples of this style. Grove House in Wharf Street (formerly the YHA hostel) has a Regency front, but its plan and underlying structure date from the seventeenth century (Figure 3). A spectacular brick merchant's house of 1691 stands on the west side of the Market Place.[7] This was the headquarters of the influential Dawson family (Figure 4). Acquila Dawson traded to places in North Yorkshire, Lincolnshire and East Anglia at the end of the seventeenth century. His son, Samuel, traded further afield - to Scandinavia - in the early years of the eighteenth century.[8] The river trade of these years also paid for the west tower of Bawtry church. According to a memorandum in the parish register, an earlier tower had collapsed on 28 April 1670. The new one was built in 1712-13, at the expense of Samuel Dawson.[9] It may be a rough copy of the earlier tower, and fits in with the medieval architecture of the rest of the church.

This church offers us further clues to the history of the town. Its medieval features date from the twelfth to the fifteenth centuries.[10] It was established as a chapel-of-ease within the ancient parish of Blyth, and so it remained until 1851 when the separate parish of Bawtry was created. Its site is not without great interest: a major parish church would probably have been built nearer the centre of town, but this

Figure 5. Crown Hotel, Market Place. Built c1780-1800 to cater for the coaching trade, eclipsed with the coming of the railways, its trade revived with twentieth century motor traffic.

chapel was away from the Market Place and near the river and wharf. Hardly surprising, it was dedicated to St Nicholas, a common dedication in communities with maritime connections. To the north of the churchyard lay Bawtry wharf, and up to the middle decades of the eighteenth century ships would have been nearly as common a sight there as railway trains are today. On the Gainsborough road is an inn called the *Ship*. Built in the 1930s, it is the successor of an earlier inn of the same on an ancient site.

All this earlier history of river trade, market town and coaching centre was overshadowed in the twentieth century by motor traffic on the Great North Road and its feeder roads. This traffic expanded greatly in the 1920s and 1930s, and reached a crescendo in the late

Figure 6. 4-6 South Parade. Elegant late Georgian houses along the Great North Road.

1950s. The motor age in Bawtry led to one or two of its buildings being converted into garages and cafes. Notable among these establishments was Sidney Barton's garage and Cafe-de-Luxe in the Market Place.[11] It led to the revival of the *Crown* and other inns (Figure 5). Bawtry's role as a stopping place on the Great North Road came to an end with the opening of the A1(M) motorway well to the west in 1960. Today, shopping, auctions and restaurants bring people to Bawtry from the surrounding areas.

Additions to the medieval town plan occurred in several phases. In the late eighteenth century grand Georgian terraces and some detached houses were built to the south of the town, along South Parade (Figure 6). To the west of this, Bawtry Hall was built in its park c1785, by Pemberton Milnes, a Wakefield woollen cloth merchant.

In the early nineteenth century the Hall became the residence of the Dowager Viscountess Galway. It later passed into the hands of Lord Crewe, and in the early twentieth century was bought be the Peake family.[12] Bawtry Hall became an RAF command centre during the Second World War. In the 1850s some houses were built along Station Road, between the old town and the isolated Great Northern Railway station to the north-east. In the 1920s and 1930s a small private residential area was developed to the north of the town. Estates of council houses were built between the Great North Road, and the railway in the 1930s and 1950s. An area of RAF housing to the north-west of the town was added in the 1950s, whilst Bawtry Hall was the headquarters of Bomber Command. Further private house building took place in a small area to the north-west of the town from the 1960s onwards. Yet at the core of Bawtry, despite these later developments, is the old town with a plan little different from that created by its Norman landowner.

Notes and References

1. Beresford M W, *New Towns of the Middle Ages* (Lutterworth Press, London 1967), pp 522-533.
2. Holland D, *Changing Landscapes in South Yorkshire* (Doncaster 1980), p 26 & 31; Holland D (ed), *New Light on Old Bawtry* (WEA, Rotherham, 1978), pp 2-3.
3. Holland D, *Bawtry and the Idle River Trade* (Doncaster Museum, Doncaster, 2nd edition, 1976).
4. Defoe D, *Tour Through England and Wales* (Everyman, London, 1959), vol 2, p 181.
5. Holland, *Bawtry and the Idle River Trade,* p 6.
6. Holland, *ibid,* p 10.
7. Holland, D (ed), *Discovering Old Bawtry* (WEA, Rotherham, 1988), I, pp 11-12.
8. Holland, *Bawtry and the Idle River Trade,* pp 3-4 & 6-9.
9. Holland (ed), *Discovering Old Bawtry,* I, p 6.
10. Pevsner N, *Buildings of England: The West Riding* (Penguin Books, Harmondsworth, 1959), see under Bawtry entry.
11. *Dunlop Guide, On the Road:* volume VI - London-Edinburgh (Burrows, Cheltenham, c1928), p 34.
12. Holland (ed), *New Light on Old Bawtry,* p 2.

14. When Buffalo Bill brought the Wild West to Doncaster

by Brian Elliott

THIS SUMMER'S EXHIBITION at the Royal Armouries, Leeds, celebrating the life and work of the legendary Buffalo Bill – including references to his Yorkshire tour of 1903-4 – serves as a fitting tribute to one of the most remarkable figures of the American West.

When Colonel W F Cody brought his Wild West Show and Congress of Rough Riders to Doncaster on 10 October 1903 he was then in his late fifties and one of the most famous men in the world. Cody's face, long white hair and goatee beard was so universally recognisable that his imminent arrival would have been obvious - even to those who couldn't read the print on posters.

The Wild West Show was often advertised with the help of impressive and colourful posters.

This contemporary woodcut of Custer's Last Stand, although totally contrary to historical and archaeological facts, for many people continues to be a real image of an American Western hero.

According to Geoffrey Ward's excellent recent interpretation, Cody had imprinted his version of the American West on an entire generation, both in America and overseas. Myth and reality fused together. Even with modern research it is not easy for historians to entirely disentangle truth and fiction regarding his frontier life. Did he really hunt and kill so many buffalo? or scalp Yellow Hand in 1876 ? and how accurate was his autobiographical account (written at the age of 32) as a pony express rider, gold-seeker and army scout ? The Show's portrayal of the events of 24 June 1876 when Lieutenant Colonel George Custer and 209 troopers of the US 7th cavalry were massacred on the grassy ridges above the Little Big Horn river helped create the myth of 'Custer's Last Stand': whooping Indians racing their war ponies in ever-tightening circles until the heroic leader, gun's smoking in both hands was alone, then mortally wounded.

Cody launched 'Buffalo Bill's Wild West' as a 'national entertainment' in 1883, an outdoor extravaganza featuring live elk and buffalo, 'genuine' cowboys in spotless outfits roping steers, 'authentic' Indians attacking a real stagecoach and a fictitious tableau where the great hero arrived at Little Big Horn too late to save Custer from death.

Chief Sitting Bull, the most famous of the Sioux Indians, born in 1834, had a brief spell with the Show. He was killed on his own reservation by Lakota (Indian) police in 1890.

In 1885 Cody recruited Chief Sitting Bull who despite getting a signing-on fee of 125 dollars and 50 dollars a week for riding slowly round the showground and afterwards signing autographs, left the show after a few months, having seen enough of the ways of the white man. Characters such as Annie Oakley, however, stayed longer. 'The most animated equestrian spectacle ever seen' included an increasingly international cast, from 'wild' Indians and Mexicans, Cossacks and Arabs to the military splendour of troops of US and English cavalries.

Cody's visit - to Town Moor - was reported in some detail in the *Doncaster Gazette*, on Friday 9 October 1903, the day before the event, under the headline BUFFALO BILL'S WILD WEST. A great deal of work would have been required to accommodate the huge open-air show, sideshows, and large crowds. An 'immense canvas pavilion' was erected 'covering the seats which extend along three sides of the vast arena' in case of bad weather.

'Exactly the same wonderful exhibition' had thrilled thousands of Londoners over fourteen weeks at Olympia the previous winter including 'their Majesties the King and Queen, their Royal Highnesses the Princesses of Wales, the Princes Louise, the Duke of Argyle, in fact the whole of the royal entourage...Queen Alexandra coming twice in four days'. But the *Gazette* reporter assured readers that the 'one bob' patron 'sees just as much for his money as those who occupy the higher price seats'.

> *We are also given some indication of what to expect: The show opens with a review of the "Rough Riders of the World". Half a dozen or more Indians, of the Brule and other branches of the great Sioux tribe* [then] *enter. On they come, riding barebacked down the arena, and uttering strange cries, that resemble nothing so much as the notes of the screech owl. Wheeling into line, they are followed in turn by other squads, until they present a solid front defending acres of the arena with Lone Bear, their chief, at their head. Next come the United States cavalry, English cavalry, Cowboys, and Cossacks. When we are all are in, the tableau is completed by the advent of Buffalo Bill who*

Despite Sitting Bull's departure there were plenty of other Indian 'personalities' willing to join the Show. Here we can see Chief Lone Bear and Laura Standing Bear. Both may well have appeared at the Doncaster Show. *Brian Elliott Collection*

> *appears reining in a handsome black steed by means of a much-cherished silver-mounted bridle, the gift of the King when* [he was] *Prince of Wales.*

Spectators would then be entertained by an exhibition of horsemanship by cowboys, Cossacks, Mexicans and 'an exposition of artillery drill' via a detachment of US veteran soldiers.

New show features were also expected, among them a demonstration of lifesaving from the United States Life-saving Corps 'who fire a line over a mast, and illustrate the use of the breeches-buoy in rescuing the shipwrecked'.

Another 'picturesque novelty' was a reconstruction of the Battle of San Juan Hill, consisting of 'two scenes', the first showing 'the bivouac' involving troops 'musing on the morrow or singing the home-songs' whilst the second illustrated 'the storming of the hill, or rather canvas partition, and is full of battle thunder and the sinister rattle of machine guns'.

A classic feature of the show was the Indians attacking the Deadwood Mail Coach, though it was pointed out that the 'old original' coach had been presented to the Smithsonian Institute in Washington.

As for 'Buffalo Bill', the *Gazette's* readers who attended were asked to take special note of Cody's legendary 'marksmanship', shooting 'upward-thrown glass balls from horseback with unerring aim' and the crackshot Johnnie Baker who 'disposes of objects standing on his head or leaning backwards over a chair with equal facility and effect'.

Finally, readers were also informed of the free sideshow 'with more or less continuous entertainment'.

Earlier, on 2 October the *Gazette* made much of Cody's long association with the Indians 'who all look upon him as their good friend'; and his 'special permit', granted by the US Government allowing him to 'take representatives' of the various tribes from their reservations for his world tours. The Cody 'publicity machine' had certainly worked well in this part of south Yorkshire.

The account of the occasion printed in the 16 October edition of the *Doncaster Gazette* was concerned with the great scale and organisation of the event rather its content. The writer who referred to himself as 'Freelance' estimated that 'at least' 20,000 people attended the afternoon and evening performance, the latter having the advantage of electric lighting, though getting to the show at night was an 'adventurous undertaking' because of the increasingly treacherous state of the Common. Cody was described as 'a fine specimen of a man' and his international cast 'a scene in itself worth the expenditure of a shilling or two'.

The logistics involved in transporting, setting up, dismantling and moving such a large show was considerable, perhaps not unlike the staging of a modern open-air pop concert. 'Freelance' estimated that the travelling cast numbered about five hundred, which had to be conveyed to Doncaster, along with all their baggage and props by means of three trains. At the showground the 'Red Indians' were camped on one side of the main show tents, each of which enclosed an area 180 feet wide and 414 feet long.

Feeding 500 must have been a mammoth undertaking, combining military-style precision mixed with considerable ingenuity for the 10 cooks and 60 waiters. There were set times for meals: breakfast between 6 and 9 am, lunch 11 am to 1pm and dinner was served from 4 to 6 pm. Each 'nationality' sat at separate tables. Thus the Cubans on one table, the Indians and Mexicans on others, and so on. This also facilitated the respective 'dietry needs' which included the provision of 1,400 lbs of meat, 700 lbs of potatoes, 800 lbs of vegetables and 450lbs of bread every day. Not surprisingly, the 'cooking car' was always one of the first of the vans to be brought on to the showground, a fire was soon lit and within thirty-five minutes breakfast served 'to large companies of the army of workers'. It was just the sort of slick organisation that enabled the Show to put on two performances in one town one day, then pack up the same evening and travel anything from twenty to a hundred miles during the night, and again play twice in another town the next day.

The 'dining tent' was divided into two sections, with the performers and 'heads of department' in one part and 'stablemen and the like' in the other. The food was prepared 'with scrupulous care and cleanliness' and we learn that 'huge urns, shining with brilliance' were used for serving tea and coffee.

After the evening performance the entire cast and workmen were conveyed to Sheffield in three sections, the first train leaving Doncaster at midnight and the last at two in the morning. On arrival at Sheffield the company and baggage moved to the show ground at Owlerton.

In November1911 William Frederick Cody announced his retirement. He was 67 years old and reputed to be worth three million dollars. But the showman couldn't get used to 'idleness'on his Wyoming ranch, so was lured back to sawdust arenas. He began to loose large amounts of money and the celebrated Wild West Show went under the auctioneer's hammer. Further come-backs occurred, mostly vignette personal

William Frederick Cody in later life, still an impressive and charismatic figure.

appearances in circus rings but his health declined. When Cody died, aged 72 in 1917 there were many columns of obituaries in the newspapers of North America and Europe. The state of Colorado ordered a public funeral in which 3,000 cars respectfully followed his coffin to its final resting place, above Denver. A Historical Centre and Museum was subsequently established in his home state of Wyoming, at Cody, the city named after him.

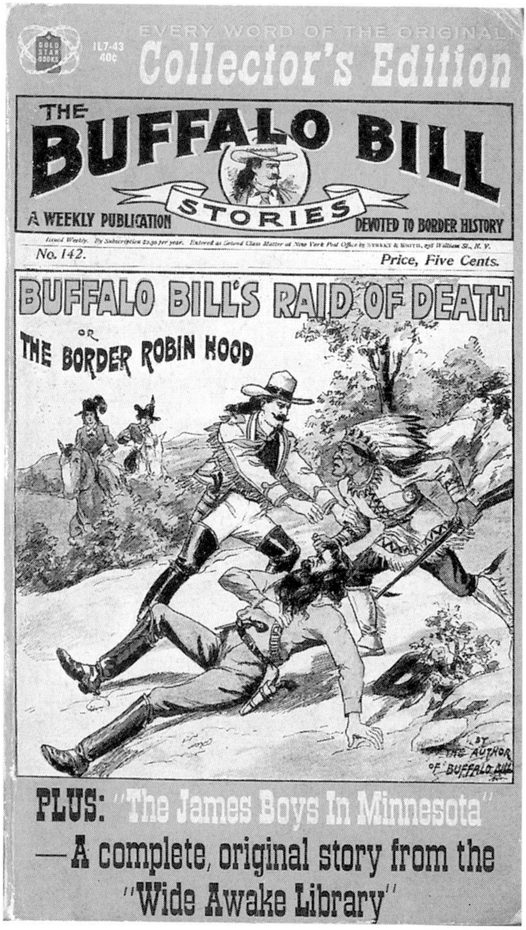

Cover of Typical 'Dime Novel', this 'Collector's Edition', originally priced at five cents, was reproduced by Gold Star Books of Derby, Connecticut, circa 1950, and part of a weekly series. The back cover 'blurb' includes the lines "Hold! Wild Wolf, I bid you hold!" sternly cried Buffalo Bill, as the Indian warrior inflamed with thirst for vengeance, was rushing upon the wounded outlaw chief...

With his touring roadshow Cody achieved a major contribution to modern social history by creating images and scenes that in turn were perfect copy for hundreds of dime novels, children's adventure books and the fast-developing silver screen. He may have been occasionally 'worse for wear' between performances, had more than a casual eye for pretty young actresses, but his contribution to the popular understanding and perception of the American West was immense if not historically accurate.

With hindsight and the benefit of modern historical research, and changed attitudes to wildlife and the Indian people, it would be easy to give a more critical assessment of Cody as a man and of his contribution to American history. But even today and for future generations his legend rather than the facts will continue to generate interest - and maybe that's how it should be. What remains absolutely uncontentious is that his Wild West Show and his intuitive ability to attract large audiences set him apart as a great and until then unequalled showman. Enterprise, flair, flamboyance and astute publicity was an essential ingredient of the razzmattazz of 'successors' such as Phineas Barnum (of Greatest Show on Earth fame) and 'Colonel' Tom Parker, manager of Elvis Presley. Cody would have admired their money-making politics.

Sources and Further Reading

William Frederick Cody, *The Life of Buffalo Bill,* 1878.
The *Independent*, 28-29 October 1986 (on Custer) and 14 August 1993 (Battle of Little Big Horn).
The *Guardian*, 18 July 1984 (ne research on 'Custer's Last Stand').
The *Daily Telegraph*, 11 July 1989 (Medal of Honour restored to Cody)
The *Doncaster Gazette,* October 1903
Brian Elliott, 'When Buffalo Bill's Wild West Show Came to Barnsley,' in *Barnsley Chronicle*, 25 September 1987: also see *Aspects of Barnsley 3,* 1995; and 'Buffalo Bill in Yorkshire,' BBC Radio Sheffield's Tony Capstick Show, recorded in July/August 1998
Geoffrey C Ward, *The West. An Illustrated History,* 1996
For a new and historically accurate profile of Sitting Bull see *The Lance and the Shield: The Life and Times of Sitting Bull,* Robert M Uttley (1999)

Acknowledgement

The Buffalo Bill Historical Center, Cody, Wyoming

CONTRIBUTORS

1. DONCASTER ROVERS, 1962-64: AN APPRENTICE'S STORY.
14. WHEN BUFFALO BILL BROUGHT HIS WILD WEST SHOW TO DONCASTER.

Brian Elliott was born and educated in the Barnsley area. After an undistinguished spell as an apprentice professional with Doncaster Rovers Football Club he obtained a proper job working for Barnsley Corporation in a Dickensian office next to the the Public Cleansing Department. His book *The Making of Barnsley* (1988) was the first published history of the town since Victorian times and in 1990 he was awarded an M Phil by the University of Sheffield for research in local history. He founded and is now the general editor of the acclaimed Aspects series, and edits the Barnsley and Doncaster volumes. Other publications include *Barnsley's History From the Air (1994) and Discovering South Yorkshire History* (1998). Brian who makes occasional contributions to BBC Radio Sheffield is Head of the School of General and Community Education at Rother Valley College and lives in Warmsworth.

2. TOM PUDDINGS AND THE WATERWAYS AROUND DONCASTER

Mike Taylor was born in Goldthorpe, educated at Wath-upon-Dearne Grammar School and the University of Liverpool, and spent his years of employment as a teacher of Chemistry. Childhood outings on the rowing boats at Hexthorpe began a lifetime involvement with the river Don and he has written about various aspects of this navigation in several national magazines such as *Waterways World* and *Archive.* He is the author of *Memories of the Sheffield and South Yorkshire Navigation* and *The River Don on Old Picture Postcards* and also gives talks on the history of the waterway to numerous societies in South Yorkshire and NE Derbyshire where he now lives. His other main interest is jazz, and he has played trombone for forty years in a variety of bands, often in the Doncaster area.

3. WADWORTH AND THE WORDSWORTH FAMILY

Ron Spensley was born in Rotherham and educated at the Grammar School there. A graduate in French of Oxford University, he subsequently carried out research in medieval literature at Keele (MA degree) and Leeds Universities, before working as a lecturer and administrator in further education in Merseyside and East Anglia. From 1987 to 1995 he was an education officer with Doncaster MBC, for whom he managed its schools reorganisation programme. Ron has published articles on medieval and modern writers in various European and American journals and magazines. He is married and (still!) a keen distance runner.

4. ELGAR'S VISIT TO DONCASTER, 1909
11. MUSIC DURING THE NAPOLEONIC WARS, 1793-1815

Philip Lloyd Scowcroft, born in Sheffield in 1933, was educated at King Edward VII Grammar School, Sheffield and Trinity Hall, Cambridge (MA, LL.M Cantab.). He was admitted as a solicitor of the Supreme Court in 1959 and from 1956 until his retirement in 1993 worked in local government in Doncaster. Philip lectures widely on music, transport history, cricket, detective fiction, military history and the law and has written hundreds of articles and reviews for fifty-seven different periodicals and for compendia like the *Oxford Companion of Railway History, Crime and Mystery Writing* and various local newspapers since 1967. He is a Member of the Council and director of the Railway & Canal Historical Society and Co-ordinator of its Rail Transport and Docks & Shipping groups. Philip has also served as Chair of Doncaster Arts & Museums Society since 1968. Independent publications include *The Law and the Teacher* , *Sidelights on Sayers* , *British Light Music* and many items on the local history of the Doncaster area, including two chapters for the first *Aspects of Doncaster* (1997).

5. Doncaster Mansion House Anniversary Tour

Brian Barber is the author of a number of articles on local government and archives including contributions to histories of modern Leeds (1980) and Sheffield (1994), and to the Society of Achivists' British Archival Practice (1996). He is, with M W Beresford, the author of the official history of the West Riding County Council (1979) and wrote the guide to the records of the West Riding quarter sessions (1984), which he catalogued whilst employed as an archivist by the West Yorkshire Archive Service. Since 1984, he has worked at Doncaster Archives, where he is now Principal Archivist. In 1994, he persuaded four distinguished historians to write *Doncaster: A Borough and Its Charters* to celebrate the eight hundredth anniversary of the first Doncaster borough charter. Brian's chapter in the previous volume of *Aspects of Doncaster* was on the landed gentry of the Doncaster area.

6. Descent into Debt: The Corporation's Finances, 1800-1838

George Owen taught sixth-form history and economics at East Barnet before moving to Mexborough School. On retirement a chance question about the *1870 Education Act* led him to investigate its consequences in Doncaster and to discover how the Borough Council successfully avoided complying with the Act's provisions. He then began to look into other aspects of the town's history, with particular reference to the activities of the old

Corporation from Elizabethan times to 1835. He has published a number of articles and is a regular contributor to the Doncaster Civic Trust *Newsletter* and the Library's *Yesterday Today*. He enjoys walking and is a keen gardener.

7. DONCASTER PLANT CHURCHES: ST JAMES AND ST JUDES

Roger Glister was born a stone's throw away from the Sheffield and South Yorkshire Navigation at Sprotbrough. The close association with the 'cut' has resulted in a life-long interest in inland waterways about which he writes extensively. He is a long-standing member of the Waterway Recovery Group, the national body for the organisation of voluntary labour for canal restoration. Lately his efforts have concentrated on the two Barnsley canals. Educated at Mexborough Grammar and the Doncaster College of Technology, he is an engineer by profession and a specialist in church heating. His other interests include fell-walking and vintage cars. Roger is a regular contributor to the Aspects Series

8. JIJGSAWS OF HISTORY: THREE PARISH CHURCHES IN THE LOWER DON VALLEY
13. BAWTRY: HISTORY IN THE TOWNSCAPE

Derek Holland specialises in the history of buildings and landscapes. A graduate of the University of Nottingham, he is a Fellow of the Ancient Monuments Society, a member of the Vernacular Architecture Group, and a member of the Medieval Settlement Research Group. He has served on the adult education panel of the Heritage Education Group and the Sheffield Diocesan Advisory Committee for the Care of Churches. Publications include *Changing Landscapes in South Yorkshire, Bawtry and the Idle River Trade,* and *Warmsworth in the Eighteenth Century.* He is a WEA Organising Tutor, has edited local history studies for WEA groups, and was founder-editor of *The South Yorkshire Historian.*

9. Remembered Forever Medieval Church Monuments in the Doncaster Area

Simeon Bennett was brought up on the Derbyshire/Staffordshire border, attending Hatton Comprehensive School where he developed an enthusiasm for medieval history and architecture. Currently working in a high street bank, he is married with a baby son and lives on the outskirts of Derby. He is an active member of the Church Monuments Society through which he met his fellow author Tony Dodsworth.

Tony Dodsworth grew up in South London before studying for a combined Geography and History degree at Birmingham University. He began teaching in London before moving north in 1974 to take up a teaching post at Pope Pius X School, Wath-upon-Dearne. He remains there today as Head of the Humanities Department. His family history research has proved that his Dodsworth ancestors moved originally from Yorkshire and so he really is a hereditary Yorkshireman! He is an enthusiastic visitor of churches, particularly as member of the Church Monuments Society. He has contributed chapters to each of the three *Aspects of Rotherham* books. Tony lives in Rotherham with his wife, Jane, and daughter, Helen.

10. Denaby Main: The Development of a South Yorkshire Mining Village

Melvyn Jones was born in Barnsley and educated at the Holgate Grammar School and the universities of Nottingham and Leeds. He taught for seven years at Myers Grove, Sheffield's first comprehensive school, and then for nine years at Sheffield City College of Education before its amalgamation into Sheffield City Polytechnic in 1976. He retired from the post of Head of

Academic Resources in the School of Leisure and Food Management at Sheffield Hallam University in 1997 He is now visiting Professor at the centre of countryside research at Sheffield Hallam University. He has written extensively on the social and economic history of South Yorkshire. Recent publications include *Chapeltown and High Green* (1996), in Chalford Publishing's Archive Photographs series and *Ecclesfield, Grenoside, High Green and Chapeltown* (1998) in Tempus Publishing's Images of England series (both with Joan Jones). He is the editor of *Aspects of Rotherham* and *Aspects of Sheffield,* volumes. He is currently working on a book on *The Making of the South Yorkshire Landscape.* Wearing another hat he is BBC Radio Sheffield's 'History Man' with a live weekly local history spot.

11. SOME WOMEN IN AUSTERFIELD WILLS AND INVENTORIES 1658-1721

Alice Rodgers was born and brought up in Burton-on-Trent. She came to South Yorkshire in the late sixties after qualifying as a teacher and, for ten years, lived and worked in Sheffield. In 1978 she and her family moved to Maltby where, in her spare time, she has been able to pursue her life-long interest on local history. In 1981 she co-founded Maltby Local History Society whose regular monthly meetings now draw people from the wider Rotherham area and beyond. She is employed as a part-time lecturer and outreach worker at Rother Valley College, Dinnington. Her contributions to the Aspects series include articles on water-powered sites in the Maltby area, on excavations at Roche Abbey, and on deer-parks of the Maltby area, all in the Rotherham volumes. She also produced an article on the Doncaster-based South Yorkshire Coalfield Church Extension Committee as a contribution to the pamphlet *God's Coal* published by the Diocese of Sheffield in 1990.

INDEX OF PEOPLE

Adam, Robert, architect, 40, 54
Anelay, William, builder, 58, 86
Anka, Paul, 13
Arne, Thomas, composer, 143, 147
Ashe, Andrew, 148
Ashley, Mr, 152
Arthur family, 36-38
Athron, Herbert, 86
Attwood, Thomas, composer, 147, 150
Baines, Edward, MP, 126
Ballagher, John, 11
Bannister, Mr, 150
Bankes, Eldon, KC, 135
Barber, Brian, 34
Barnham, Phineas, 182
Bartholomew, W H, 23, 25, 27, 29, 31
Barton, Sydney, 174
Bassani, Miss, vocalist, 52
Basendales, George, 167
Battie family, 36-38
Beckett, Sir Edmund (Denison), MP, 66-67, 84, 86, 88
Bestall, Jackie, 10
Billings, John, 11, 17
Bletcher family, 46
Bolts, William, 45
Bond, Mr, 150
Booth, Colin, 12-14, 16-17
Boughton, Rutland, pianist, 52
Boyce, William, composer, 153
Bradbury, Mr, 152
Bradford, William, Mayflower pilgrim, 155-56
Braham, John, composer, 149
Brailsford, Isaac, 145, 151-52
Bratt, Harold, 9, 11
Briggs family, of Austerfield, 160-61
Britten, Benjamin, pianist, 52
Broadbent, Albert, 12, 17
Brooke, William, mercer, mayor, 67
Broomhead, Sarah, 166
Browne, Sir Anthony, 120-21
Buck, Samuel, 37
Buffalo Bill (see Cody)
Burgess, Frederick, 115
Burks, George, steward, 69-75
Bury, Edward, 84
Busoni, Ferruccio, pianist, 52
Butt, Clara, 52
Bycroft, Syd, 10
Callcott, composer, 150
Campion, Rev J, 85
Carr, John, architect, 56, 77
Carter, composer, 150
Chadbourne family, of Austerfield, 159
Chaminade, Cecil, pianist, 52
Chapman, Alice, 162-65
Charles I, 61
Chaworth, Thomas, 113
Childers, Leonard Wallbank, 78
Chorley, Dr, 78
Clarkson, Master, 153
Clayton, Lewis, 10-11, 17
Clifford, Mr, 152
Clive, Robert, 44-45
Cody, Colonel William Frederick, 175-82
Collinson C, 64
Conwell, Tony, 11-13
Cook, B, 14
Cooke, Sir William Bryan, of Owston Hall, 66
Copley family, 36-38, 128
Corelli, composer, 150, 152
Cresacre family of Barnburgh, 115-16
Crewe, Lord, 174
Crompton, Dennis, 15
Crossley, Joseph, MP, 126
Crosthwaite, Rev R J, 87
Custer, Lt Col George, 176
Davaux, composer, 153
Davy, John, composer, 150
Dawson family, 172
Defoe, Daniel, 170
Deincourt, Isobel, 111
Deincourt, Sir William, 111
Dibdin, Charles, composer, 143, 149, 151
Dodsworth, Roger, antiquary, 120
Doherty, Peter, 10
Downie, 16
Eardley, Lord, 65, 149
Edward IV, 61, 99
Edward VI, 111
Edward VII, 66
Egleton, Charles, 42
Elgar, Sir Edward, composer, 50-52
Elliott, Brian, 8-19
Elizabeth II, 66
Ellis, Mr, 149, 152
Ellis, John (Austerfield), 160
Erskine, Mr, 151, 153
Ewbank, Rev Andrew, 47
Ewbank, Rev William, 47
Fairburn, Rev Thomas, of Fishlake, 98
Fairhurst, John, 11, 17
Fellows, Harry, 14
Feron, Miss, 151
Fish, Mary, 166
Fisher F W, town clerk, 66
Fisher, Frederick, solicitor, 63
Fitzwilliam, Edmund, 95, 110, 117-18, 120
Fitzwilliam, 5th Earl, 65
Fitzwilliam, 6th Earl, 65
Fitzwilliam, Maud, 118
Fitzwilliam, Sir Richard, 119
Fitzwilliam, Sir Roger, 120
Fitwilliam, Sir William, 110-13
Foljambe family, 48
Foster, Gordon, 10
Fowler, C Hodgson, architect, 95
French, Thos & Judith, 162
Fryer, Alfred, 116
Galliard, composer, 153
Galway, Dowager Countess, 174
Garnet, Tom, 10
Garnham, Jack, 8
George III, 65
George IV, 57
Girouard, Marc, 37
Glover, Ron, 9, 14, 17
Goddard, Henry, architect, 85
Grainger, Colin, 17
Greathead, Canon Ted, of Hatfield, 104
Green, James, 46
Greenhoff, Jimmy, 9
Griffin, composer, 152
Grindall, Mary, 166
Grindall, Thomas, 166
Gryowetz, composer, 151-52
Hale, Alfie, 12-13, 16-17
Halifax, Viscount, of Hickleton Hall, 66
Hall family, of Austerfield, 157, 167
Hallifax, George, clockmaker, 58, 63-64
Handel, composer, 52, 147, 151-53
Hardwick, Ken, 14-15
Harty, Hamilton, 52
Haspell, Alan, 15
Hatfield, Joseph, 143
Haydn, composer, 147, 150, 152-53
Hayman, Francis, 54
Helliwell, Keith, 11
Henderson, John, 17
Henry VII, 102-03
Herbert family, 45
Herrington, Eric, 11
Higgins family, 36-38, 48
Hildreth, Stuart, 11, 13
Hinton, Ron, 11
Hobson, John, 9
Holbein, Hans, artist, 116

Hold, Oscar, 8,11-12,16
Holderness, Earl of, 44-45
Holgate/Holdgate/Houlgate family, of Austerfield,159,162-63, 165-66
Holt, Richard, 64
Hook, composer, 150
Horsley, William, composer, 151
Hotham, John, 118
Hunter, Rev Joseph, historian, 34, 107-08, 110, 115, 117, 120, 155
Huntriss, Joseph,126
Huntsman, Benjamin, clockmaker, 59
Hurst, William, architect, 56-57, 78, 80
Hyde, Mr, 153
Hyde, B, 14
Inigo Jones, architect, 61-62, 65
Jackson, James, 78
Jacobs, Miss, 151
James I, 61
Jeffery, Thomas, surveyor, 157
Jeffrey, Alick, 11, 15-16-17, 19
Jennings, Elizabeth, 74
Jennings, Richard, 74
Johnson, Mike, 11-12
Jommeli, composer, 151-53
Jordan, Clarrie, 10
Julien, Louis, 50
Kempe, CE, stained glass designer, 103
Kent family, 42-43, 46
Keyser, Charles, 96
Kozeluch, composer, 152
Lambton, Colin, 15
Laura Standing Bear,178
Leach, Peter, 39
Lees, Mr, 152
Leivers, Bill, 16-19
Lett,Phyllis, contralto, 52
Lilley, William, 58, 63-64
Lindley, William, architect, 56-57
Liszt, Franz, composer, 50, 52
Lockwood, W F, 52
Lone Bear, Chief, 178
Lovell, Mick, 9, 11, 14, 17
Lumley, Sir William, 46-47
McCall, David, 11
McMinn, Robert, 9-11, 14, 17
MacFarlane, Jim, 138, 142
Machin, George, 15
Maclagan, Dr, 87
Marcello, composer, 153
Margerum, Mrs, 152
Marriott, Thomas, 73
Marsden, Jack, 17
Marshall, Frank, 10-11, 17
Marshall, Dr J D, 125
Marshall, Rev Richard, of Fishlake, 97
Martini, composer, 151
Mason, T B, town clerk, 66
Mather, Mr, 149, 151-52
Mauleverer, Rev Richard, of Fishlake, 97
Mazzinghi, Joseph, composer, 147, 150
Meadows, Bob,12
Melvin, Mr, 150
Micklethwaites of Swaithe (Worsbrough), 35
Miller, Edward, historian/musician, 36, 60,143-47, 149, 151
Milnes, Pemberton, 174
Mitchell, Richard,167
Montagu, Andrew, 129
Moore family, of Austerfield, 159, 162, 166
Moore, Brian,15
More, John, 116
Morini, 153
Mozart, composer, 153
Mulligan, Mick, 8
Mulligan, Peter, 8
Napoleon,154
Neville, Lady Lucy, 119
Nibloe, John, 12-13, 15
Oakley, Annie, 177
Ogley, Alan, 9
Ornsby, Rev George, of Fishlake, 98-99
Owen, James, 48
Oxford, Ken,17
Pace, George, architect, 94, 103
Paganini, Niccolo, violinist, 50, 52
Paine, James, architect, 39-40, 54-55, 60-62, 64-66
Palmer, Robert (& his widow),161
Parker, 'Col', Tom, 182
Parkinson, Michael, 8
Parkinson, Thomas, 46
Parry, John Orlando,52
Pearson,Richard,126
Peel, Sir Robert, PM, 67
Pembroke, Earl of, 65
Pergolesi, composer, 153
Perritt, Thomas, plasterer, 58
Pevsner, Nikolas, architectural historian, 115,117
Pickard, Henry, 29
Pitt, William (the Younger),46
Platt family (mason-architects), 39-40
Pleyel, composer, 150-51
Pope. John Buckingham, 126
Pope, Richard, 125
Potter, Fred,11,13,16
Presley, Elvis, popular singer, 12, 182
Purcell, composer,147
Purvis, Willie,12
Raine, David,11-12
Ravenscroft, Thomas, composer, 147
Reeve, William, composer, 150
Reynolds, Sir Joshua, artist, 66
Richter, Hans, 50
Rickard, William, carpenter, 58
Ricketts, Graham, 17
Ripley, Keith, 17
Rockingham, Marquis of, PM,65
Robinson family, 39
Robinson George, 80
Robinson, John, 80, 82
Robinson, Phil, 11, 16-17
Robinson, Robert,74
Rokeby, Rev John, of Kirk Sandall, 92
Rokeby, Rev William of Halifax(& Bishop of Meath), 92
Romney, George, 44
Rose, Joseph, plasterer, 58
Routh, Pauline,121
Rovalla, composer,153
Ripley, Keith,12
Russell, Miss, 153
Ryder, Peter F, 107
Salmon, Mrs, 152-53
Sambrook, Ray, 11
Sampall, Anne, 162
Sampall, Thomas,160-62
Sampieri, composer,153
Savage, Thomas, Archbishop of York, 102
Scovell, Sir George, 47
Seels, Joseph, 46
Shaw, John, 46
Shaw, K, 14
Shaw, Thomas, 46
Shield, William, composer, 143, 150-51
Siddons, Sarah, actress, 66
Simpson, Mr,150
Simms,Ronald, architect,103
Sitting Bull, Chief,177,182
Skinner, George, 166
Smith, Lawrence, 46
Sousa, John Philip, conductor, 52
Spofforth, composer,152
Squire, W H, cellist, 52
Stamitz, composer, 147
Steele, Miss, vocalist, 52
Stirling, David, 9-11, 14, 17

Storace, Stephen, composer,143
Suett, Mr,152
Surr, Joseph, 46
Sutton, Edward, 167
Swales, John,161
Sweed, Rev John, of Hatfield, 103-04
Tait, Alex, 17
Taylor, Fred,11
Taylor, Rev, 94
Taylor, Sir Robert, architect, 54
Tchaikovsky, composer,52
Teale, J M, architect, 93
Tew, Edward, 78
Thalberg, 52
Thomas, John, harpist, 52
Thompson,Eric,11
Thompson, John, 'bricklayer', 58
Tindall, Bert, 10
Tomlinson, John, 127
Travis, Mr, 152
Vanhal, composer, 151
Verelst family, 39, 43-47
Vessey family, of Austerfield, 162, 166
Vieuxtemps, Henri, violinist, 52
Wainwright, John,37
Wales, Tony, 11
Walker family, of Austerfield,167-68
Wallace, Willie, 12
Walpole, Sir Robert, 36
Watton, James, 16
Ward, Geoffrey, 176
Webbe, composer, 150
Weber, composer, 51
Wederburn-Webster family, 45
Westlake, Brian,15
Whitaker, John, Mayor, 64
White, Dick,12-13
White, Mr, 151-52
Whiteley, D, 14
Willis,T, 14
Wilson, Edward, composer, 145, 150
William IV(Duke of Clarence), 57
Williams, Danny, 14
Williams, Charlie, 10
Winn, Sir Rowland, of Nostell, 54
Windross, Dennis, 11-12
Winterbotham, Sarah, 73
Wofindin, P, 14
Woodward, Alan, 9
Wordsworths of Penistone & Wadworth, 34-48
Wragg, Mr, 153
Wright, Joseph, artist, 67
Wright, T, 147
Yellow Hand,176

INDEX OF PLACES

Acaster (Lincs), 85-86
Accrington, 6
Accrington Stanley FC, 11
Angel Inn, Bawtry, 170
Angel Inn, Doncaster, 147
Aire & Calder Navigation (A&CN), 20, 23, 25, 29, 31, 57
Armthorpe, 90
Aston (Roth), 47
Aston Hall (Roth), 44-45
Aston Villa FC, 11
Austerfield, 7,155-168
Balby, 63, 69, 86
Barnsley, 6, 8-9, 58,153
Barnsley FC, 10
Battle Abbey (Sussex), 120-21
Bawtry, 7, 13, 48, 146, 150, 155, 158, 166, 169-174
Bawtry Carr,157
Bawtry Hall, 174
Bawtry Town AFC, 15
Baxtergate (Don), 61
Bengal (India), 43-45
Bermuda, 46
Beverley, 87
Birmingham, 6
Blackburn, 6
Blackpool FC, 9
Blyth(Notts), 108, 158, 169, 172
Boat Inn, Sprotbrough, 27
Bolton Percy, 47
Boston (Lincs), 66, 85
Boulogne (France), 45
Bradford, 6
Brancroft,158
Bridgewater (Somerset), 45
Bristol, 53, 80
Bristol City FC, 16-17
Bromley, 87
Burnley FC, 15
Bury St Edmonds(Suffolk), 43
Cadeby Main Colliery, 23, 126, 129, 133, 135, 139
Cambridge City FC, 11
Cantley Hall, 56
Carlisle United FC, 17
Carlton, nr Barnsley, 8,123
Carmelite Priory (Don), 54
Conisbrough, 25,27-28, 32, 124, 128 (also see St Peter's Church)
Corn Exchange (Don), 51-52
Castleford, 20
Chesterfield Canal, 171
Chesterfield FC, 14
Christchurch (Don), 57,152
Church Fenton, 113
Clifton Park Museum, Rotherham, 44
Cody, Wyoming (USA), 181-82
Crewe Alexandra FC, 16
Crown Inn/Hotel, Bawtry, 170, 173-74
Cusworth Hall, 39, 54, 58
Darlington FC, 12, 16-17
Dearne & Dove Canal, 23, 123
Dearne Valley Colliery, 15
Denaby /Denaby Main,7, 23, 25, 27-30, 32-33, 123-142
Denver, Colorado (USA), 180
Derby, 67
Derby County FC, 11-12, 17
Dewsbury, 126
Dolphin Inn, Doncaster, 81
Dome Leisure Complex (Don), 10
Doncaster Plant Works, 84,86
Doncaster Rovers FC, 8-19
Dublin, 92
Duke Street (Don), 54
Dunscroft Miners' Welfare, 9
Dutch House, Bawtry, 170,172
Edenthorpe, 90-91,94
Elba (island), 154
Elsecar, 123
Felixchurch, 113
Finningley, 13,157-58
Fishlake, 6 (also see St Cuthbert's Church)
Fornham St Genevieve (Suffolk), 42-43
Frenchgate, Doncaster, 150
Fulham FC, 12
Goole, 20-21, 23, 30-31, 57
Grantham, 72
Great North Road, 158,169,173-74
Great Northern Railway, 21, 28, 84-85
Grimsby Town FC, 12,14
Grove House, Bawtry, 171
Halifax, 92, 126
Hallgate (Don), 56, 59-60, 145
Hatfield, 6, 30-32 (also see St Lawrence's Church)
Hexthorpe, 69, 84, 86
Hexthorpe, manor of, 155
Hickleton Hall, 54, 66
High Street (Don), 52, 54, 60
Holywell House, Southampton, 45
Hooton Pagnell Hall, 56
Huddersfield, 6
Hull, 6
Hyde Park Flats (Don), 64

Keadby, 21-22
Ketton, 94
Kirk Bramwith, 23,30
Kirklington, 47
Kirk Sandall, 6, 21, 25, 27-29, 31-32, 69 (also see St Oswald's Church)
Leeds, 6, 20, 25, 71, 82, 87, 126, 153, 175
Leeds United FC, 9, 16
Leigh House, Bawtry, 169-70
Levitt Hagg, 90
Lincoln, 80
Lincoln City FC, 12
Little Big Horn River(USA), 176
Liverpool FC, 9, 12
London,32, 35, 38-39, 42-43, 48, 53, 64, 171, 177
Londesbrough, 47
Long Sandall, 90-91
Lundhill, 15
Maltby, 124
Manchester, 13, 52,147
Manchester City FC, 16
Manchester Ship Canal, 23
Manchester United FC, 9
Mansion House (Bristol), 53
Mansion House (Don), 7, 50, 52-68, 73-74, 77, 144, 153
Mansion House (London), 53
Mansion House (Newcastle), 53
Mansion House (York), 53, 77
Manvers Main, 27
Marr, 90
Meath (Ireland), 92
Mexborough, 123,126
Middlesbrough FC, 14, 16
Milethorn, 25, 29
Misson(Notts/Lincs), 158, 160
Misterton,167
Monk Bretton, 8-9
Muckross (County Kerry, Ire), 45
New Bentley, 124
New Edlington, 124
New Junction Canal, 23-24,31
New Rossington, 124
Newark (Notts), 64
Newcastle-upon-Tyne, 53
Newcastle United FC, 14-15
North Road Bridge (Don), 28-29
Northwich Victoria FC, 12
Nostell Priory, 54
Nottingham, 74
Notts County FC, 9,15-16
Notts Forest FC, 13
Old Windsor, 45
Ormsby Hall (Middlesbrough), 40
Owston Hall & estate, 56, 66
Parkgate, Rotherham, 124
Patricroft, 84
Penistone, 34-35, 46
Penistone Cloth Hall, 40
Peterborough FC, 12, 84
Plant Works (see Doncaster)
Pontefract, 6
Poynton House (Lincs), 48
Priory Place (Don), 59
Priory Place Chapel (Don), 57
Racecommon (Don), 7
Racecourse (Don), 6,77
Rawmarsh, 124,153
Red Lion Inn, Doncaster, 147
Reigate, 36
River Don, 20-21, 27, 29-30, 38, 76, 90, 95, 99, 126, 171
River Dun Company, 70
River Idle, 158,170
River Trent, 21-22, 171
Rossington, 58-59, 64, 69, 71, 73-75, 78, 80-82
Rotherham, 6, 32, 44, 124
Rotherham United FC, 13-14, 17
Royal Armouries, Leeds, 175
Sandall Beat, 10
Sandbeck Park, 7, 46, 54, 58
Scot Lane (Don), 54
Scrooby (Notts), 103
Scunthorpe United FC, 9, 14
Selby, 20,153
Sevenscore (Thanet), 36
Sheffield, 6, 22, 33, 35, 59, 149, 180
Sheffield & South Yorkshire Navigation (S&SYN), 22-23, 25, 28-33
Sheffiled United FC, 9, 12, 15
Sheffield Wednesday FC, 12
Ship Inn, Gainsborough Road, Bawtry, 173
Shurton Court, Bridgewater, Somerset, 45
Skegness Town FC, 15
Snaith, 153
South Parade (Don), 56-57, 66
South Yorkshire Railway, 85, 123
Southampton, 45
Sprotbrough, 25-28, 32-33 (also see St Mary's Church)
St Alban's Catholic Church, Denaby, 130, 141
St Cuthbert's Church, Fishlake, 89, 95-99
St George's Church (Don), 31, 85
St Helena's Church, Austerfield, 156
St George's Church (London), 43
St Oswald's Church, Kirk Sandall, 89-95
St James & St Judes Churches (Don), 6, 84-88
St John's Church, Wadworth, 41-42, 47, 106, 117-118, 121
St John's Church, Wakefield, 56
St Katherine's Church, Loversall, 106, 113-15
St Lawrence's Church, Hatfield, 90, 99-104
St Mary Magdalene Church (Don), 53
St Mary's Church, Sprotbrough, 106, 108-113,120-21
St Mary's Church, Tickhill, 106, 119-21, 144
St Nicholas's Church, Bawtry, 172-73
St Peter's Church, Barnburgh, 106-7, 115-17
St Peter's Church, Conisbrough, 106, 108-9
Stainforth & Keadby Canal, 22-23, 30-31
Stockport County FC, 12,14-15
Stoke City FC, 13,15
Subscription Rooms (Don), 57
Sunderland, 39
Sunderland FC, 14,16
Sutton-cum-Lound (Notts), 97
Swaithe Hall, Worsbrough, 35
Sydney (Australia), 15
Sykehouse, 24, 31, 95
Thorncliffe, nr Sheffield,123
Thorne, 21, 31, 81, 99
Thyrbergh, 126
Tickhill, 37,166 (also see St Mary's Church)
Town Moor, Doncaster, 177
Tranmere Rovers FC, 16,19
Tunstall (Staffs), 87
Wadworth (& Wadworth Hall), 6, 34-49, 54
Water Hall, Penistone, 34-35
Wath-upon-Dearne, 123
Wakefield, 6, 20, 56, 174
Wentworth, 85
Wentworth Woodhouse, 65
West Stockwith (Notts)
Westfield House, Balby, 63
Wilton House, Dorset, 65
Wolverhampton Wanderers FC, 13-14
Wombwell, 15,123-24
Woodlands, 124
Worsbrough,35
Worsbrough Bridge, 123
Wragby, 54
Wyoming (USA), 180-81
York, 53, 56, 58, 66, 71, 73, 77, 80